French 1 for Christian Schools®

Bruce A. Byers

Robert D. Loach

French 1 for Christian Schools®

Bruce A. Byers

Robert D. Loach

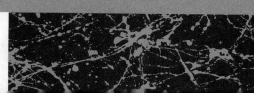

Bob Jones University Press, Greenville, SC 29614

NOTE:

The fact that materials produced by other publishers may be referred to in this volume does not constitute an endorsement of the content or theological position of materials produced by such publishers. Any references and ancillary materials are listed as an aid to the student or the teacher and in an attempt to maintain the accepted academic standards of the publishing industry.

FRENCH I for Christian Schools®

Bruce A. Byers, Ph.D.
Robert D. Loach, M.A.

Produced in cooperation with the Bob Jones University Department of Modern Languages of the College of Arts and Science and the School of Religion.

for Christian Schools is a registered trademark of Bob Jones University Press.

© 1982, 1999 Bob Jones University Press
Greenville, South Carolina 29614

ISBN 1-59166-647-3

15 14 13 12 11 10 9 8 7 6 5 4 3 2 1

Table of Contents

viii

to the student

France: A Mission Field?

When the average person thinks of France, he thinks of art, the Eiffel Tower, fine dining, perfume, designer clothing, and more. Does France, with so much refinement, civilization, and centuries of tradition really need missionaries? Most French people would call themselves Catholics, but few actively practice their professed religion. Most are indifferent to religion, some are antagonistic, and others are actively involved in the occult. Those who claim to be Bible-believing, born-again Christians represent a very small portion of the population. In a poll taken in the late 1980s, nearly half of the French people interviewed said they had no Bible in their home. Accordingly, one of the purposes of this book is to help equip young people to be used of the Lord in meeting the spiritual needs of the people in France and of French-speaking people around the world.

The dialogues and readings in this book will center on an American family arriving in France for missionary service. With the Dupont family, you, as a student, will encounter the various experiences of everyday life in an unfamiliar setting and the adjustments that every missionary in a foreign culture must make. Certainly this will not include every facet of life in France; however, this presentation is from the perspective of a newcomer who is eager to adapt in order to reach the lost more effectively. Of course, you may not be called to foreign missionary service, but at least you will be made aware not only of French language and culture but also of the spiritual needs of the French people.

The Dupont family has a natural interest in France since, as is obvious from the name Dupont, their family heritage is French. Mr. Dupont studied French for several years in high school, and he will now need some further training in language school in France to increase his fluency. However, his wife studied French in high school and college and, therefore, will not need to attend language school. They have taught their children some basic sentences during deputation so that they would be at least somewhat familiar with a few expressions. The children will have very little difficulty learning the language and in a relatively short time will be quite fluent. During the time of language school and adjusting to life in France, the Dupont family will be working with a French pastor, Philippe Plouvin, and his family, none of whom speak English. Thus they will try to communicate in French right from the start. This will help them become involved in the ministry of the church in Toulouse, the city where Mr. Dupont will also be attending language school.

FRANCE

Saint Omer
Etoples
Eu
Armentières
Berek
Fourmies
Fécamp
Beauvais
Sedan
Saint-Lô
Lisieux
Louviars
Creil
PARIS
Bar-le-Duc
Hennebort
Saumur
Beaune
Nevers
Les Sables
d' Olonne
Autun
Lons-le-Saunier
Montluçon
Oyonnax
Angoutême
Thiers
Royan
St. Just-
Cognac
St. Rambert
Roussillon
Tulle
Le Puy
Villeneuve
Sur Lot
Cahors
Decazeville
Abenas
Millau
Dax
Manasque
Cavaillon
Saint Jean de Luz
Beaucalre
Toulouse

A Gallup poll taken last September in France found that 31% of the people are "non-religious," and 13% more are "convinced atheists." In a time of crisis, three-fourths said they would talk with a friend or family member, and only 7% would consult a clergyman. Nearly half said they did not believe in sin, and 48% had no Bible in their home or among family members. Three-fourths placed their hope for the future in the ability of science to conquer sickness and misery.

(Emerging Trends, 4/87)

The cities on this map, except for Paris and Toulouse, are cities of over 18,000 with no gospel witness. In addition, there are over 35,000 towns and villages without a gospel witness.

chapitre un

faire connaissance

Marc 16, 15 Allez par tout le monde, et prêchez la bonne nouvelle à toute la création.

1 1 1 1 1 1 1 1 1 1

Philippe and Sophie Plouvin and their sons Jean-Luc and Denis are meeting Robert and Alice Dupont and their children Anne and Paul at the airport. Although they have corresponded and exchanged pictures in preparation for the arrival of the Dupont family, there are still some formal introductions which must be made as they meet for the first time and become acquainted.

M. Plouvin:	Bonjour, M. Dupont. Bienvenue en France.
M. Dupont:	Merci, monsieur. Comment allez-vous?
M. Plouvin:	Je vais très bien, merci, et vous?
M. Dupont:	Un peu fatigué, mais pas mal.
M. Plouvin:	Voici ma femme, Sophie.
M. Dupont:	Enchanté, madame.
Mme Plouvin:	Ravie, monsieur.

supposons . . .

The adults in the above dialogue already know each other, and they have a brief encounter on the street. The conversation would then be less formal.

M. Dupont:	Bonjour, M. Plouvin. Comment ça va?
M. Plouvin:	Ça va bien, merci. Et vous?
M. Dupont:	Comme ci, comme ça.

(After a bit of small talk, they say good-bye.)

M. Plouvin:	Eh bien, au revoir.
M. Dupont:	A bientôt.

supposons . . .

Sometime after becoming friends, two of the children meet on the street.

Denis:	Salut, Paul. Ça va?
Paul:	Oui, ça va. Et toi?
Denis:	Bien, merci.

(Their good-byes might go something like this.)

Paul:	Bon, à tout à l'heure.
Denis:	A tout à l'heure.

maintenant en anglais . . .

Mr. Plouvin:	Hello, Mr. Dupont. Welcome to France.
Mr. Dupont:	Thank you, sir. How do you do? (idiomatic)
Mr. Plouvin:	I am doing (idiomatic) very well, thank you, and you?
Mr. Dupont:	A little tired, but not bad.
Mr. Plouvin:	This is my wife, Sophie.
Mr. Dupont:	Pleased (to meet you), ma'am.
Mrs. Plouvin:	Delighted, sir.

let us suppose . . .

Mr. Dupont:	Hello, Mr. Plouvin. How are you doing? (idiomatic)
Mr. Plouvin:	I'm doing well, thanks. (idiomatic) And you?
Mr. Dupont:	So-so.
Mr. Plouvin:	Well, good-bye.
Mr. Dupont:	See you later. (idiomatic)

let us suppose . . .

Denis:	Hi, Paul? How's it going? (idiomatic)
Paul:	(Yeah), fine. (idiomatic) And you?
Denis:	Well, thanks.
Paul:	Good, see you soon.
Denis:	See you soon.

faire connaissance

formal and informal

French, like English, has formal and informal levels of expression. A speech given by a political figure would differ somewhat from a conversation between friends. In the conversation between M. Dupont and M. Plouvin, who were meeting for the first time, more formal structures were used, such as *Bonjour, monsieur* and *Comment allez-vous?* In the exchanges which followed, much less formal structures were used, such as *Salut, ça va?* and *Comment ça va?* The student learning French will need to keep these distinctions in mind in order to avoid causing an uncomfortable situation by what he says.

A. Match the remark or question with the correct response. Some responses may be used more than once.

1. Salut.
2. Ça va bien?
3. Bonjour, monsieur.
4. Enchanté.
5. Comment allez-vous?
6. Au revoir.
7. Voici ma femme.

a. A bientôt.
b. Bonjour, madame.
c. Je vais très bien, merci.
d. Salut.
e. Non, ça va mal.
f. Bonjour, mademoiselle.
g. Ravi.

B. How would you respond to each of these remarks or questions?

1. Comment allez-vous?
2. Bonjour, monsieur/madame/mademoiselle.
3. Ça va?
4. A tout à l'heure.
5. Ça va bien, merci, et toi?
6. Salut.

C. Construct a brief conversation to fit each of these situations:

1. You greet a friend in the hall after the weekend.
2. You meet your teacher in the mall.
3. You are a businessman meeting a new client.
4. You are a missionary greeting a young person from your church.
5. You say good-bye to a classmate after a basketball game.
6. You say good-bye to your pastor after a church service.

Since the Dupont children are still timid about trying to speak French, Mme Dupont initiates a conversation with the Plouvin children.

Mme Dupont:	Comment t'appelles-tu?
Jean-Luc:	Je m'appelle Jean-Luc.
Mme Dupont:	Et lui, comment s'appelle-t-il?
Jean-Luc:	Il s'appelle Denis. *(to Anne)* Et toi, comment t'appelles-tu?
Anne:	Je m'appelle Anne.

supposons . . .

Mme Dupont and Anne make the acquaintance of a young lady after church. Since adults are meeting for the first time, the conversation will be more formal.

Mme Dupont:	Bonsoir, mademoiselle. Je m'appelle Alice Dupont. Comment vous appelez-vous?
Mlle Lafond:	Je m'appelle Suzanne Lafond. *(pointing to Anne)* Et elle, comment s'appelle-t-elle?
Mme Dupont:	Elle s'appelle Anne.

maintenant en anglais . . .

Mrs. Dupont:	What's your name? (idiomatic)
Jean-Luc:	My name is Jean-Luc. (idiomatic)
Mrs. Dupont:	And him, what's his name? (idiomatic)
Jean-Luc:	His name is Denis. (to Anne) And you, what's your name? (idiomatic)
Anne:	My name is Anne. (idiomatic)

let us suppose . . .

Mrs. Dupont:	Good evening, miss. My name is Alice Dupont. What's your name? (idiomatic)
Miss Lafond:	My name is Suzanne Lafond. (pointing to Anne) And her, what is her name? (idiomatic)
Mrs. Dupont:	Her name is Anne. (idiomatic)

faire connaissance

5

les prénoms . . .

The following is a list of common French names. See if you can find one similar to your own.

Elle s'appelle . . .

Adèle	Diane	Jacqueline	Nathalie
Agathe	Dominique	Janine	Nicole
Alberte	Edith	Jeanne	Odette
Alice	Elisabeth	Jeannette	Odile
Amélia	Elise	Joëlle	Olive
Andrée	Ella	Joséphine	Pascale
Anne	Emilie	Judith	Patricia
Anne-Marie	Emma	Julienne	Paulette
Annick	Estelle	Laure	Pauline
Annie	Eugénie	Liliane	Raymonde
Bérénice	Eve	Line	Renée
Berthe	Evodie	Lise	Rosalie
Blanche	Fabrice	Louise	Rose
Blondine	Félicité	Lucie	Ruth
Brigitte	Florence	Lucienne	Sandrine
Catherine	Françoise	Lydie	Sarah
Chantal	Gabrielle	Madeleine	Simone
Charlotte	Geneviève	Margot	Solange
Christel	Georgette	Marguerite	Sophie
Christine	Germaine	Marie	Suzanne
Claire	Gilberte	Marie-Ange	Sylvie
Clarisse	Gisèle	Marie-Claire	Thérèse
Claudette	Hélène	Mariette	Véronique
Claudine	Héloïse	Marthe	Virginie
Clémence	Henriette	Martine	Vivienne
Colette	Ida	Michèle	Yvette
Danielle	Inès	Monique	Yvonne
Débora	Irène	Nadine	Zita
Denise	Isabelle	Natacha	

Il s'appelle . . .

Adam	Clément	Gérard	Kévin	Prosper
Adolphe	Daniel	Gilbert	Léo	Quentin
Alain	David	Gilles	Léon	Régis
Albert	Denis	Grégoire	Laurent	Rémi
Alexandre	Didier	Guillaume	Louis	Raoul
Alexis	Dominique	Gustave	Luc	Raymond
Alfred	Edmond	Guy	Lucien	Robert
Alphonse	Edouard	Henri	Marc	Roger
André	Emile	Hervé	Marcel	Roland
Antoine	Eric	Honoré	Martin	Samuel
Armand	Ernest	Hubert	Matthieu	Serge
Arnaud	Etienne	Hugues	Maurice	Siméon
Arthur	Eugène	Jérémie	Maxime	Simon
Auguste	Fabrice	Jérôme	Michel	Théodore
Benoît	Félix	Jacques	Nathan	Thibault
Bernard	Ferdinand	Jean	Nicolas	Thierry
Bertrand	Fernand	Jean-Claude	Noël	Thomas
Blaise	Francis	Jean-Marc	Olivier	Timothée
Boris	François	Jean-Philippe	Pascal	Valéry
Bruno	Frédéric	Jean-Pierre	Patrice	Victor
Charles	Gabriel	Joël	Patrick	Vincent
Christian	Gaston	Joseph	Paul	Xavier
Christophe	Gauthier	Jules	Philippe	Yves
Claude	Geoffroy	Julien	Pierre	Yvon
Claude-Marie	Georges	Justin	Pierrick	

tu and *vous*

When French people speak to each other, they use two different words for *you.* If they are speaking to family members, to friends, to children, or even to pets, they use *tu.* In other situations they use *vous,* which is considered more formal. In speaking to the Lord in prayer, born-again French Christians have traditionally used *tu* whereas all other religious groups have customarily used *vous.* Can you think of any reasons for this difference?

D. If you were a(n) _____ speaking to a(n) _____, which would you use, *tu* or *vous?*
   1. child . . . teacher
   2. adult . . . child
   3. teacher . . . university student
   4. pastor . . . adult member of your church
   5. elementary teacher . . . child in your class
   6. grown-up . . . dog
   7. patient . . . doctor

E. Answer each question according to the partial response in parentheses.
   modèle: Comment s'appelle-t-il? (Pierre) *Il s'appelle Pierre.*
   1. Comment vous appelez-vous? (Gustave)
   2. Comment s'appelle-t-elle? (Louise)
   3. Tu t'appelles Odette? (Non, . . . Annick)
   4. Il s'appelle Hugues? (Oui, . . .)
   5. Comment t'appelles-tu? (your French name)

F. Ask your classmate his name. He will answer your question, and then he will ask the next person the same question, and so on all around the room.

G. Give the question that would elicit the following responses.
   modèle: Je m'appelle Paulette. *Comment t'appelles-tu?*
   1. Je m'appelle Solange.
   2. Elle s'appelle Line.
   3. Il s'appelle Jacques-Yves.
   4. Non, je m'appelle Hubert.
   5. Je m'appelle M. Boulanger.
   6. Non, elle s'appelle Charlotte.

H. Construct a brief conversation with another person in which you greet each other, find out how the other person is doing, find out each other's name, and say good-bye. How would this conversation differ for each of these situations?
1. two students
2. two adults
3. an adult and a student

prononciation

/i/, /u/, and /y/

The three French vowel sounds introduced in this chapter are presented as symbols surrounded by slashes (/ /). The slashes are used as a reminder that the symbols between them represent sounds rather than actual French spelling. In many cases you will find that the sound symbols and the letters used in spelling are identical; in other cases, however, they are not. While it is necessary for us to use these symbols in order to focus discussion on a particular sound and to describe that sound precisely, you will not be required to memorize the sound symbols. Rather, you should concentrate on articulating the sounds accurately and on learning how to spell them correctly in French.

The /i/ sound, spelled in French with the letters *i* or *y,* is pronounced much like the letters *ee* in *feet* in English. In French the lips are spread in a smiling position and the jaw remains motionless during the production of the /i/ sound. The tongue is forward in the mouth. Observe the /i/ sound in these words.

rav*i*	*il*
merc*i*	S*y*lvie
Al*i*ce	fat*i*gué

The sound /u/ is spelled in French with the letters *ou*. Its pronunciation is similar to *oo* in the English word *moose*. During the articulation of the French /u/ sound the lips are tightly rounded and the tongue is in the back of the mouth. Note the /u/ sound in the following words.

v*ou*s	L*ou*ise
Pl*ou*vin	t*ou*t
bonj*ou*r	B*ou*langer

The sound /y/ has no equivalent in English. It is spelled in French with the letter *u*. Its articulation combines those of /i/ and /u/. That is, the lips are tightly rounded as in /u/, but the tongue is forward as in /i/. Thus the sound can be produced by pronouncing the /i/ sound with the lips rounded. The /y/ sound can be heard in the following words.

L*u*c	sal*u*t
D*u*pont	bienven*u*e
t*u*	S*u*zanne

Pronounce the following pairs of words.

Louis–Luc	Plouvin–Dubois
bonjour–salut	Louise–Suzanne
vous–tu	tout–tu

culture

Normally, when French people greet one another and take leave of each other, they shake hands, give each other a kiss on the cheek, or both. There is physical contact, which is usually missing when Americans say, ''Hi'' or ''Bye'' and give a quick wave of the hand. Whenever and wherever acquaintances meet or part, they will exchange *la poignée de main* (handshake). The closer the relationship or friendship, the more likely will be *la bise* (kiss). This practice is not very comfortable for most Americans who visit France, particularly when they see or experience this between men. However, since the French do not find this at all unusual, a missionary may feel it necessary to avoid offending someone by making some adjustments in his effort to make friendships.

la famille

Proverbes 1, 8 Ecoute, mon fils, l'instruction de ton
père, Et ne rejette pas l'enseignement de ta mère.

2 2 2 2 2 2 2 2 2 2

Now that we have met the Plouvin and the Dupont families, let's read about them in French.

M. et Mme Plouvin ont deux fils. Ils s'appellent Jean-Luc et Denis. Jean-Luc a neuf *ans* et son frère quinze ans. M. et Mme Dupont ont deux *enfants*—un fils et une fille. Le fils s'appelle Paul et sa sœur Anne. Il a neuf ans et elle a quatorze ans.

years

children

Plouvin

Philippe

Sophie

Jean-Luc

Denis

Dupont

Robert

Alice

Anne

Paul

A. Complete the description of the Dupont family tree using the description of the Plouvin family tree as a model.

1. M. Plouvin est le mari de Mme Plouvin.

   M. Dupont est le _____ de _____.

2. Mme Plouvin est la femme de M. Plouvin.

   Mme Dupont est la _____ de _____.

3. M. Plouvin est le père de Jean-Luc et Denis.

   M. Dupont est le _____ de _____ et _____.

4. Mme Plouvin est la mère de Jean-Luc et Denis.

   Mme Dupont est la _____ de _____ et _____.

5. Jean-Luc est le fils de M. et Mme Plouvin.

   Paul est le _____ de _____ et _____.

   Anne est la _____ de _____ et _____.

6. Denis est le frère de Jean-Luc.

   Paul est le _____ d' _____.

   Anne est la _____ de _____.

gender and definite articles

In French, as in English, nouns referring to people are considered either masculine or feminine. For example, the father is spoken of as "he" and the mother as "she," just as we have already learned in French with *il s'appelle* and *elle s'appelle*. Unlike English, however, French has a masculine and a feminine word for the definite article *the*. The father, for instance, is *le* père, but the mother is *la* mère. *Le* and *la* are called definite articles because they refer to definite or specific nouns. Consider the difference in meaning implied in these two questions:

Who has a book?

Who has the book?

The person asking "Who has *the* book?" has a specific book in mind, while the first question could be referring to any book.

B. Give the masculine or feminine counterpart for each of these family relationships.
   modèle: le fils   *la fille*
   1. le père
   2. la fille
   3. le frère
   4. la femme
   5. la mère
   6. la sœur

C. Replace the underlined words in the sentences with the words in parentheses. Be sure to use the appropriate definite article.
   modèle: Voici le père de Jean-Luc. (mère)
           Voici la mère de Jean-Luc.
   1. Voici la sœur de Paul. (père)
   2. Mme Dupont est la mère de Paul. (femme de M. Dupont)
   3. Anne est la fille de M. et Mme Dupont. (Paul . . . fils)
   4. Mme Plouvin est la femme de M. Plouvin. (M. Plouvin . . . mari de Mme Plouvin)
   5. Voici le fils de M. Dupont. (fille)

D. Answer the following questions based on the family trees.
1. Comment s'appelle le père de Jean-Luc?
2. Qui est la sœur de Paul?
3. Anne est la fille de Mme Plouvin? (Non, Anne est . . .)
4. Denis est le fils de Jean-Luc?
5. Comment s'appelle la femme de M. Dupont?
6. Qui est la mère de Paul?

dialogue

supposons . . .

If the Plouvin and Dupont families had not previously met, the children's conversations could sound like this:

Paul: Combien de frères as-tu?
Jean-Luc: J'ai un frère. Et toi, tu as un frère?
Paul: Non, j'ai une sœur. Elle a 14 ans. Quel âge a ton frère?
Jean-Luc: Mon frère a 15 ans. Et toi, quel âge as-tu?
Paul: J'ai 9 ans.
Jean-Luc: Tiens! J'ai 9 ans aussi.

maintenant en anglais . . .

Paul: How many brothers do you have?
Jean-Luc: I have one brother. And you, do you have a brother?
Paul: No, I have a sister. She is 14 years old. (idiomatic) How old is your brother?
Jean-Luc: My brother is 15 years old. And you, how old are you?
Paul: I am 9 years old.
Jean-Luc: Hey! I'm 9 years old, too.

les nombres

zéro	0						
un	1	six	6	onze	11	seize	16
deux	2	sept	7	douze	12	dix-sept	17
trois	3	huit	8	treize	13	dix-huit	18
quatre	4	neuf	9	quatorze	14	dix-neuf	19
cinq	5	dix	10	quinze	15	vingt	20

E. Comptez.
1. Count from 1 to 10.
2. Count from 11 to 20.
3. Count from 2 to 20 using even numbers.
4. Say all the numbers divisible by three from 0 to 20.
5. Count from 1 to 19 using odd numbers.
6. Count backwards from 20 to 0.

F. Express the following problems in words.

modèle: 1 + 1 = 2
Un et un font deux

1. 2 + 3 = _____
2. 4 + 6 = _____
3. 5 + 7 = _____
4. 8 + 3 = _____
5. 10 + 4 = _____
6. 9 + 9 = _____
7. 10 + 7 = _____
8. 6 + 13 = _____
9. 11 + 9 = _____
10. 15 + 1 = _____

possessive adjectives

Consider the following sentence from the reading on page 15: Quel âge a **ton** frère? *How old is your brother?* If Paul had wanted to ask ''How old is your sister?'' he would have said, ''Quel âge a **ta** sœur?''

Notice that there are two different words for *your: ton* and *ta*. These possessive adjectives reflect the different genders, just as *le* and *la* do. Likewise to say *my,* it is necessary to choose *mon* or *ma,* depending on the gender of the noun following.

G. Express the following in French.
   1. my brother
   2. your sister
   3. my son
   4. my daughter
   5. your wife
   6. my mother
   7. your father
   8. my sister
   9. your husband
   10. my husband

H. Looking at the family tree on page 12, pretend that you are Paul, and answer the following questions from his perspective.
   modèle: Ta mère s'appelle Sophie? *Non, ma mère s'appelle Alice.*
   1. Comment s'appelle ton père?
   2. Ta sœur s'appelle Anne?
   3. Comment s'appelle ta mère?

Now pretend you are M. Plouvin.
   1. Comment s'appelle ta femme?
   2. Denis est ton frère?

Now pretend you are Jean-Luc.
   1. Comment s'appelle ton frère?
   2. Comment s'appellent ton père et ta mère?

Now consider the following sentences from the reading on page 12:

Jean-Luc a neuf ans et **son** frère quinze ans.
Jean-Luc is nine years old and his brother fifteen.

Le fils s'appelle Paul et **sa** sœur s'appelle Anne.
The son's name is Paul and his sister's name is Anne.

There are two different words for *his—son* and *sa.* Since *frère* is masculine, it is preceded by *son,* the masculine form of the possessive adjective. *Sa,* the feminine counterpart, is used with *sœur. Son* and *sa* mean not only *his* but also *her.* Therefore, *son frère* means either "his brother" or "her brother," depending on the context and the antecedent. This is not a problem for the French since to use *son frère* out of context would be just as confusing as to do so in English. For example, if someone asked you, "Do you know his brother?" you would have to ask, "*Whose* brother?" since there is no antecedent in your conversation.

la famille

I. Express the following in French.
   1. his father
   2. her father
   3. his mother
   4. her mother
   5. her sister
   6. his son
   7. her husband
   8. his wife

J. Referring to the family trees on page 12, give the names of Paul's family members.

   modèle: mère *Sa mère s'appelle Alice Dupont.*
   1. père
   2. sœur

Now give the names of Mme Dupont's family members.

révision

	masc.	fem.	
definite articles	le	la	*the*
possessive adjectives	mon	ma	*my*
	ton	ta	*your*
	son	sa	*his*
	son	sa	*her*

dialogue

supposons . . .

A conversation between two of the parents could sound like this:

Mme Dupont:	Combien d'enfants avez-vous?
Mme Plouvin:	Nous avons deux fils. Et vous?
Mme Dupont:	Nous avons un fils et une fille.

maintentant en anglais . . .

Mrs. Dupont:	How many children do you have?
Mrs. Plouvin:	We have two sons. And you?
Mrs. Dupont:	We have a son and a daughter.

subject pronouns

In the sentence, *Nous avons deux fils,* from the dialogue, the subject of the sentence is *nous* (we). The other subject pronouns in English are *I, you, he, she, it,* and *they.* Perhaps a clearer way of seeing how these pronouns relate to one another is in the form of a table indicating the person and number:

	singular	plural
1st person	I	we
2nd person	you	you
3rd person	he, she, it	they

The first person is the speaker (I), or the speaker and others (we).
The second person is the person or persons spoken to (you).
The third person is any other person(s) or thing(s) spoken about (he, she, it, they, and the nouns they would replace).
In French this table looks like this:

	singulier	pluriel
1ère personne	je	nous
2e personne	tu, vous	vous
3e personne	il, elle	ils, elles

Note the following:

- The subject pronoun *je* is capitalized only when it is the first word in a sentence.
- You have already learned that *vous* is used as a singular pronoun in formal address. Here you see that it also serves as the second person plural pronoun. In the plural there is no distinction between formal and informal address.
- The lack of a separate pronoun for *it* in French will be discussed in Chapter 4.
- There are two words for *they. Elles* replaces two or more feminine nouns. *Ils* replaces two or more masculine nouns or a mixed group containing at least one masculine noun.

K. Match the French sentence with its English translation in the list below, using your knowledge of **subject pronouns.**
   1. Il ne veut pas manger les escargots.
   2. Je crains les ours.
   3. Elles aiment jouer avec leurs amis.
   4. Nous voudrions aller dans la lune.
   5. Tu prends du café.
   6. Ils feront un bonhomme de neige.
   7. Vous comprenez la leçon.
   8. Elle décroche le téléphone.

   a. They (fem.) like to play with their friends.
   b. You (singular informal) are having coffee.
   c. He does not want to eat the snails.
   d. She picks up the phone.
   e. We would like to go to the moon.
   f. I am afraid of bears.
   g. They (masc.) will make a snowman.
   h. You (plural) understand the lesson.

L. Tell which subject pronoun you would use to begin each sentence if you were writing the pronoun in French.
   modèle: He rides the train. *il*
   1. *We* spend a long time at the table.
   2. M. and Mme Dupont, *you* are sitting in the wrong seats.
   3. *She* is going to Toulouse.
   4. *They* are handsome.
   5. *I* forgot to send the letter.
   6. Paul, *you* are my best friend.

avoir (to have)

When we speak about subject/verb agreement or verb conjugations, we are referring to the manner in which a verb changes its form in accordance with its subject (noun or pronoun). In the readings and dialogues of this chapter, you have seen all the forms of the conjugation of the verb *avoir* in the present tense. Here they are in a table.

j'ai *(I have)*	nous avons *(we have)*
tu as *(you have)*	vous avez *(you have)*
il, elle a *(he, she has)*	ils, elles ont *(they have)*

Notice that the form *avez* is always used with *vous* whether *vous* is plural or singular-formal. The verb *avoir* means "to have." However, in some idiomatic expressions in French, *avoir* is used where in English we would use "to be." In this chapter we have seen one such idiom:

Quel âge as-tu? (literally, *What age do you have?*)
J'ai 9 ans. (literally, *I have 9 years.*)

M. Write the correct form of the verb *avoir* in the blank.
1. Quel âge est-ce que tu _____?
2. J' _____ treize ans.
3. Combien d'enfants est-ce que vous _____?
4. Nous _____ deux enfants.
5. Mon frère _____ neuf ans.
6. Ils _____ un fils et une fille.
7. M. et Mme Plouvin _____ deux fils.

N. Answer these questions about the Dupont and Plouvin families.
1. Quel âge a Jean-Luc?
2. Combien d'enfants ont M. et Mme Plouvin?
3. Est-ce que Denis a un frère?
4. Quel âge a Anne?
5. Combien de fils ont M. et Mme Dupont?
6. Quel âge a Paul?

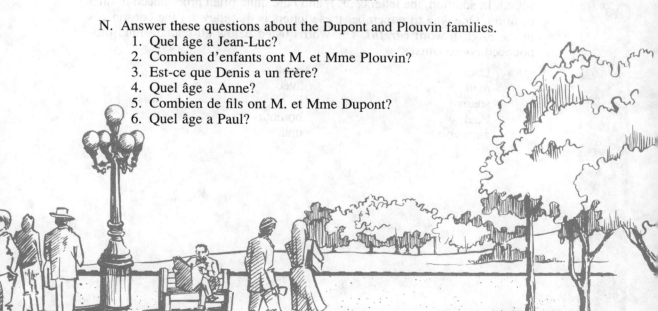

O. What about your family?
   1. Quel âge est-ce que tu as?
   2. Combien de frères et de sœurs est-ce que tu as?
   3. Comment s'appelle ton frère? Et ta sœur?
   4. Quel âge a ton frère? Et ta sœur?
   5. Combien de sœurs a ton père? Et ta mère?

P. In French, ask a classmate his age. Then ask about his family—number, names, and ages of brothers and sisters. Write down your findings to report to the rest of the class.

prononciation

final consonants

Most consonants, when found at the very end of a word, are not pronounced in French. Observe the final consonants in these words:

ans	Plouvin
et	ton
enfant	Denis
comptez	combien
vous	deux

There are some exceptions to this general pattern. In this chapter, for example, you have learned that the word *fils* is pronounced with a final /s/ sound. In addition, the letters *c, r, f,* and *l* are quite often pronounced in final position. One way to remember these letters is that they are the consonants in the English word **careful.** The words listed below all contain final pronounced consonants.

Luc	quel
neuf	avec
sœur	il
Paul	bonjour
au revoir	mal

Occasionally, some final consonants, which are not normally pronounced, are pronounced when the next word begins with a vowel sound. This phenomenon is known as *liaison*. Liaison occurs only in limited grammatical contexts. In this chapter, two such contexts can be observed. The first is liaison between subject pronouns and verbs beginning with a vowel:

nous$_{(z)}$avons ils$_{(z)}$ont
vous$_{(z)}$avez elles$_{(z)}$ont

The second is liaison after numbers. Compare the following:

un un$_{(n)}$enfant
deux deux$_{(z)}$ans
trois trois$_{(z)}$escargots

Numbers follow their own set of pronunciation rules. You may have noticed that in counting, the numbers *cinq, six, sept, huit, neuf,* and *dix* have pronounced final consonants. Before a word beginning with a vowel sound, the *x* of *six* and *dix* is pronounced with a /z/ sound, and the *f* of *neuf* is pronounced with a /v/ sound. Compare the following:

six six$_{(z)}$enfants
neuf neuf$_{(v)}$ans
dix dix$_{(z)}$escargots

In general, French families are very closely knit. Most people in France place family as their number one priority. Many French mothers do not work outside the home, and their time is spent mostly for the family in doing housework, grocery shopping, and cooking. Families in which the mother works, even part-time, still try to have one meal a day where they can all sit around the table to share and discuss ideas at length. The French consider this time an essential part of family life. French young people who go away to a university in France usually pick the one that is closest to their parents so that they can go home as many weekends as possible. There is great family loyalty and a desire to preserve family values and traditions. Although divorce is on the increase in France, it is much less common than in America. In 1989, for example, the percentage of marriages in America that ended in divorce was 50%, compared to only 15% in France. Many couples in France are choosing to remain childless or to have only one child. The French government, recognizing the potential for future economic problems this tendency may cause, has begun to give incentives to couples to have more children. These are in the form of *allocations familiales* (money allotments) and various reductions in expenses and fares for large families.

chapitre trois

chez la famille Plouvin

Actes 16, 31 Crois au Seigneur Jésus, et tu seras sauvé, toi et ta famille.

3 3 3 3 3 3 3 3 3 3

Shortly after their arrival in Toulouse, the Dupont family is invited to the Plouvins' house for dinner. After their meal, the Dupont family, the Plouvin family, and Mme Plouvin's parents, M. et Mme Boulanger, retire to the living room to visit. They are looking at a family photo album.

	Mme Plouvin:	Voici une photo de mon frère. Il s'appelle André.
	Mme Dupont:	Tiens, un frère? Quel âge a ton frère?
right?	Mme Plouvin:	Il a 25 ans. Il est **jeune**, *n'est-ce pas*?
	Anne:	Est-ce qu'il est **marié**?
this is	Jean-Luc:	Oui, et voici une **photo** de sa femme. *C'est* ma tante Margot.
	Anne:	Elle est **petite**.
	Jean-Luc:	Voici une **autre** photo de Margot.
is this?	Anne:	*Est-ce* son **bébé**?
	M. Boulanger:	Ah oui, c'est ma **petite-fille**. Elle s'appelle Georgette, *après moi*, George Boulanger.
after me		

Try to guess the meaning of the boldfaced words from their context without consulting the glossary.

vocabulaire

les parents

Georges 68 Boulanger   Marie 67

Philippe 41 Plouvin   Sophie 39

André 25 Boulanger   Margot 23

Denis 15   Jean-Luc 9   Georgette 1

Georges est le grand-père de Jean-Luc.
Marie est la grand-mère de Denis et de Georgette.
Denis est le petit-fils de Georges.
André est l'oncle de Denis.
Margot est la tante de Denis.
Georgette est la nièce de Philippe.
Jean-Luc est le neveu d'André.
Denis est le cousin de Georgette.
Georgette est la cousine de Jean-Luc.

A. Complete the statements about the family tree using the statements under the tree as a model.

1. Sophie est _____ de Georgette.
2. Marie est _____ de Jean-Luc.
3. Jean-Luc est _____ de Georgette.
4. Georgette est _____ de Georges.
5. Denis est _____ de Margot.
6. Philippe est _____ de Georgette.

B. Répondez.
1. Qui est le grand-père de Georgette?
2. Comment s'appelle la nièce de Sophie?
3. Qui est le petit-fils de Marie? (choose one)
4. Comment s'appelle le frère de Sophie?
5. André est le mari de Marie, n'est-ce pas?
6. Qui est la cousine de Denis?

acquaintances

le voisin   *the neighbor (m.)*
la voisine   *the neighbor (f.)*
l'ami   *the friend (m.)*
l'amie   *the friend (f.)*
le garçon   *the boy*
la jeune fille   *the girl*

more family relationships

le beau-père   *the father-in-law or the stepfather*
la belle-mère   *the mother-in-law or the stepmother*
le beau-frère   *the brother-in-law or the stepbrother*
la belle-sœur   *the sister-in-law or the stepsister*
le beau-fils   *the son-in-law or the stepson*
la belle-fille   *the daughter-in-law or the stepdaughter*

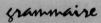

grammaire

possessive of nouns

In English, you can express possession in two ways:

- by adding *'s* to the noun–for example, my father*'s* brother.
- with the preposition *of* and the noun–for example, the brother of my father.

In French, however, nouns can show possession only with the preposition *of* and the noun–for example, *le frère de mon père.*

When *de* is followed by the definite article *le,* the two words are always contracted to form *du:*

la mère de la fille   **but**   la mère *du* garçon

C. Express the following in French.
   modèle: Robert's sister   *la sœur de Robert*
   the brother's friend   *l'ami du frère*
   1. my father's neighbor
   2. the sister's friend
   3. Daniel's cousin
   4. Colette's brother
   5. the (masc.) neighbor's mother
   6. the boy's grandfather
   7. the girl's grandmother
   8. the uncle's wife

D. **Qui est . . . ?** A small child is asking you questions so that he can better understand family relationships. Answer his questions clearly.

modèle: Qui est le père de mon père? *C'est ton grand-père.*
Qui est ma tante? *C'est la sœur de ta mère (de ton père).*
ou *C'est la femme de ton oncle.*

1. Qui est la fille de ma tante?
2. Qui est le frère de mon père?
3. Qui est mon cousin?
4. Qui est ma belle-sœur?
5. Qui est la mère de ma cousine?
6. Qui est ma grand-mère?
7. Qui est la femme de mon père?
8. Qui est la fille de mon frère?
9. Qui est mon neveu?

chez la famille Plouvin

les nombres

20	vingt	25	vingt-cinq
21	vingt et un	26	vingt-six
22	vingt-deux	27	vingt-sept
23	vingt-trois	28	vingt-huit
24	vingt-quatre	29	vingt-neuf

30   trente, 31 trente et un, 32 trente-deux . . .
40   quarante . . .
50   cinquante . . .
60   soixante . . .

E. Comptez.
     1. Comptez de 0 à 65 par cinq.
     2. Comptez de 20 à 68 par les nombres pairs.
     3. Comptez de 21 à 69 par les nombres impairs.

F. Express the following problems in words.
     modèle:
        25 + 9 = 34
     Vingt-cinq et neuf font trente-quatre.
        25 − 9 = 16
     Vingt-cinq moins neuf font seize.

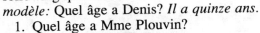

1. 10 + 20 =	6. 28 − 7 =
2. 17 + 6 =	7. 34 − 12 =
3. 15 + 29 =	8. 52 − 27 =
4. 26 + 36 =	9. 66 − 13 =
5. 41 + 18 =	10. 51 − 14 =

G. *Quel âge . . . ?* Refer to the family tree on page 26 to answer the following questions.
     modèle: Quel âge a Denis? *Il a quinze ans.*
     1. Quel âge a Mme Plouvin?
     2. Quel âge a Georgette?
     3. Quel âge a Marie Boulanger?
     4. Quel âge a Philippe?
     5. Quel âge a André Boulanger?
     6. Qui a neuf ans?
     7. Qui a soixante-huit ans?
     8. Qui a vingt-trois ans?

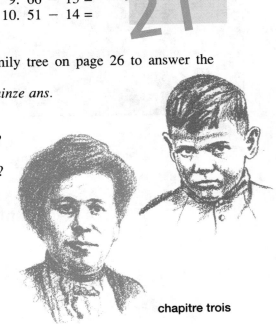

chapitre trois

H. Tell the relationship, name, and age of three members of your extended family.

modèle: Mon oncle Paul a quarante-deux ans.

plural of nouns

Most plural nouns in French are spelled with a final *s* just as they are in English: *frère–frères, sœur–sœurs.* Words that already end with an *s* remain unchanged in the plural: *fils–fils.* However, since final consonants are usually not pronounced in French, that *s* is not heard in the spoken language. Instead, the oral signal that a noun is plural is often the article that precedes it:

le frère–les frères (/lø frɛr/–/le frɛr/)
la sœur–les sœurs (/la sœr/–/le sœr/).

The third way of saying *the* in French is *les,* the plural of both *le* and *la.*

I. Make the following nouns plural.
   modèle: la cousine   *les cousines*
   1. le père
   2. la mère
   3. la voisine
   4. le fils
   5. le cousin

Just as there is a plural form for *le* and *la,* there is also a plural form for each pair of masculine and feminine possessive adjectives.

mon père	ma mère	mes parents
ton père	ta mère	tes parents
son père	sa mère	ses parents

J. Pretend you are showing pictures to your friends. Answer their questions with *c'est* (there is) or *ce sont* (there are), according to the model.
   modèle: C'est ton oncle? *Oui, c'est mon oncle.*
            Qui est-ce? (cousins) *Ce sont mes cousins.*
   1. C'est ta mère?
   2. C'est ton père?
   3. Ce sont tes frères?
   4. Ce sont tes cousins?
   5. C'est ta sœur?
   6. Qui est-ce? (voisins)
   7. Qui est-ce? (oncles)
   8. Qui est-ce? (nièce)
   9. Qui est-ce? (tantes)
   10. Qui est-ce? (belle-sœur)

Noun phrases are another grammatical context in which liaison takes place. Thus the final *s* of *les, mes, tes, ses* is pronounced as a /z/ sound before a noun beginning with a vowel. Say these words aloud:

les(z)adultes
mes(z)amis
tes(z)enfants
ses(z) oncles

être (to be)

The verb *être* like *avoir* is an irregular verb and is one of the most frequently used verbs in the French language. Here is its conjugation:

	singulier	pluriel
1ère	je suis *(I am)*	nous sommes *(we are)*
2ème	tu es *(you are)*	vous êtes *(you are)*
3ème	il, elle est *(he, she is)*	ils, elles sont *(they are)*

K. Georges Boulanger is talking to one of his family members about the family. (Refer to the family tree on page 26.) Complete each sentence with the proper form of *être* as you determine the identity of the family member who is speaking.

1. Marie et moi, nous _____ les parents de ton oncle.
2. Ton oncle _____ André.
3. Sa fille _____ Georgette.
4. Georgette _____ ta cousine.
5. Philippe et Sophie _____ tes parents.
6. Ton frère et toi, vous _____ mes petits-fils.
7. Tu _____ le frère de Denis.
8. Qui es-tu? «Je _____.»

predicate adjectives

The verb *être* is often followed by an adjective describing the subject. Such adjectives are called predicate adjectives. An example from the dialogue is "Elle est *petite*." If we were talking about several women, the sentence would read "Elles sont *petites*." Here the word *petites* is spelled with an *s* since it is describing a plural word. Adjectives in French change their form according to the words that they modify. When the noun or pronoun is singular, the adjective is singular also; when the noun or pronoun is plural, the adjective is plural. Thus the adjective is said to "agree in number" with the word it modifies. This is one type of **adjective agreement**.

Adjectives also show agreement in gender. If we were talking about a man, the sentence above would read: Il est *petit*.

Notice two things about the word *petit*:

- The final *e* has been dropped.
- The second *t* is now in final position and is, therefore, not pronounced. /pøti/

As a general rule, feminine adjectives end with the letter *e*. Therefore, if there is a consonant before the *e*, the consonant is pronounced. To form the masculine adjective, the letter *e* is dropped, and any preceding consonant is not pronounced. If we were talking about two or more men, the adjective would be plural and the sentence would read:

Ils sont petits.

Words already ending in *s* or in *x* remain unchanged in the plural:

Il est gros.   *Ils sont gros.*
Il est sérieux. *Ils sont sérieux.*

Both final *s* and final *x* are silent. The word *little*, therefore, has two spoken forms and four different spellings, depending on the word it describes:

/pøti/–*petit, petits* and /pøtit/–*petite, petites*.

Here are some other adjectives that work the same way:

feminin		masculin		
singulier	**pluriel**	**singulier**	**pluriel**	
grande	grandes	grand	grands	*big, tall*
laide	laides	laid	laids	*ugly*
bavarde	bavardes	bavard	bavards	*talkative*
blonde	blondes	blond	blonds	*blonde-haired*
intelligente	intelligentes	intelligent	intelligents	*smart*
amusante	amusantes	amusant	amusants	*funny*
intéressante	intéressantes	intéressant	intéressants	*interesting*
brune	brunes	brun	bruns	*brunette*
taquine	taquines	taquin	taquins	*fond of teasing*

Other adjectives following the same pattern have an additional spelling change in the masculine:

feminin		masculin		
singulier	**pluriel**	**singulier**	**pluriel**	
rousse	rousses	roux	roux	*red-haired*
grosse	grosses	gros	gros	*fat*
sérieuse	sérieuses	sérieux	sérieux	*serious*
silencieuse	silencieuses	silencieux	silencieux	*quiet*
heureuse	heureuses	heureux	heureux	*happy*
ennuyeuse	ennuyeuses	ennuyeux	ennuyeux	*boring*
sportive	sportives	sportif	sportifs	*athletic*

Another group of adjectives has no difference in the pronunciation of the feminine and masculine forms. This group may be divided into two types:

- The masculine form ends in a pronounced vowel.

mariée	marié	*married*
sauvée	sauvé	*saved*
âgée	âgé	*old, aged*
enchantée	enchanté	*pleased*
ravie	ravi	*delighted*
jolie	joli	*pretty, good-looking*
têtue	têtu	*stubborn*

- The masculine form already ends in an unpronounced *e*. Thus the masculine and feminine forms are identical.

jeune	jeune	*young*
riche	riche	*rich*
pauvre	pauvre	*poor*
mince	mince	*thin*
timide	timide	*shy*
bête	bête	*stupid*
triste	triste	*sad*
sympathique	sympathique	*nice*
célibataire	célibataire	*unmarried*

chapitre trois

L. Tell the same characteristic of the masculine counterpart of the person in each of these sentences.

modèle: Ma mère est petite.   *Mon père est petit aussi.*
1. Ma sœur est bavarde.
2. Sa grand-mère est grande.
3. La voisine est silencieuse.
4. Ta cousine est sportive.
5. Ma petite-fille est sauvée.
6. La belle-sœur est têtue.
7. Sa mère est timide.
8. Ma tante est jeune.

M. Say that the person in the sentence has the opposite characteristic. Be sure to make proper adjective agreement.

modèle: Mon oncle est grand.   *Mon oncle est petit.*
1. Mon frère est bête.
2. La cousine est jolie.
3. Ma fille est triste.
4. Son oncle est silencieux.
5. Ton voisin est jeune.
6. Sa sœur est riche.
7. Le fils est gros.
8. Ta nièce est mariée.

chez la famille Plouvin

N. Make the original sentences in exercise M plural.
   modèle: Mon oncle est grand.   *Mes oncles sont grands.*

O. Make plural the sentences that are singular, and make singular the sentences that are plural.
   modèle: Je suis grand.   *Nous sommes grands.*
            Vous êtes sportives.   *Tu es sportive.*
   1. Je suis petit.
   2. Tu es intéressante.
   3. Ils sont têtus.
   4. Nous sommes rousses.
   5. Elle est sympathique.
   6. Vous êtes amusants.
   7. Il est ennuyeux.
   8. Elles sont blondes.
   9. Vous êtes bavard.
   10. Je suis sportive.

P. Describe yourself using the structure, "Je suis . . ." Use as many different adjectives as you can.

Q. Bring in pictures of your family, friends, or neighbors. Be prepared to give a brief description of each person.

36

final consonant sounds and mute e

The presence or absence of a consonant sound at the end of a word in French is often an oral signal of the word's gender–for example, *petit–petite*. The masculine adjective ends in a silent consonant that is pronounced in the feminine form. The addition of a mute *e* (silent *e*) in the spelling reflects this pronunciation change. A French person clearly articulates all final consonant sounds with a crisp release that is much more distinctly heard than final consonant sounds in English. Compare the pronunciation of the words in each of these pairs:

laid	laide
gros	grosse
silencieux	silencieuse
petit	petite
bavard	bavarde

In fact, as long as it is followed by a mute *e*, a final consonant sound is always precisely articulated, even in those words not involving gender distinctions:

soixante	fille
rose	bête
Philippe	monde
tante	âge

Now consider the pronunciation difference between each of these masculine and feminine pairs:

voisin /vwazɛ̃/	voisine /vwazin/
cousin /kuzɛ̃/	cousine /kuzin/
taquin /takɛ̃/	taquine /takin/
brun /brɛ̃/	brune /bryn/

In these words the addition of the mute *e* indicates more than a gender change. Notice that the vowel quality also changes from a nasal vowel to a

non-nasal (or oral) vowel. Nasal vowels will be discussed in greater detail in Chapter 9; but for now, there are several important principles to learn. The letter *n* at the end of a word is not pronounced, but the letter *n* followed by a mute *e* is pronounced. The vowel preceding a silent *n* is nasal, but the vowel preceding a pronounced *n* is oral. Practice with these words, some of which you have not seen before:

nasal vowel

bon	son
mon	garçon
Jean	an
bien	Plouvin
combien	un

oral vowel + n

jeune	téléphone
Simone	âne
Martine	cuisine
mène	scène
une	lune

You may have already noticed that many French words are similar or identical to English words in spelling. Many French words became a part of the English language after 1066 when William the Conqueror *(Guillaume le Conquérant)* defeated England. This defeat is known as the Norman Conquest. As the conquerors, the French made their language the official language of England. Any public or official business had to be transacted in French. The Anglo-Saxons adopted the French vocabulary in the areas of government, the judicial system, education, the military, and professions known only to the upper classes. Whenever the Anglo-Saxon commoners addressed the French nobility, they were forced to speak French; however, they continued to speak among themselves in their own dialects, which were Germanic in origin. Hence they would refer to their animals in Old English, but when they, as servants, placed the food on the nobleman's table they would use the French word. Therefore, in many cases words from both languages are part of modern English:

of Germanic origin	of French origin
hen	poultry *(poulet)*
sheep	mutton *(mouton)*
calf	veal *(veau)*
cow	beef *(bœuf)*
swine	pork *(porc)*

chez la famille Plouvin

Students of French are at a great advantage in being aware of this because they will often be able to figure out what a French word means by recognizing its similarity to an English word. Try to guess the English equivalent for the following French words.

le juge
le gouvernement
le tailleur
la classe
l'armée

However, there exist between French and English many "false cognates" (*faux amis*) which look alike, but are not related in meaning. Therefore, to assume that *all* words that look alike in French and English mean the same thing can cause some problems in understanding and in communication. Here are some examples:

in French	in English
le coin	the corner, not "coin"
le collège	the middle school, not "college"
la lecture	the reading, not "lecture"
sensible	sensitive, not "sensible "
impair	odd number, not "to impair"
joli	pretty, not "jolly"

dans le salon

Psaume 119, 105 Ta parole est une lampe à mes pieds, Et une lumière sur mon sentier.

dialogue

The Dupont family is still at the home of the Plouvins. At times the conversation is a little difficult as the members of the Dupont family try to say something and are not sure of the French word or as the Plouvins use words that the Duponts do not yet know. Paul is interested in photography and asks Mr. Plouvin what kind of *caméra* he uses. Mr. Plouvin explains to him that a *caméra* is used in making movies or videos, but for photographs or slides one uses an *appareil photographique,* more commonly called just an *appareil.* The Dupont children feel much less awkward now about asking the names of different objects around them.

What's this?	Anne:	*Qu'est-ce que c'est?* (pointing to a chair)
	Jean-Luc:	C'est une chaise.
	Paul:	C'est aussi une chaise? (pointing to the armchair)
there is our dog in	Denis:	Non, c'est un fauteuil. Ah, *voilà notre chien dans le fauteuil.*
mean	Anne:	Comment s'appelle-t-il? Il a l'air *méchant.*
but	Denis:	Il s'appelle Milou. Il est grand, *mais* il n'est pas
ferocious		*féroce.*

appareil pho

Qu'est-ce que c'est?

un mur
une radio
un rideau
un coin
une pendule
une fenêtre
un tableau
une porte
une télévision
une lampe
une chaise
une cage
une étagère
une table
un chien
un divan
un chat
un fauteuil
un tapis
une plante

Here are some useful prepositions to answer the question *Où est . . . ?* (Where is . . . ?):

dans	*in*	entre	*between*
sur	*on*	devant	*in front of*
sous	*under*	derrière	*behind*

A. Tell where the following items are located according to the drawing above.

   modèle: Où est la lampe? *Elle est sur le plancher.*

   1. Où est la radio?
   2. Où est la télévision?
   3. Où est la chaise?
   4. Où est l'oiseau?
   5. Où est la pendule?
   6. Où est le chat?

graphique

dans le salon

grammatical gender

In Chapter 2 we saw that biological gender (male and female) determines the article or possessive adjective (e.g., *le père/mon père* and *la mère/ma mère)*. French has not only biological gender but also grammatical gender. *All* nouns, whether referring to people, places, things, or ideas have gender. That means that *every* inanimate object in French is masculine or feminine. For example, *curtain* (le rideau) is always masculine whereas *table* (la table) is always feminine. There is no logical reason for considering one word masculine and another feminine. The association of gender with particular nouns is a result of the historical development of the French language and not of some characteristic of the noun itself. For instance, the French word for *purse* (le sac) is masculine, while the word for *necktie* (la cravate) is feminine. The closest thing to gender of nonliving objects in English would be to refer to a car or a boat as "she." For an English-speaking person learning French, it is important to learn the gender of a noun along with the noun itself.

indefinite articles

When not referring to a specific noun, the French use the indefinite articles *un* and *une:*

C'est un chien.   *This is a dog.*
C'est une photo.   *This is a picture.*

B. Dans le salon . . . Tell what is in your living room by substituting the noun in parentheses for the underlined noun in the sentence, making any necessary changes in the article.

modèle: Nous avons un <u>divan</u> dans le salon. (chaise)
        Nous avons une chaise dans le salon.

1. Nous avons un <u>tableau</u> derrière le divan. (fauteuil)
2. J'ai un <u>rideau</u> devant la fenêtre. (table)
3. J'ai une <u>étagère</u> sous la fenêtre. (radio)
4. Une <u>lampe</u> est sur le plancher. (tapis)
5. Un <u>oiseau</u> est sur la table. (télévision)
6. Nous avons un <u>tableau</u> entre la porte et la fenêtre. (pendule)

The plural of *un* and *une* is *des*. In English we can express the plural of indefinite articles in the following ways:

I have *a* book. (singular)
I have books. (plural)
I have *some* books. (plural)

Except in idiomatic expressions in French (some of which you will learn later in this chapter), there will always be some sort of determiner (article, possessive adjective, etc.) before a noun. Therefore, the plural of *J'ai un livre* must have a determiner and can be only *J'ai des livres*.

C. Express the following sentences in the singular.
    modèle: Il a des photos. *Il a une photo.*
      1. Elle a des frères.
      2. Nous avons des chiens.
      3. Ils ont des lampes.
      4. J'ai des plantes.
      5. Tu as des fauteuils.
      6. Vous avez des pendules.
      7. Elles ont des cousins.

dans le salon

D. Express the following sentences in the plural.
   modèle: J'ai une sœur. *J'ai des sœurs.*
   1. J'ai une Bible.
   2. Jérôme a un cousin.
   3. Nous avons un divan.
   4. Tu as une fenêtre.
   5. Elles ont un chat.
   6. Vous avez une tante.

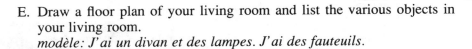

E. Draw a floor plan of your living room and list the various objects in your living room.
   modèle: J'ai un divan et des lampes. J'ai des fauteuils.

some idiomatic uses of *avoir*

You have learned many ways to describe people in French using the verb *être* and a predicate adjective. You have also learned that age is expressed in French with the verb *avoir;* and therefore, a Frenchman does not say, "I am 15," but rather "I have 15 years." The French also use the verb *avoir* where we would use forms of the verb *to be* plus a predicate adjective. For example, in English we would say, "I am hungry" whereas the French would say, *J'ai faim,* which translates literally, "I have hunger." Here are some common idiomatic uses of *avoir* which you will be using:

avoir faim	*to be hungry*
avoir soif	*to be thirsty*
avoir sommeil	*to be sleepy*
avoir peur (de)	*to be afraid (of)*
avoir raison	*to be right*
avoir tort	*to be wrong*
avoir froid	*to be cold*
avoir chaud	*to be warm*

F. Answer the following questions affirmatively.
   modèle: Tu as faim? *Oui, j'ai faim.*
   1. Tu as soif?
   2. Elle a raison?
   3. Tu as froid?
   4. Vous avez sommeil?
   5. Anne a peur du chien?

G. Express the following in French.
   modèle: He is wrong. *Il a tort.*
   1. I am sleepy.
   2. She is warm.
   3. We are afraid.
   4. You are right.
   5. They are hungry.

H. Put the correct form of *avoir* or *être* in the blank.

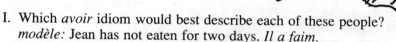

   1. Il _____ raison.
   2. Nous _____ timides.
   3. Elles _____ amusantes.
   4. Tu _____ faim.
   5. Vous _____ peur du chat.
   6. Elle _____ petite.
   7. Ils _____ soif.

I. Which *avoir* idiom would best describe each of these people?
   modèle: Jean has not eaten for two days. *Il a faim.*
   1. I think that Toulouse is the capital of France.
   2. It is −3°F, and Céleste is not wearing an overcoat.
   3. We were studying for final exams and slept for only three hours last night.
   4. You have been eating but have had nothing to drink.
   5. It is 90°F in the shade, and my air conditioning unit is broken.
   6. Jean-Pierre says that the French word *joli* and the English word *jolly* are false cognates.
   7. The neighbors hear a strange sound in their basement and think it is a burglar.

negation

Sentences can be made negative in French by placing *ne* before the verb and *pas* after the verb:

   Nous sommes bavards.   *We are talkative.*
   Nous **ne** sommes **pas** bavards.   *We are not talkative.*

• *Ne* becomes *n'* before a verb beginning with a vowel:

   Il est féroce.
   Il **n'**est pas féroce.

J. Pretend you are talking to a person who answers all your questions
negatively. Tell what he would say.

modèle: Le chien est méchant? *Non, le chien n'est pas méchant.*

Tu es petit? *Non, je ne suis pas petit.*

1. Tu as sommeil?
2. Le chat est joli?
3. Tu es têtu?
4. Ta sœur est timide?
5. Tu as peur?

- The indefinite determiners–*un, une,* or *des*–become *de* or *d'* following
a negative verb:

J'ai un frère. *Je n'ai pas de frère.*
Nous avons des livres. *Nous n'avons pas de livres.*

K. Make the following sentences negative.

1. J'ai une sœur.
2. Nous avons des enfants.
3. Ils ont un téléphone.
4. Paul a des cousins.
5. Vous avez une télévision.

L. Answer the following questions about yourself negatively or affirmatively, according to your own situation:

modèle: Tu as une tante? *Non, je n'ai pas de tante.*

Toi et ton père, vous êtes grands? *Oui, nous sommes grands.*

1. Tu as soif?
2. Tu t'appelles Raoul?
3. Tu as un chien?
4. Tu as un frère (une sœur)?
5. Toi et ta mère, vous êtes blonds?
6. Toi et ton ami(e), vous êtes bavards?
7. Toi et ton voisin, vous avez peur de mon chien?

chapitre quatre

possessive adjectives (cont.)

Until now we have used possessive adjectives indicating that only one person is expressing possession. For instance, if I (je) am the owner, I say *mon chien, ma tante,* or *mes livres.* But consider this line from the dialogue:

> Voilà notre chien dans le fauteuil.

Who is the owner of the dog? Denis is speaking, yet he does not say *mon chien.* Since Denis is speaking for his whole family, he uses *notre,* the French word for *our.* Here is a complete table of the possessive adjectives. The sentences to the left indicate the owner(s).

		masc.	fem.	plural
J'ai un frère, une sœur, et des cousins.	Voici	**mon** frère	**ma** sœur	**mes** cousins.
Tu as un frère, une sœur, et des cousins.	Voici	**ton** frère	**ta** sœur	**tes** cousins.
Il a un frère, une sœur, et des cousins.	Voici	**son** frère	**sa** sœur	**ses** cousins.
Elle a un frère, une sœur, et des cousins.	Voici	**son** frère	**sa** sœur	**ses** cousins.
Nous avons un frère, une sœur, et des cousins.	Voici	**notre** frère	**notre** sœur	**nos** cousins.
Vous avez un frère, une sœur, et des cousins.	Voici	**votre** frère	**votre** sœur	**vos** cousins.
Ils ont un frère, une sœur, et des cousins.	Voici	**leur** frère	**leur** sœur	**leurs** cousins.
Elles ont un frère, une sœur, et des cousins.	Voici	**leur** frère	**leur** sœur	**leurs** cousins.

Notice that *notre, votre,* and *leur* do not have separate masculine and feminine forms.

M. Substitute the correct form of the possessive adjective in parentheses for the article in italics in the sentences below. (Change the form of the possessive adjective, if necessary.)

modèle: Elle est dans *le* fauteuil. (son) *Elle est dans son fauteuil.*

1. Voilà *le* livre sur la chaise. (son)
2. *Le* chien est derrière le divan. (votre)
3. *La* pendule est grande. (ton)
4. C'est *la* Bible devant la fenêtre. (notre)
5. Elle a une photo de *la* mère. (mon)
6. Pascal et René sont dans *les* fauteuils. (leur)

N. As shown in the sentences and the table above, say in French, ''Here is . . .'' plus whatever noun the person in the given sentence owns.

modèle: J'ai un chien. *Voici mon chien.*

1. Bruno a une Bible.
2. Nous avons un tapis.
3. Tu as des plantes.
4. Il a un chat.
5. Elle a un chat.
6. Elles ont un chat.
7. Il a des chats.
8. Vous avez des lampes.
9. Suzanne et Hélène ont un oiseau.
10. J'ai une radio.
11. Nous avons une radio.
12. Nous avons des radios.

O. Pretend that you are Anne or Denis speaking for your family. Answer the following questions about your living room by referring to the drawing below.

modèle: Est-ce votre salon? *Oui, c'est notre salon.*

1. Comment est votre salon? (Il est . . .)
2. Votre chat est sous la table? (Non, . . .)
3. Le tapis est sur le plafond?
4. Vous avez deux fenêtres?
5. Où est la pendule?
6. Le fauteuil est derrière la fenêtre?
7. Où est la télévision?
8. Où est la lampe?
9. Le livre est entre la radio et la pendule?
10. Qu'est-ce que c'est là-bas, dans le tableau?

P. Give a brief description of your own living room, limiting yourself to the grammatical structures and vocabulary you have learned to this point.

elision

Certain one-syllable words lose their final vowel when followed by a word that begins with a vowel sound. This "elision" occurs regularly in only eleven words in French, seven of which you have already seen: *je, ne, ce, de, le, la,* and *que.* Compare these sentences:

Je suis blonde.	*J'ai* deux frères.
Ils *ne* sont pas grands.	Ils *n'ont* pas de télévision.
Ce sont mes voisins.	*C'est* ma femme.
Voici une photo *de* Denis.	Voici une photo *d'Anne.*
Voilà *le* chat.	Voilà *l'oiseau.*
Où est *la* radio?	Où est *l'étagère?*
Est-ce *que* Paul est marié?	Est-ce *qu'il* est marié?

Notice that the elision in these sentences involves dropping a final *e,* except for the word *la.*

liaison

The /z/ sound of liaison is heard after the definite article *les,* the indefinite article *des,* and all the possessive adjectives ending in *s,* when any of these articles or adjectives are followed by a vowel sound. Compare these phrases:

les cousins	les$_{(z)}$escargots
des voisins	des$_{(z)}$amis
mes frères	mes$_{(z)}$autos
tes Bibles	tes$_{(z)}$oncles
ses livres	ses$_{(z)}$amies
nos chaises	nos$_{(z)}$enfants
vos sœurs	vos$_{(z)}$églises
leurs filles	leurs$_{(z)}$étagères

Liaison also occurs with the indefinite article *un* and the singular possessive adjectives ending in *n,* only here it is an /n/ sound that is heard rather than a /z/. Notice the difference in these phrases:

un tapis	un$_{(n)}$an
mon fauteuil	mon$_{(n)}$ami
ton livre	ton$_{(n)}$oncle
son chien	son$_{(n)}$enfant

This liaison form of the singular possessive adjective is *always* used before a vowel sound, even if the word that follows is feminine:

une étagère	mon$_{(n)}$étagère
une amie	ton$_{(n)}$amie
une église	son$_{(n)}$église

culture

Frenchmen love their privacy. They want to feel secure in their own quiet, little world. This private nature manifests itself in a number of ways. Most French people write their return address on the *back* of the envelope, and some do not even write a return address at all. A Frenchman sending a post card will often mail it in an envelope so that no one can read its message. It is not at all uncommon in apartment buildings to find only a last name or a last name with initials on a Frenchman's mailbox. Many people are neighbors for years without ever knowing each other's names. When a Frenchman buys land to build a house, the first thing he builds is a fence around the property. A missionary to France must cope with this private nature that makes meeting and getting to know people difficult. Missionaries may become discouraged as they walk by stone and wrought-iron fences block after block in a French city. In spite of their great desire to become acquainted with people and to give them the gospel, they often find it difficult to penetrate the walls that Frenchman have built around themselves to insure their privacy and security.

Those fences usually have huge dogs behind them, too. When Americans try to imagine the kind of dog a Frenchman would own, they usually think of a nicely trimmed French poodle. However, few French people have miniature poodles. Many of them prefer large dogs—German shepherds, Dobermans, etc.—and they love to spoil their dogs. Dogs accompany their masters just about anywhere—to the market, to museums, even to restaurants, and no one thinks twice about it. Some Frenchmen even take their dogs to dog beauty parlors.

aller en ville

Jean 14, 6 Jésus lui dit: Je suis le chemin, la vérité, et la vie. Nul ne vient au Père que par moi.

5 5 5 5 5 5 5 5 5 5

dialogues

Part of the adjustment that the Duponts make is learning their way around Toulouse without the use of a car, since they have not yet been able to purchase one. Mr. Dupont wants to go to the university to register for language school in the fall. Before leaving he gets some advice from Mr. Plouvin.

M. Dupont: Pour aller à l'université, je vais en taxi?

M. Plouvin: Ah, non, le taxi est bien trop cher. Prenez plutôt l'autobus ou le métro. C'est beaucoup moins cher.

M. Dupont: Quel est le numéro de l'autobus?

M. Plouvin: C'est le bus numéro 21.

M. Dupont: Et pour l'université, quel est l'arrêt?

M. Plouvin: C'est l'arrêt après la poste.

M. Dupont: Merci beaucoup.

M. Plouvin: De rien.

Mr. Dupont has taken the bus as Mr. Plouvin suggested, but he got off at the wrong stop. He decides to go the rest of the way on foot. He asks a passer-by for directions.

M. Dupont: Pardon, monsieur. Où est l'université, s'il vous plaît?

Le passant: C'est par là. Montez la rue, tournez à gauche au coin et allez tout droit. Et puis passez par la poste et tournez à droite à la première rue.

M. Dupont: C'est donc près de la poste?

Le passant: Mais non. Descendez la rue et traversez le pont. L'université n'est pas loin de l'église St. Pierre.

M. Dupont: Vous êtes très gentil. Merci bien, monsieur.

Le passant: Il n'y a pas de quoi.

chapitre cinq

maintenant en anglais . . .

Mr. Dupont: In order to go to the university, do I go by taxi?
Mr. Plouvin: Oh no, the taxi is too expensive. Take the bus or the subway. It's much less expensive.
Mr. Dupont: What is the number of the bus?
Mr. Plouvin: It's bus number 21.
Mr. Dupont: And for the university, what is the bus stop?
Mr. Plouvin: It's the stop after the post office.
Mr. Dupont: Thank you very much.
Mr. Plouvin: You're welcome. (idiomatic)

Mr. Dupont: Excuse me, sir. Where is the university, please?
The passer-by: It's that way. Go up the street, turn left at the corner, and go straight ahead. And then go past the post office and turn right at the first street.
Mr. Dupont: So it's near the post office?
The passer-by: Why, no. (Literally, ''but no'') Go down the street, and cross the bridge. The university is not far from the St. Pierre church.
Mr. Dupont: You are very kind. Thanks a lot, sir.
The passer-by: Think nothing of it. (idiomatic)

vocabulaire

des moyens de transport

Comment est-ce que vous allez à l'école?
Je vais . . . en voiture/en auto. (I go . . . by car.)

en taxi.

en autobus.

en métro.

en moto.

en vélomoteur.

à vélo.

à pied.

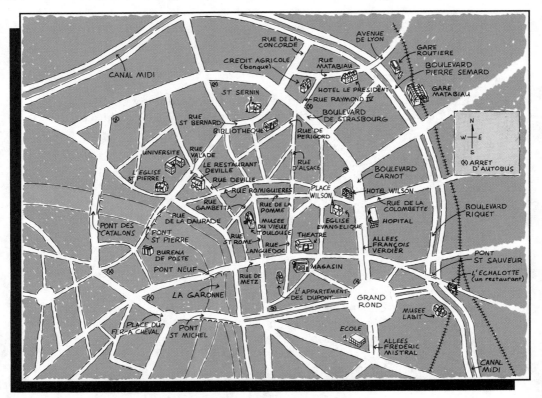

A. You are at the place given, and someone asks you how to get somewhere else. Give directions according to the **plan de Toulouse**.

modèle: l'université . . . Où est le musée du vieux Toulouse?

> *Montez la rue Deville. Tournez à gauche à la deuxième rue. Montez la rue Gambetta. Tournez à droite à la rue Saint Rome et descendez. Le musée est à droite.*

1. le Restaurant Deville . . . Où est le Pont Neuf?
2. la gare routière . . . Où est l'église St. Sernin?
3. le magasin . . . Où est la banque?
4. l'école . . . Où est l'hôpital?
5. le Musée Labit . . . Où est l'Hôtel Wilson?
6. l'église évangélique . . . Où est l'université?
7. l'Hôtel le Président . . . Où est l'arrêt d'autobus?
8. la bibliothèque . . . Où est le Restaurant Deville?

question formation

You have seen several ways to ask questions:

- With intonation alone–In speech this is simply the voice rising at the end of the question. This is an informal method of asking questions in conversation.

    C'est donc près de la poste?

- With *n'est-ce pas?*–The words *n'est-ce pas?* can be added to the end of any statement to change it to a question.

    Il est jeune.
    Il est jeune, n'est-ce pas?

- With *est-ce que*–The words *est-ce que* can be added to any sentence to change it to a question.

    Il est marié.
    Est-ce qu'il est marié?

- With inversion–Inversion is switching the subject with the conjugated verb.

    Combien d'enfants avez-vous?

Since inversion is the most formal of all the methods, you will not hear inversion often in informal conversation. Its usage will be restricted mostly to questions with these situations:

    with *vous*: Quel âge avez-vous?
    in certain idioms: Comment t'appelles-tu?
    with subject nouns in short sentences: Où est le chien?

In informal conversation *est-ce que* is usually used in the place of inversion:

    Comment est-ce que vous allez à l'école?

B. Make the following sentences into questions three different ways: using intonation, *n'est-ce pas,* and *est-ce que.*
   1. C'est mon bus.
   2. L'hôtel est près de la banque.
   3. Nous allons en taxi.
   4. Tu as quinze ans.
   5. Mme Dupont a peur des chats.

C. Change these questions with inversion into questions using *est-ce que*.
   modèle: Combien de frères as-tu? *Combien de frères est-ce que tu as?*
   1. Comment allez-vous à l'école?
   2. Allons-nous à pied?
   3. Où vas-tu?
   4. Est-il célibataire?
   5. As-tu faim?

D. In pairs, find out the following information from your partner by asking
   appropriate questions.
   1. his/her age
   2. if he/she is shy
   3. if he/she is hungry
   4. where he/she is going tonight *(ce soir)*
   5. how he/she goes to school
   6. if he/she has a dog or cat
   7. if he/she is afraid of dogs or cats

ordinal numbers

The French word for *first* has two forms:

   premier (masc.) and *première* (fem.)

To form the other ordinal numbers (second, third, fourth, etc.), add *-ième* to
the last consonant of the cardinal number (*deux, trois, quatr-*, etc.). Only
premier/première shows gender distinction. Here are the cardinal numbers
from one to ten with their corresponding ordinal numbers:

un, une	premier, première (1er, 1ère)
deux	deuxième (2e)
trois	troisième (3e)
quatre	quatrième (4e)
cinq	cinquième (5e)
six	sixième (6e)
sept	septième (7e)
huit	huitième (8e)
neuf	neuvième (9e)
dix	dixième (10e)

Notice the *u* after the *q* in cinquième and the *v* in *neuvième*.

E. Give the equivalent ordinal number.
   1. sept
   2. deux
   3. huit
   4. cinq
   5. une
   6. quatre

F. Tell how each of these students ranks in his class according to the number indicated.
   modèle: Pauline (3ᵉ)   *Pauline est la troisième.*
           Claude (7ᵉ)   *Claude est le septième.*
   1. Marcel (2ᵉ)
   2. Pascal (1ᵉʳ)
   3. Suzanne (9ᵉ)
   4. Alain (10ᵉ)
   5. Elisabeth (4ᵉ)

the preposition *à* and the definite article

Observe the preposition *à* (at, to) followed by the definite article in the following directions:

   Allez au musée.
   Allez à la poste.
   Allez à l'église.
   Allez aux magasins.

Two of the situations require the contraction of à and the article: *au musée* and *aux magasins.* In English, contractions are optional. We can say, "I am here," or "I'm here." However, in French the contractions *au* and *aux* are obligatory. The right-hand side of the following table shows what *à* plus a definite article will look like before a noun.

   à + le = au
   à + la = à la
   à + l' = à l'
   à + les = aux

The letter *h* in French is silent. Since the first sound you hear in *hôtel* and *hôpital* is a vowel sound, there will be elision and liaison, just as though the *h* were not even there:

   à l'hôtel   aux₍z₎hôtels

G. Six people are preparing to distribute tracts. As each person suggests where he or she might begin, the pastor, who has already decided who will go where, gives them each an assigned destination:

modèle: Maurice: Je vais à l'école. (magasin)

        Le pasteur: *Non, allez au magasin.*

1. Janine: Je vais à l'université. (poste)
2. Alexis: Je vais à l'hôtel. (églises)
3. Jean-Pierre: Je vais au théâtre. (hôpital)
4. Pauline: Je vais à la gare. (restaurant)
5. Lydie: Je vais au musée. (banques)
6. Adolphe: Je vais aux magasins. (métro)

H. Suppose that a person expresses the following needs or wishes to you. Tell him where he can have them fulfilled.

modèle: I am hungry. *Allez au restaurant.*

1. I need some stamps.
2. I want to cash a check.
3. I want to catch a train.
4. I need to catch a bus.
5. I would like to see a play.
6. I want to learn French.
7. I need to talk to a pastor.
8. I need to see a doctor.

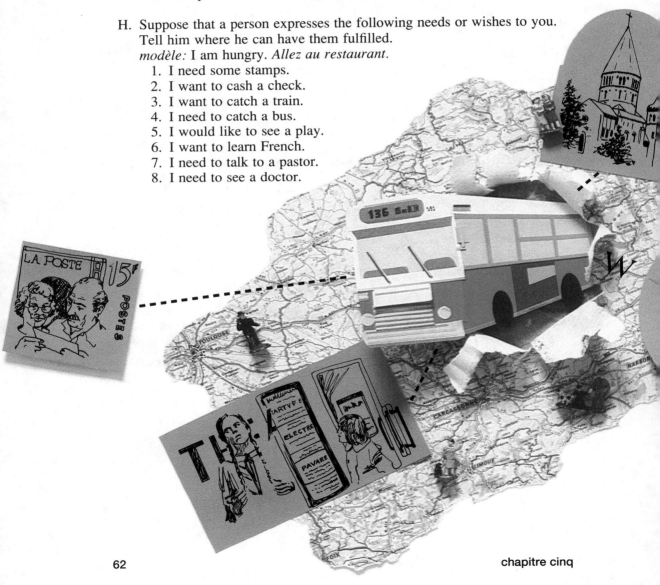

aller (to go)

You have already learned parts of this verb: *Comment allez-vous?*; *Je vais bien*; *Ça va*; and commands like *Allez au restaurant*. Here is the complete conjugation of *aller:*

je vais	nous allons
tu vas	vous allez
il, elle va	ils, elles vont

There are three possible translations for any of these present tense forms. Consider the following translations of *tu vas:*

Tu vas à l'école chaque jour.	*You go to school every day.*
Tu vas à l'école maintenant.	*You are going to school now.*
Est-ce que tu vas à l'école?	*Do you go to school?*

The context will determine the exact meaning.

I. Substititute the subject in parentheses for the subject in the sentence, making any necessary changes.

1. Je vais à la maison. (elles)
2. Georges va à pied. (nous)
3. Vous allez au théâtre. (Pierre)
4. Tu vas mal. (je)
5. Elle va en métro. (vous)
6. Les Dupont vont à Toulouse. (tu)

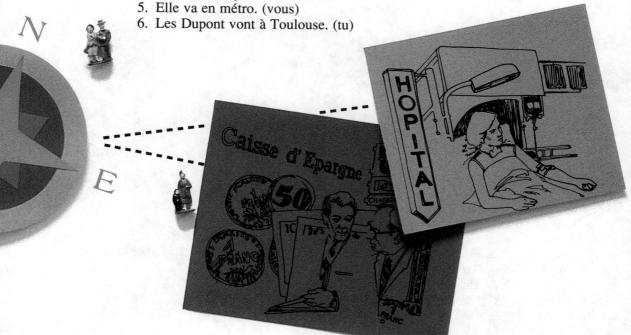

J. Tell where each person is going this weekend.

modèle: Monique . . .
Monique va au restaurant.

1. Alfred . . .

2. Nadine . . .

3. Jeanne . . .

4. Roland . . .

5. Hervé . . .

6. Judith . . .

K. Answer the following questions with the cues given.
   modèle: Où est-ce que tu vas? (je . . . université) *Je vais à l'université.*
   1. Comment allez-vous? (nous . . . très bien)
   2. Comment est-ce que Georges va à l'école? (. . . vélo)
   3. Où est-ce que Marie et Brigitte vont maintenant? (. . . hôpital)
   4. Tu vas à pied? (Non, . . . moto)
   5. Où est-ce que nous allons? (vous . . . église)
   6. Maman, comment est-ce que je vais à l'école? (tu . . . pied)

chapitre cinq

prepositions of location

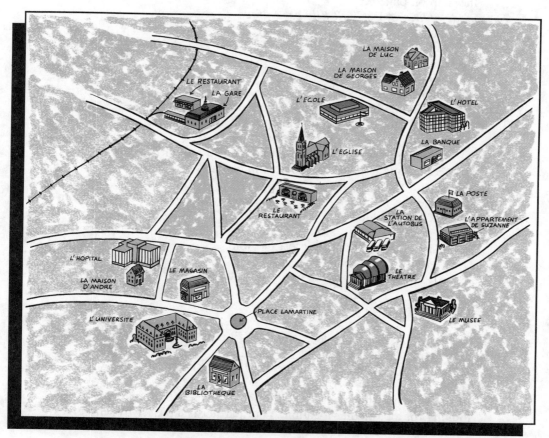

L'église est en face du restaurant.
   The church is across from the restaurant.
L'hôtel est à côté de la banque.
   The hotel is beside the bank.
L'hôpital est loin du musée.
   The hospital is far from the museum.
Le magasin est près de l'université.
   The store is near the university.
Le restaurant est derrière la gare.
   The restaurant is behind the train station.
La banque est au coin de la rue.
   The bank is at the corner of the street.
La maison de Georges est devant la maison de Luc.
   George's house is in front of Luke's house.

L. Tell where the building is in relation to another building according to the map on page 65.

modèle: Où est l'église? *Elle est en face du restaurant.*

1. Où est l'appartement de Suzanne?
2. Où est l'université?
3. Où est la maison d'André?
4. Où est le théâtre?
5. Où est la gare?
6. Est-ce que l'hôtel est près de la gare?
7. Est-ce que la maison de Georges est en face de l'école?
8. Est-ce que l'église est à côté de la poste?
9. Est-ce que la bibliothèque est près du restaurant?
10. Est-ce que la poste est derrière la banque?

M. Complete the following dialogue between you and a passer-by whom you ask for directions.

toi:	_____, s'il vous plaît?
le passant:	La gare? Elle n'est pas loin.
toi:	Comment _____?
le passant:	Montez la rue et tournez au coin.
toi:	_____?
le passant:	Non, à gauche.
toi:	_____?
le passant:	Non, à la deuxième rue. Et puis voilà l'université.
toi:	La gare est _____?
le passant:	Oui, elle est en face de l'université.

N. In pairs, using the map of Toulouse (on page 65), pretend you are looking for a particular location. Your partner is a passer-by who gives you directions. Ask questions as needed.

prononciation

l'alphabet

a	/a/	g	/ze/	m	/ɛm/	s	/ɛs/	y	/i grɛk/
b	/be/	h	/aš/	n	/ɛn/	t	/te/	z	/zɛd/
c	/se/	i	/i/	o	/o/	u	/y/		
d	/de/	j	/zi/	p	/pe/	v	/ve/		
e	/ø/	k	/ka/	q	/ky/	w	/dublø ve/		
f	/ɛf/	l	/ɛl/	r	/ɛr/	x	/iks/		

French uses three accent marks:

l'accent aigu (the acute accent): église
l'accent grave (the grave accent): père, à, où
le circonflexe (the circumflex): bête, hôpital, théâtre

These accent marks do not indicate emphasis or stress, but are part of the correct spelling of a word. In the case of the accented *e*, the accent marks also reflect pronunciation distinctions, as shown in the examples above. Sometimes, they even indicate differences in meaning. For example, you have seen that *à* (with the grave accent) is a preposition meaning "at" or "to" whereas *a* (without the grave accent) is a verb meaning "has." Thus accent marks are a crucial part of the French writing system, and the student of French must learn them as part of the correct spelling of a word.

Another important mark is the cedilla *(la cédille)*. It is placed under a *c* to indicate that the letter is pronounced with an /s/ sound:

garçon /garsɔ̃/   ça /sa/

When a *c* is followed by an *e* or an *i*, it is always pronounced /s/:

Alice /alis/   voici /vwasi/

But when followed by an *a, o,* or *u,* the letter *c* is pronounced as a /k/ sound, unless the cedilla is present:

Pascal /paskal/   cousin /kuzɛ̃/   culture /kyltyr/

France has a highly developed system of public transportation. Many French people are dependent on public mass transit–buses, subway, and commuter trains. Many families have only one car; some do not own a car at all; and others who have a car choose not to drive it in the cities in order to avoid the heavy traffic. French people are more willing to walk than Americans are and think nothing of walking some distance to catch a bus or a train. People of every age group have bicycles, and teens and young adults have motorbikes instead of cars. More and more people are buying cars in France, but having an automobile is much more expensive than in America because of soaring gasoline prices, inflation, and insurance costs.

chapitre six

faire des courses

Jean 6, 35 Jésus leur dit: Je suis le pain de vie.

It is Wednesday, a market day in Toulouse. Mrs. Plouvin takes Mrs. Dupont grocery shopping to acquaint her with the neighborhood. Mrs. Dupont is surprised to learn that although the larger French cities boast of supermarkets and giant department stores, the traditional small specialty shops and the street market are still very much a part of French life. Mrs. Plouvin points out a variety of places specializing in food items and explains some of the products found in each.

After visiting a number of shops, the two women go into a grocery shop *(une épicerie)* to buy a few things for today's evening meal.

L'épicier:	Bonjour, mesdames. Vous désirez?
Mme Plouvin:	Bonjour, monsieur. Oui, je *cherche* un kilo de *sucre* et des *œufs*.
L'épicier:	Du sucre? . . . voilà.
Mme Plouvin:	Et les œufs, c'est combien?
L'épicier:	8 F 20 *la dizaine*.
Mme Plouvin:	Bien. Avez-vous aussi du *sucre vanillé?*
L'épicier:	*Voyons* . . . ah oui, *c'est là-bas.* Et c'est *tout?*
Mme Plouvin:	Oui, merci.
L'épicier:	Bon, un kilo de sucre, une dizaine d'œufs, et trois sachets de sucre vanillé. Ça fait 33 F 60.
Mme Plouvin:	Avez-vous *la monnaie de* 50 F, s'il vous plaît?
L'épicier:	Certainement. Voilà, madame.
Mme Plouvin:	Merci, monsieur.

am looking for
sugar/eggs

a group of ten
vanilla sugar
Let's see/it's over there/all

change for

A la boulangerie on trouve du pain:
At the bakery one finds bread:

une baguette

une brioche

un croissant

A la pâtisserie on trouve des pâtisseries:

un gâteau

une tarte

une religieuse

A la boucherie on trouve de la viande:

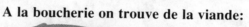

un gigot d'agneau

un bifteck

un poulet

A la boucherie chevaline on trouve de la viande de cheval:

A la charcuterie on trouve de la viande de porc:

du lard

des saucissons

du jambon

A. Où est-ce que tu vas . . . ?
   modèle: Où est-ce que tu vas pour acheter (*to buy*) du fromage?
           Je vais à la crémerie.
   1. pour acheter un gâteau?
   2. pour acheter du jambon?
   3. pour acheter du poivre?
   4. pour acheter un croissant?
   5. pour acheter des crevettes?
   6. pour acheter des tomates?
   7. pour acheter un bifteck?
   8. pour acheter une boîte de sardines?
   9. pour acheter du beurre?

A la poissonnerie on trouve du poisson et des fruits de mer:

une truite

des crevettes

A l'épicerie on trouve des épices, des produits en boîtes, des fruits et des légumes, du fromage, des boissons, et des condiments:

des oignons

du sel

du poivre

des tomates

des pommes

de l'eau minérale

une boîte de sardines

chapitre six

B. Qu'est-ce qu'on trouve . . . ?
  modèle: Qu'est-ce qu'on trouve à la boucherie?
  On trouve de la viande. ou *On trouve un gigot d'agneau.*
  1. à la pâtisserie
  2. à la crémerie
  3. à la boucherie chevaline
  4. au marché
  5. à la boulangerie
  6. à la charcuterie
  7. à l'épicerie?
  8. à la poissonnerie?

**A la crémerie on trouve
des produits laitiers:**

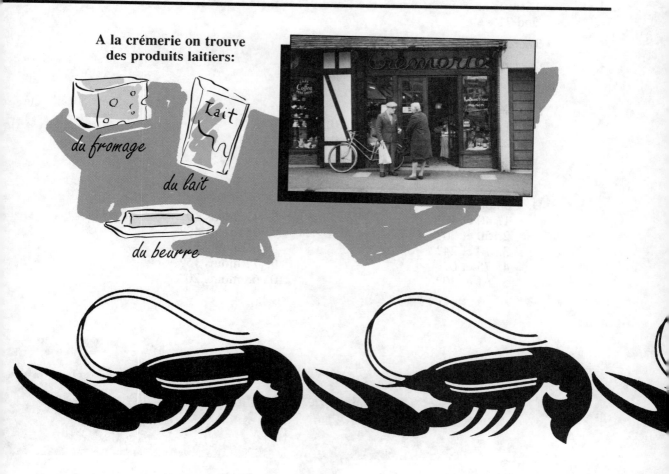

du fromage

du lait

du beurre

les nombres

The numbers from 70 to 99 are:

70 soixante-dix	80 quatre-vingts	90 quatre-vingt-dix
71 soixante et onze	81 quatre-vingt-un	91 quatre-vingt-onze
72 soixante-douze	82 quatre-vingt-deux	92 quatre-vingt-douze
73 soixante-treize	83 quatre-vingt-trois	93 quatre-vingt-treize
74 soixante-quatorze	84 quatre-vingt-quatre	94 quatre-vingt-quatorze
75 soixante-quinze	85 quatre-vingt-cinq	95 quatre-vingt-quinze
76 soixante-seize	86 quatre-vingt-six	96 quatre-vingt-seize
77 soixante-dix-sept	87 quatre-vingt-sept	97 quatre-vingt-dix-sept
78 soixante-dix-huit	88 quatre-vingt-huit	98 quatre-vingt-dix-huit
79 soixante-dix-neuf	89 quatre-vingt-neuf	99 quatre-vingt-dix-neuf

- There is no *et* in the numbers 81 and 91, as there is in 21, 31, 41, 51, 61, and 71.

- There is liaison after quatre-vingts:

    quatre-vingts ans /katrœ vɛ̃$_{(z)}$ ã/

C. Comptez en français.
   1. Comptez de 10 à 90 par 10.
   2. Comptez de 11 à 91 par 10.
   3. Comptez de 5 à 95 par 5.
   4. Comptez à rebours de 99 à 60.

D. Combien font:
   1. 40 et 40?
   2. 50 et 20?
   3. 70 et 24?
   4. 75 et 6?
   5. 61 et 30?
   6. 41 moins 10?
   7. 95 moins 40?
   8. 86 moins 11?
   9. 77 moins 15?
   10. 68 moins 20?

The numbers higher than 99 continue as follows:

100 cent	200 deux cents	300 trois cents
101 cent un	201 deux cent un	301 trois cent un
102 cent deux	202 deux cent deux	302 trois cent deux
103 cent trois	203 deux cent trois	303 trois cent trois

1.000 mille   2.000 deux mille
1.100 mille cent   2.200 deux mille deux cents

3.459 trois mille quatre cent cinquante-neuf

- In French numbers, the decimal point is used where Americans would place a comma, and *vice versa:*

    1.450 in French = 1,450 in American numbers
    1,45 in French = 1.45 in American numbers

- *Cent* has an *s* to show plural in *deux cents, trois cents,* etc., but there is no *s* if *cent* is followed by another number.

- *Mille* never has an *s.*

- When a number follows *cent,* there is no liaison:
    cent un /sã ɛ̃/

    However, there is liaison if a word other than a number follows, provided that word begins with a vowel:

    cent₍ₜ₎ans

E. Read the following numbers aloud:

1. 67	6. 342
2. 125	7. 2.719
3. 566	8. 4.683
4. 982	9. 6.874
5. 238	10. 9.999

79

*Pêches
abricots
7
kilo* 9F90

SUPERPLUS
4.85
Super
5.46
Gazole   F. le litre
3.69

72

money: *le franc*

The general word for money in French is *argent* (m); the word *monnaie* (f) is used mainly for change received in a transaction. *Le franc* is the basic French monetary unit. In recent history its value has ranged from 5 to over 10 francs per American dollar. At the writing of this book, the *franc* is worth approximately 16 cents. Like the dollar the *franc* is divided into hundredths (centimes), with coins and bills of various denominations, as pictured below.

When prices of items in French stores are listed, they appear in this form: 3,45 F or 3 F 45. Both are read: *trois francs quarante-cinq* (centimes).

F. C'est combien? Tell the prices of the items shown below.
1. Le sucre, c'est combien?
2. Le gâteau, c'est combien?
3. La table, c'est combien?
4. Le vélo, c'est combien?
5. La télévision, c'est combien?
6. La pendule, c'est combien?
7. Le pain, c'est combien?
8. Le chien, c'est combien?

G. You are a customer at the charcuterie. Fill in what you say.

Charcutier:	Bonjour, _____.
Toi:	_____. (Respond appropriately.)
Charcutier:	Vous désirez?
Toi:	_____. (Tell him what you are looking for.)
Charcutier:	Ah, voilà.
Toi:	_____. (Ask him the price.)
Charcutier:	Ça fait 8,65 F. C'est tout?
Toi:	_____. (Tell him that that's all. Ask him if he has change for 10 F.)
Charcutier:	Oui, voici 1,35 F.
Toi:	_____. (Thank him, and take leave.)

the partitive

The partitive *(le partitif)* is equivalent to the English word "some." In French it takes several different forms:

I am looking for *some* sugar and *some* eggs.
  Je cherche *du* sucre et *des* œufs.
She wants *some* cream, too.
  Elle désire *de la* crème, aussi.

The different forms are combinations of the word *de* and the appropriate definite article *le, la, l'*, or *les*. This table summarizes those combinations.

	"some"	
masculine	du	sucre
feminine	de la	viande
before a vowel	de l'	eau
any plural	des	pommes

You have already seen these same forms in sentences such as the following:

Il a peur du chien.
  He is afraid of the dog.
L'école est au coin de la rue.
  The school is on the corner of the street.

The only difference now is that as a partitive, the meaning is "some" rather than "of the."

In English, the partitive idea is often conveyed without the word "some":

I'm looking for sugar.   Je cherche *du* sucre.

However, in French, the partitive word must always be present when the partitive idea is understood.

H. Give the correct form of the partitive.
   modèle: Je désire _____ œufs. *des*
   1. Il cherche _____ sucre.
   2. Nous avons _____ crevettes.
   3. Elles achètent _____ orangeade.
   4. Victor cherche _____ pain.
   5. Vous désirez _____ tarte?
   6. Elle a _____ oignons.
   7. Tu désires _____ beurre?
   8. Il achète _____ viande de cheval.

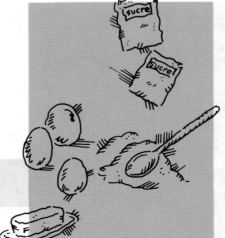

I. Tell the shopkeeper what you are looking for.

modèle: Je cherche du bifteck.

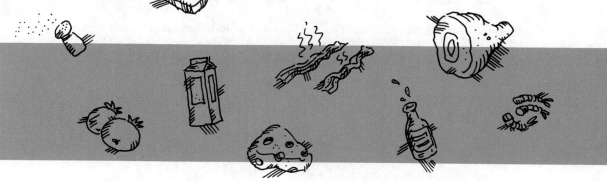

The partitive, like the indefinite articles *un, une,* and *des,* becomes *de* after a negative verb:

Il a *du* pain.   Il n'a pas *de* pain.
Elle cherche *de* la viande.   Elle ne cherche pas *de* viande.
Nous avons *des* croissants.   Nous n'avons pas *de* croissants.

J. Pretend that you are a shopkeeper, who is out of everything that his customers want.

modèle: Je cherche du pain.   *Je regrette, je n'ai pas de pain.*
  1. Je cherche du sucre.
  2. Je cherche de l'eau minérale.
  3. Je cherche de la viande de cheval.
  4. Je cherche des pommes.
  5. Je cherche du sel.
  6. Je cherche une tarte.
  7. Je cherche de la crème.
  8. Je cherche un gâteau.

Another context in which *de* is used rather than the full partitive is after an expression which tells an amount, such as a kilogram, a dozen, or a packet:

J'achète de la viande.	. . . un kilo de viande
Je cherche des œufs.	. . . une dizaine d'œufs
Je cherche du sucre vanillé.	. . . un sachet de sucre vanillé

Other "expressions of quantity," as they are called, include the following:

une tranche	*a slice*
une bouteille	*a bottle*
une boîte	*a box, a can*
un morceau	*a piece*
un litre	*a liter*

K. Tell how much you want of each item, using the cues provided.
   modèle: Vous cherchez du sucre? (un kilo)
      Oui, un kilo de sucre, s'il vous plaît.
   1. Vous cherchez du jambon? (deux tranches)
   2. Vous cherchez de l'eau minérale? (trois bouteilles)
   3. Vous cherchez des sardines? (une boîte)
   4. Vous cherchez une tarte? (un morceau)
   5. Vous cherchez du bifteck? (un kilo)
   6. Vous cherchez de la crème? (une boîte)
   7. Vous cherchez des œufs? (une dizaine)
   8. Vous cherchez du Coca-Cola? (deux litres)

regular -er verbs

Mrs. Plouvin tells the grocer:

> Je *cherche* un kilo de sucre et des œufs.

The word *cherche* is the first person singular of the verb *chercher*. Here is the entire conjugation in the present tense:

chercher *(to look for)*

je cherche		nous cherchons	
tu cherches		vous cherchez	
il		ils	
elle	} cherche	elles	} cherchent
on			

This table not only shows the conjugation of *chercher,* but also represents the pattern for conjugating an entire class of verbs called the *regular -er verbs*. Named for the last two letters in their infinitive (the "to" form of the verb in English–for example, to look for, to eat, to buy, etc.), the -er verbs constitute the largest class of verbs in the French language. Since their conjugation forms a regular pattern, once you learn how to conjugate one verb in the class, you can do all of them. Note carefully these details:

- The written endings are

-e	-ons
-es	-ez
-e	-ent

These are added to the stem after the *-er* of the infinitive is dropped.

- The yellow-shaded forms on the conjugation table above are all pronounced alike, since their endings are silent. The nous form of the verb (first person plural) ends in the sound /ʒ/; and the vous form, ending in the /e/ sound, sounds exactly like the infinitive. Thus in the spoken language, there are three different forms in the present tense of any -er verb.

  ending in /ʒ/ (cherchons)
  ending in /e/ (chercher, cherchez)
  with no pronounced suffix (cherche, cherches, cherchent)

- These verbs, like most present-tense verbs, can be translated three different ways, depending on the context. Note the three possible meanings of *nous cherchons:*

we are looking for:	Nous cherchons un livre. *We are looking for a book.*
we look for:	Nous cherchons la réponse à chaque question. *We look for the answer to each question.*
we do look for:	Nous ne cherchons pas les questions, mais nous cherchons les réponses. *We do not look for the questions, but we do look for the answers.*

- The subject pronoun *on* may be translated several different ways, but its verb form is always third person singular.

> On tourne à gauche. *You turn left.*
> On va à l'église? *Shall we go to church?*
> On trouve de la viande à la boucherie.
>   *One finds meat at the butcher shop.*
> On parle français en France. *They speak French in France.*

- Other regular -er verbs include those in the following chart.

trouver	*to find*	On trouve le musée près de l'église.
aimer	*to like, to love*	Il aime son appartement.
détester	*to hate*	Elle déteste les sardines.
regarder	*to look at*	Nous regardons le plan de Toulouse.
désirer	*to desire*	Désirez-vous un bifteck?
tourner	*to turn*	Tu tournes à gauche là-bas.
monter	*to go up*	Ils montent la rue Claude Monet.
traverser	*to go across*	Je traverse le pont pour aller au zoo.
passer (par)	*to pass (by)*	Nous passons par la gare.
acheter	*to buy*	Vous achetez du pain; moi, j'achète des croissants.
entrer (dans)	*to enter (into)*	Elle entre dans le musée.
rentrer	*to return (home)*	Je rentre en taxi.

L. Change the singular subject to the plural in these sentences.
   modèle: Il regarde la télévision. *Ils regardent la télévision.*
   1. Je traverse la rue au coin.
   2. Elle tourne à droite.
   3. Tu aimes les oignons?
   4. Le garçon cherche des saucissons.
   5. Je passe par son appartement.
   6. Tu achètes du sel à l'épicerie.
   7. Ma fille déteste les escargots.
   8. Il parle français.

M. Fill in the blank with the correct present tense form of the verb.
   1. Nous _____ un appartement. (chercher)
   2. Claire _____ Jean-Paul. (aimer)
   3. Je _____ un croissant sur la table. (trouver)
   4. Vous _____ des tartes à la pâtisserie. (acheter)
   5. Ils _____ dans l'église. (entrer)
   6. Tu _____ par la poste. (passer)
   7. On _____ la rue pour aller à la poste. (traverser)

N. Mme Plouvin goes to the open-air market.
   1. Elle _____ acheter des pommes. (désirer)
   2. Elle _____ la rue Labeda. (monter)
   3. Elle _____ la place Wilson. (traverser)
   4. Elle _____ au marché en plein air. (aller)
   5. Elle _____ les supermarchés. (détester)
   6. Elle _____ avec le marchand de pommes. (parler)
   7. Elle _____ deux kilos de pommes. (acheter)
   8. Elle _____ à pied. (rentrer)

O. Pretend that you go along with Mme Plouvin to the market. Retell exercise N in the first person plural *(Nous . . .).*

the partitive and the definite article

The partitive is used to indicate a *part* of a quantity, rather than the entire quantity. For example, to say, *Vous acheter du pain* means "You are buying *some* bread," not all bread in general. Now compare the meaning when the definite article is used in the following two ways:

to indicate something in general.
> J'aime le pain. *I like bread (in general).*
> Je déteste les escargots. *I hate snails (in general).*

to indicate a specific object pointed out by a given context.
> J'achète le pain que tu aimes.
> *I buy the bread that you like.*
> J'ai les escargots que tu cherches.
> *I have the snails you are looking for.*

In English, the definite article, like the partitive, may be omitted in some situations:

> I like bread.
> Do you eat snails?

However, in French, these situations require the definite article.

P. Use a verb from the line below to express your general opinion about these items.

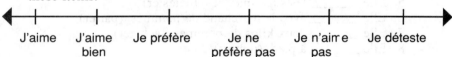

J'aime J'aime bien Je préfère Je ne préfère pas Je n'aime pas Je déteste

modèle: les sardines *Je déteste les sardines.*
1. les escargots
2. les chats
3. le fromage
4. la truite
5. l'eau minérale
6. le Coca-Cola
7. l'école
8. le lait

Q. Decide whether to use the partitive or the definite article in these sentences. Explain your decision.

   modèle: Je déteste _____escargots. (les/des)

   > *Je déteste les escargots.*
   > *You can detest snails in general.*

   1. Vous désirez _____ pain? (le/du)
   2. Il aime _____ chats. (les/des)
   3. Je trouve _____ boîte de tomates que tu cherches. (la/de la)
   4. Nous achetons _____ croissants. (les/des)
   5. Tu préfères _____ eau minérale? (l'/de l')
   6. Ils ont _____ fromage. (le/du)
   7. Elle cherche _____ crème. (la/de la)
   8. Je désire _____ eau. (l'/de l')

R. Tell what you want, buy, do, or think, etc., in these situations.

   modèle: You have a craving for seafood.

   > *J'achète de la truite.*
   > *Je mange des crevettes.*
   > *Je vais à la poissonnerie.*
   > *Je désire du poisson. etc.*

   1. You feel like eating cheese.
   2. You want to buy some horse meat.
   3. You have a yearning for a French pastry.
   4. You express your opinion about French bread.
   5. You crave a French meal.
   6. You tell how you like shrimp.
   7. You need to buy a stamp.
   8. You tell your name and age.
   9. You ask how to get to some particular store.
   10. You tell how many brothers and sisters you have.

Now read about Mrs. Plouvin's and Mrs. Dupont's grocery shopping in French:

Today is Wednesday — *C'est aujourd'hui mercredi.* Mme Plouvin et Mme Dupont vont
do some errands/first — *faire des courses. D'abord* elles vont à la boulangerie pour
then — acheter des croissants et du pain. *Ensuite,* elles vont à la charcu-
gooseliver paste/finally — terie. Elles y achètent du jambon et du *pâté de foie gras. Enfin,*
elles entrent dans l'épicerie. Mme Plouvin y cherche du sucre,
then — des œufs et des sachets de sucre vanillé. *Puis,* elles rentrent à
after their morning/tired — pied. *Après leur matinée* au marché, elles sont très *fatiguées.*

S. Answer in a complete sentence.
1. Où vont Mme Plouvin et Mme Dupont pour chercher du pain?
2. Qu'est-ce qu'elles achètent à la charcuterie?
3. Est-ce qu'elles trouvent des croissants à l'épicerie?
4. Comment est-ce qu'elles rentrent?
5. Est-ce qu'elles sont fatiguées ou énergiques?

grammaire

the pronoun *y*

The pronoun *y* replaces a prepositional phrase of location:

Elles vont à la boulangerie.	Elles *y* vont.
Le chien est dans le fauteuil.	Le chien *y* est.
On trouve la poste derrière la gare?	Non, on n'*y* trouve pas la poste.

The best way to translate *y* in sentences such as these is with the word *there.*
Notice the placement of *y* immediately before the verb. Although this word
order may at first be bewildering to an American learning French, it is
important to master early the principle that in French all object pronouns
precede the verb. When the verb is negative, the *ne (n')* precedes *y.*

T. Replace the prepositional phrases of location with the pronoun *y*.
1. Nous allons à la banque.
2. On trouve le livre sur l'étagère.
3. Je ne suis pas au coin.
4. Elle cherche du pain à la boulangerie.
5. La maison n'est pas à côté du restaurant.
6. Vous entrez dans le musée.

U. Answer the questions using *y* in your answer.
modèle: Est-ce que tu vas à la boucherie chevaline? (Oui)
 Oui, j'y vais.
1. Est-ce que Dominique va à l'hôpital? (Oui)
2. Vous entrez dans la poste? (Non, nous . . .)
3. Est-ce qu'elle achète des religieuses à la pâtisserie? (Oui)
4. Tu vas à l'église? (Oui)
5. Est-ce que Gabrielle trouve son chien sous la table? (Non)
6. Je trouve du sel à la boulangerie? (Non, tu . . .)

V. Write a short paragraph describing a shopping trip with a friend. Tell where you go, what you buy, and how much it costs.

faire des courses

French oral vowel sounds (part I)

	Front		Central	Back
	unrounded	rounded	unrounded	rounded
high	/i/	/y/		/u/
higher mid	/e/	/ø/		/o/
lower mid	/ɛ/	/œ/		/ɔ/
low			/a/	

There are ten oral (that is, non-nasal) vowel sounds in French:
- The labels *front, central,* and *back* refer to the location of the highest part of the tongue.

- The labels *high, higher mid, lower mid,* and *low* refer to the relative height of the tongue.

- The labels *rounded* and *unrounded* refer to the position of the lips. Thus in articulating the /i/ sound, the tongue is high and toward the front of the mouth, and the lips are unrounded. By contrast, in articulating the /o/ sound, the tongue is slightly lower and pulled back in the mouth, and the lips are rounded.

- All the sounds are pure vowels; that is, they are produced without the slight change in vowel quality that might accompany them in English. To produce pure vowel sounds, the jaw, tongue, and lips remain immobile during the articulation of the vowel. Note these contrasts:

English		**French**	
day	/de^y/	des	/de/
bow	/bo^w/	beau	/bo/
too	/tu^w/	tout	/tu/
see	/si^y/	si	/si/

Some of the common spellings of these sounds are listed below, along with an illustrative word for each spelling.

/i/	i, y	si, Yves
/e/	é, ai	zéro, j'ai
/ɛ/	e, è, ê, ai	elle, mère, bête, aime
/y/	u	tu
/ø/	eu,e	deux, le
/œ/	eu, œ	neuf, sœur
/a/	a	la
/u/	ou	vous
/o/	o, ô, au	vélo, hôpital, chaud
/ɔ/	o	école

In small towns and villages in France, the only stores available are the specialty shops and the street market. The street merchants normally come to a particular town only two days a week. Therefore, housewives must make their purchases for several days at a time when they go to the street market. The selection is usually quite good, and the prices vary from one stand to the next. Some people return to the same merchants time after time if they are satisfied with their wares, if the prices are good, and if they have become acquainted with individual merchants. The specialty shops are open daily, and some housewives will go to them every day or every other day, depending on the types of goods they need. For instance, Frenchmen buy their bread every morning, and sometimes several times during the day because they want their bread to be fresh. Bread in France is relatively inexpensive because the prices have been regulated by the government since the French Revolution in 1789. At that time bread was so expensive that the common man could not afford to buy it. It was decided that any Frenchman should be able to afford bread and that the prices would thereafter be regulated to insure that he could.

In addition to the specialty shops and street market, larger towns and cities also have *supermarchés* and *hypermarchés*. The *supermarchés* are similar to our supermarkets, while the *hypermarchés* (also called *grandes surfaces*) have clothing, hardware, sporting goods, and toys in addition to the food items available in the *supermarchés*. These types of stores are increasing in popularity because of the variety, convenience, and excellent prices they offer the shopper. Yet many French people like the individual, personal attention in smaller shops. They also feel a loyalty to the *petits commerçants* (independent shopkeepers) who could eventually go out of business as a result of not being able to compete with the larger stores. Some of the missionaries, pastors, and their church members like to frequent the smaller shops as a contact for witnessing to the shopkeepers in spite of the higher prices there. However, since missionaries need to be careful about their expenditures, they are also drawn to the *supermarchés, hypermarchés,* and *grandes surfaces* in order to economize. It is often a difficult decision.

aller au restaurant

Esaïe 55, 1 Vous tous qui avez soif, venez aux eaux, Même celui qui n'a pas d'argent! Venez, achetez et mangez; venez, achetez du vin et du lait, sans argent, sans rien payer!

7 7 7 7 7 7 7 7 7 7

dialogue

Mr. Dupont goes to *L'Echalotte,* a restaurant in Toulouse, with a young man he is trying to disciple.

M. Dupont:	Est-ce un bon restaurant, Serge?
Serge:	Oui, je dîne souvent ici. Les plats sont très très bons.

Le garçon donne une carte* aux deux clients.

le garçon:	Que prenez-vous comme entrée?
Serge:	La soupe du jour, qu'est-ce que c'est?
le garçon:	C'est une soupe à l'oignon.
Serge:	Bien, je prends la soupe du jour.
le garçon:	Et comme plat principal?
Serge:	Je voudrais du rôti de bœuf et des pommes frites.
le garçon:	Et vous prenez le rôti de bœuf saignant?
Serge:	Non, à point, s'il vous plaît.
le garçon:	(à M. Dupont) Et vous, monsieur, que désirez-vous?
M. Dupont:	Je prends le menu* à 45 F avec une côtelette de veau.
le garçon:	Et comme boisson? Je suggère un vin rouge.
Serge:	Monsieur ne prend pas d'alcool. Nous allons prendre du Coca.

*Notez bien: In French the written menu is called *la carte*. From this French word we get the expression *à la carte* in English to describe a method of ordering—"from the menu." The French word *menu* refers not only to the written menu but also to a dinner special proposed by the restaurant.

maintenant en anglais . . .

Mr. Dupont:	Is this a good restaurant, Serge?
Serge:	Yes, I eat dinner here often. The food is very good.

The waiter gives a menu to the two customers.

the waiter:	What are you having for your entree?
Serge:	What is the soup of the day?
the waiter:	It is onion soup.
Serge:	Well, I'll have the soup of the day.
the waiter:	And for the main dish?
Serge:	I would like roast beef and French fries.
the waiter:	Would you like the roast beef rare?
Serge:	No, medium, please.
the waiter:	(to Mr. Dupont) And you, what would you like?
Mr. Dupont:	I'll have the 45 F dinner with veal cutlet.
the waiter:	And for drinks? I suggest a red wine.
Serge:	The gentleman does not drink alcohol. We'll have Coke.

A. Answer the following questions about the dialogue. Answer in complete sentences.
1. Où est-ce que M. Dupont et Serge dînent?
2. Comment sont les plats dans le restaurant?
3. Est-ce que Serge prend la soupe du jour?
4. Qu'est-ce que Serge prend comme viande?
5. Comment est-ce qu'il prend son rôti de bœuf?
6. Qu'est-ce qu'il prend comme légume?
7. Est-ce que M. Dupont prend le menu à 55 F?
8. Qu'est-ce qu'il prend comme boisson?

aller au restaurant

Qu'est-ce qu'on mange aux repas?

What does one eat at meals?

au petit déjeuner

un bol de café au lait

du thé

un croissant

une biscotte

du pain

au déjeuner

un sandwich au fromage

un croque-monsieur

une omelette

du yaourt

un sandwich au jambon

au goûter

une tartine avec de la pâte à tartiner

un pain au chocolat

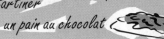

une boisson de sirop

du fruit

un sandwich au fromage ou au jambon

au dîner

des hors d'oeuvre

des huîtres

des escargots

du pâté

des crudités

de la soupe

du pâté maison

la viande

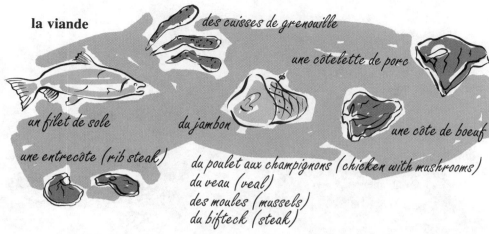

des cuisses de grenouille

une côtelette de porc

un filet de sole   du jambon

une côte de boeuf

une entrecôte (rib steak)

du poulet aux champignons (chicken with mushrooms)
du veau (veal)
des moules (mussels)
du bifteck (steak)

les légumes (m.)

des carottes

des haricots (verts)

des pommes de terre

des (pommes) frites

des asperges

du maïs

des petits pois

des artichauts

du chou

du chou-fleur

de la salade verte

de la salade niçoise (a salad of tomatoes and other vegetables with tuna
and anchovies in an olive oil dressing)

les fruits

une poire

une banane

une pomme   une pêche   une orange   des raisins

les fromages

du camembert

du brie

du chèvre

les desserts

de la tarte

de la glace

du yaourt

du gâteau

une pâtisserie

du fromage

du fruit

les boissons

du jus de fruit

du café

de l'eau minérale

du Coca-Cola

du thé

de la grenadine

methods of food preparation

saignant(e)	*rare*
à point	*medium*
bien cuit(e)	*well done*
sauté(e)	*fried in butter*
au beurre	*in butter*
au jus	*in its own juices*
au gratin	*in cheese*
maison	*house style*
grillé(e)	*grilled*
cru(e)	*raw, uncooked*

verbs associated with food

manger	*to eat*
dîner	*to eat dinner*
déjeuner	*to eat lunch*

B. At which meal might each of the following be eaten in France?
   modèle–une biscotte *On mange une biscotte au petit déjeuner.*
   1. du poulet aux champignons
   2. un croissant
   3. un sandwich au fromage
   4. un pain au chocolat
   5. un bol de café au lait
   6. des frites
   7. une côtelette de porc
   8. un croque-monsieur

C. *Vous êtes au restaurant.* Choose from among the items listed under *le dîner* to tell what you are having for each course.
   Qu'est-ce que tu prends . . .
   1. comme hors d'œuvre?
   2. comme plat principal?
   3. comme légume?
   4. comme dessert?
   5. comme boisson?

grammaire

prendre (to take)

je prends	nous prenons
tu prends	vous prenez
il, elle, on prend	ils, elles prennent

The verb *prendre* means literally "to take," but in the case of food and drink the French use it where we would use the verbs "to eat," "to drink," or even "to have." Another verb conjugated like *prendre* is *comprendre* (to understand). Simply place the prefix *com-* in front of each form of *prendre;* for example, *je prends–je comprends.*

D. Fill in the blank with the appropriate form of *prendre* or *comprendre* as indicated.
   1. Je _____ un taxi pour aller en ville. (prendre)
   2. Les enfants _____ de la glace. (prendre)
   3. Vous _____ la question? (comprendre)
   4. Alice _____ le métro pour rentrer. (prendre)
   5. Je ne _____ pas votre réponse. (comprendre)
   6. Nous _____ une tasse de café, s'il vous plaît. (prendre)
   7. Tu _____? (comprendre)
   8. On _____ le menu à 50 F? (prendre)

aller au restaurant

E. Tell what each of these people is having at the restaurant.
modèle: Monique (du fromage) *Monique prend du fromage.*
1. M. Vincent (du jus d'orange)
2. tu (de la salade niçoise)
3. les deux femmes (des moules)
4. je (du pâté maison)
5. vous (des asperges)
6. on (une omelette)
7. ils (des huîtres)
8. nous (un bifteck bien cuit)

F. Ask a friend in the class the following questions. Take notes in French and report to the class in French.
1. Qu'est-ce que tu prends pour le petit déjeuner?
2. Où est-ce que tu prends le déjeuner?
3. Qu'est-ce que tu prends pour le déjeuner aujourd'hui?
4. Est-ce que tu dînes souvent au restaurant?
5. Est-ce que tu prends un goûter après l'école?

adverbs of time

toujours	*always*	souvent	*often*
quelquefois	*sometimes*	ne . . . jamais	*never*

- Adverbs of time generally follow the verb they modify.

  Je vais souvent au restaurant.
  I often go to the restaurant.
  Nous mangeons quelquefois chez nous.
  Sometimes we eat at home.

- The adverb *jamais* requires the *ne* of negation before the verb when it means *never*.

  Ma mère ne mange jamais d'escargots.
  My mother never eats snails.

- The adverb *jamais* without the *ne* means *ever* in questions. If the response is affirmative, another adverb is used; *jamais* is not used.

  Tu manges jamais de la soupe?   *Do you ever eat soup?*
  Oui, je mange de la soupe.   *Yes, I eat soup.*
  Oui, je mange souvent de la soupe.   *Yes, I often eat soup.*

chapitre sept

G. Using an adverb from the continuum below, tell how often you do each of these activities.

toujours	souvent	quelquefois	rarement	ne . . . jamais

modèle: Tu vas à la bibliothèque? *Oui, j'y vais quelquefois.*

1. Tu vas à l'église?
2. Tu vas au restaurant?
3. Tu manges jamais du chou-fleur?
4. Tu dînes chez un ami?
5. Tu es timide?
6. Tu es bavard(e)?
7. Tu parles français?
8. Tu prends jamais des cuisses de grenouille?

adverbs of quantity

beaucoup *much, many, a lot*
(un) peu *(a) little*
assez *enough*
trop *too much, too many*
tant *so much, so many*

- Like adverbs of time, these adverbs generally follow the verb that they modify.

  Mon chien mange trop.
  My dog eats too much.
  Son père achète très peu au marché.
  Her father buys very little at the market.

- These adverbs can be used alone as in the examples above, or they can be used with a noun to tell the amount.

  Je prends beaucoup de café. *I drink a lot of coffee.*
  Vous mangez un peu de gâteau. *You eat a little cake.*

- As with the quantities you learned in Chapter 6 (*une bouteille, un kilo, deux litres,* etc.), the adverbs of quantity will change the partitive to just *de* or *d'*.

du jus	une bouteille de jus	assez de jus
de la tarte	une tranche de tarte	trop de tarte
des pommes	un kilo de pommes	tant de pommes

- A quantity of a beverage can be expressed in other ways as well.

un bol de café au lait	*a bowl of coffee with milk*
une tasse de thé	*a cup of tea*
un verre d'eau	*a glass of water*

H. Using the clue provided with each question, give an answer that tells *how much*.

modèle: Tu manges de la soupe? (beaucoup)
   Oui, je mange beaucoup de soupe.

1. Tu manges du pain? (un peu)
2. Tu prends du café? (une tasse)
3. Tu achètes des pommes? (un kilo)
4. Tu as de l'argent? (assez)
5. Tu manges des escargots? (très peu)
6. Tu as de la patience? (tant)
7. Tu prends de la tarte? (une tranche)
8. Tu prends du jus de raisin? (un verre)

lecture

orders
requests the bill/included
tip

Au restaurant M. Dupont et son ami Serge dînent bien. Serge *commande* du rôti de bœuf et M. Dupont prend le menu à 45 F. Serge mange des frites, mais M. Dupont n'en mange pas. Il préfère le chou-fleur et les petits pois. Après la salade, ils prennent du fromage. M. Dupont en mange un peu, mais Serge en mange beaucoup. La nourriture à *L'Echalotte* est délicieuse. Après le repas M. Dupont *demande l'addition*. Le service est *compris*, c'est pourquoi il ne donne pas de *pourboire* au garçon.

grammaire

the pronoun *en*

The pronoun *en* replaces a partitive and the noun that follows:

Je prends du veau.	→ J'en prends.
Elle a de l'orangeade.	→ Elle en a.

In this context, *en* means "some," "some of it," or "some of these." Like *y*, the pronoun *en* precedes the verb. In negation an *n'* precedes *en*.

Je ne prends pas de pain.	→ Je n'en prends pas.
Il ne mange jamais d'œufs.	→ Il n'en mange jamais.

Here the meaning of *en* is "any," "any of it," or "any of them."

chapitre sept

I. Answer the following questions affirmatively or negatively, according to your own personal situation or preferences.

modèle: Tu manges des oignons au petit déjeuner?

> *Oui, j'en mange au petit déjeuner.*
> *Non, je n'en mange pas au petit déjeuner.*
> *Non, je n'en mange jamais au petit déjeuner.*

1. Tu prends de la soupe au restaurant?
2. Tu manges jamais des escargots?
3. Tu prends du café au dîner?
4. Tu achètes de l'eau minérale?
5. Tu cherches du pain?
6. Tu manges du pâté au déjeuner?
7. Tu prends des crudités au dîner?
8. Tu achètes des légumes au marché?

The pronoun *en* also replaces the partitive *de* and the noun phrase that follow expressions of quantity.

Il mange un peu de fromage. → Il en mange un peu.
Je prends une tasse de café au lait. → J'en prends une tasse.

In this context, the meaning of *en* is "of it," or "of them."

J. Answer the following questions affirmatively, using *en* in your answer.

modèle: Est-ce que le chat mange beaucoup de poisson?

> *Oui, il en mange beaucoup.*

1. Est-ce que Serge mange beaucoup de fromage?
2. Est-ce que l'enfant mange assez de légumes?
3. Est-ce que le chien mange trop de viande?
4. Tu prends un morceau de gâteau?
5. Vous achetez une bouteille d'eau minérale?
6. Est-ce que les filles cherchent une boîte de maïs?
7. Tu as un peu de café?
8. Est-ce qu'il a un verre de lait?

aller au restaurant

K. Using *en* and an expression of quantity from the line below, tell how much of these foods you normally eat per week.

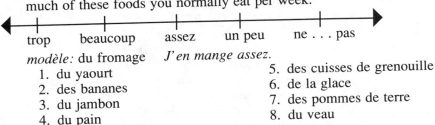

trop   beaucoup   assez   un peu   ne . . . pas

modèle: du fromage   *J'en mange assez.*

1. du yaourt
2. des bananes
3. du jambon
4. du pain

5. des cuisses de grenouille
6. de la glace
7. des pommes de terre
8. du veau

the adjectives *beau, nouveau,* and *vieux*

As you have seen, an adjective must agree in both number and gender with the noun it modifies:

Le restaurant est bon.
La nourriture est bonne.
Les raisins sont bons.
Les pommes sont bonnes.

Now notice the changes that occur in these adjectives:

Le garçon est beau.   *The boy is handsome.*
Sa sœur est belle.   *His sister is beautiful.*

Some other adjectives have a feminine form that is quite different from the masculine. Here are two other common adjectives with irregular forms:

Le vélo est nouveau.   *The bike is new.*
La moto est nouvelle.   *The motorcycle is new.*
Le restaurant est vieux.   *The restaurant is old.*
La maison est vieille.   *The house is old.*

Here is a table of these three adjectives in all their forms:

masculine		*feminine*	
beau	beaux	belle	belles
nouveau	nouveaux	nouvelle	nouvelles
vieux	vieux	vieille	vieilles

The plural forms of *beau* and *nouveau* are spelled with an *x instead* of an *s*. The same thing will be true of all French words ending in *-au*.

chapitre sept

L. Answer each question based on the previous statement.
   modèle: Les garçons sont beaux. Et les filles?
       Elles sont belles aussi.
   1. Les croissants sont bons. Et les tartines?
   2. Les cathédrales sont belles. Et le musée?
   3. La grand-mère est vieille. Et le grand-père?
   4. Le tapis est nouveau. Et les rideaux?
   5. Les autobus sont vieux. Et la voiture?
   6. Mon cousin est beau. Et ta cousine?
   7. Notre table est nouvelle. Et vos chaises?
   8. Ses pâtisseries sont bonnes. Et son pain?

M. Write a sentence of description using each of the following adjectives. Make sure that your subject is the same person and number as the adjective form you are given.
   modèle: vieilles   *Nos voitures sont vieilles.*
   1. belle   4. vieux
   2. nouveaux   5. beaux
   3. bon

N. Pretend you are in a French restaurant. Construct a conversation between you and a waiter as you order from the menu.

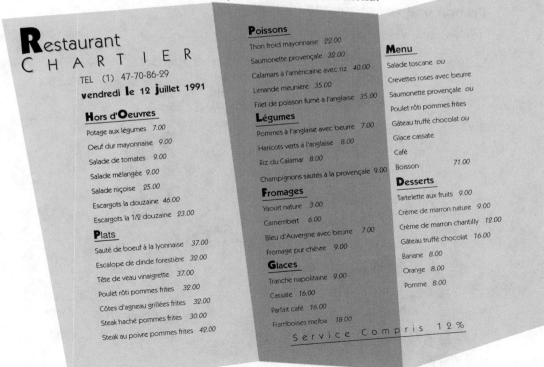

Restaurant
C H A R T I E R
TEL (1) 47-70-86-29
vendredi le 12 juillet 1991

Hors d'Oeuvres
Potage aux légumes 7.00
Oeuf dur mayonnaise 9.00
Salade de tomates 9.00
Salade mélangée 9.00
Salade niçoise 25.00
Escargots la douzaine 46.00
Escargots la 1/2 douzaine 23.00

Plats
Sauté de boeuf à la lyonnaise 37.00
Escalope de dinde forestière 32.00
Tête de veau vinaigrette 37.00
Poulet rôti pommes frites 32.00
Côtes d'agneau grillées frites 32.00
Steak haché pommes frites 30.00
Steak au poivre pommes frites 42.00

Poissons
Thon froid mayonnaise 22.00
Saumonette provençale 32.00
Calamars à l'américaine avec riz 40.00
Limande meunière 35.00
Filet de poisson fumé à l'anglaise 35.00

Légumes
Pommes à l'anglaise avec beurre 7.00
Haricots verts à l'anglaise 8.00
Riz du Calamar 8.00
Champignons sautés à la provençale 9.00

Fromages
Yaourt nature 3.00
Camembert 6.00
Bleu d'Auvergne avec beurre 7.00
Fromage pur chèvre 9.00

Glaces
Tranche napolitaine 9.00
Cassate 16.00
Parfait café 16.00
Framboises melba 18.00

Menu
Salade toscane ou
Crevettes roses avec beurre
Saumonette provençale ou
Poulet rôti pommes frites
Gâteau truffé chocolat ou
Glace cassate
Café
Boisson   71.00

Desserts
Tartelette aux fruits 9.00
Crème de marron nature 9.00
Crème de marron chantilly 12.00
Gâteau truffé chocolat 16.00
Banane 8.00
Orange 8.00
Pomme 8.00

S e r v i c e   C o m p r i s   1 2 %

aller au restaurant

103

h aspiré

You have already seen that the letter *h* is never pronounced in French.

l'hôtel	/lotɛl/
l'hôpital	/lopital/
les huîtres	/lezɥitr/

However there are some *h*'s which, though not pronounced, do not allow elision and liaison.

le hors d'œuvre	/løɔdœvr/
les haricots	/leariko/
le héros	/løero/ (the hero)
les héros	/leero/ (contrast with les zéros /lezero/)

This type of *h* is known as aspirate h *(h aspiré)*. You must memorize which *h*'s are aspirate and which are not, just as a person learning English must learn to pronounce correctly phrases such as *a house* and *an hour*. Most dictionaries will indicate that an *h* is aspirate with a symbol such as an asterisk (*).

French oral vowel sounds (part II)

The front vowel sounds are as follows:

	Front unrounded	rounded
high	/i/	/y/
higher mid	/e/	/ø/
lower mid	/ɛ/	/œ/

In Chapter 1 you studied the formation of the high front vowels:

/i/   petit
/y/   tu

The higher mid front vowels are articulated with the jaw slightly more open. To practice the /ø/ sound, start by pronouncing the /e/ sound and gradually round the lips keeping the tongue toward the front of the mouth.

/e/ ———gradually round the lips——— /ø/

Practice these words containing the /ø/ sound.

eux	Matth*ieu*
l*e*	D*ieu*
j*e*	ennuy*eux*
n*eveu*	Mons*ieu*r
p*eu*	délic*ieux*

The /œ/ is produced with the jaw even more open than with the /ø/ sound. To practice the /œ/ sound, start by saying the /ɛ/ sound and gradually round the lips.

/ɛ/ ———gradually round the lips——— /œ/

Practice these words containing the /œ/ sound. Notice that in each word the /œ/ sound is followed by a pronounced consonant.

n*euf*	s*œu*r
j*eu*ne	l*eu*r
faut*eui*l	h*eu*reux
b*eu*rre	p*eu*r
profess*eu*r	b*œu*f

culture

Mealtimes in France are in many ways different from their counterparts in America. Breakfast is a relatively small meal in France. Some people drink only a bowl of *café au lait,* which is coffee and heated milk in equal proportions. Others will eat a slice or two of bread with jam or *pâte à tartiner* along with their *café au lait. Pâte à tartiner,* available in many brands, is a paste of chocolate and finely ground hazelnuts which is very popular in Europe.

Lunch is the principal meal of the day for families that can be together at home from work and school. For them it is a large sit-down meal served in courses. First there will be some sort of appetizer, next the main course, then a salad (usually just leaf lettuce and vinaigrette), then cheese, dessert, and finally coffee. Some workers in large cities and even some students are not able to return home for lunch. Instead they eat in *une cantine* (a cafeteria), go to a self-service or a fast-food restaurant, or eat a lunch they have brought from home.

The French generally eat dinner later than we do in America. Since the children go to school most of the afternoon and since the father does not usually arrive from work until 6:00 or even 7:00, it is not unusual to begin dinner at 8:00. Since the children get very hungry before then, they are allowed *un goûter* (an afternoon snack) when they get home from school. Dinner is a small meal similar to our American lunch if the family has eaten their main meal at noon. Those who eat lunch at work and school will have their large meal in the evening. The evening meal is a time when most families spend several hours together at the table just talking and sharing the day's events with one another.

French table etiquette is somewhat different from ours. It is considered proper to have both hands, but not the elbows, on the table while eating. Parents scold their children for not having both hands on the table. Many French people eat left-handed, cutting their meat with the knife in the right hand and the fork in the left, but not transferring the fork to the right hand after cutting the meat. Some people eat their entire meal left-handed all the time.

For dining out there are many choices of cafés and restaurants in France. People go to a café for a light meal or for just a cup of coffee or some other beverage. For a more substantial meal, they go to a restaurant. It is customary and expected to leave *un pourboire* (a tip of 15 per cent) unless the menu specifies *service compris* (the tip is included in the price). If it is not included, the menu may not say anything about it or may specify *service non-compris*. In either case it is the responsibility of the customer to take note of this and act accordingly. Not leaving a tip is a serious breach of restaurant etiquette. One other word of caution to an American dining in a French restaurant concerns the method by which meat is cooked. Most French people prefer their red meat very rare, and they would almost never order it *bien cuit* (well done). Even if the customer specifies *bien cuit*, it will most likely arrive medium, not well done.

Quel temps fait-il?

Colossiens 3, 23 Tout ce que vous faites, faites-le de bon cœur, comme pour le Seigneur et non pour des hommes.

8 8 8 8 8 8 8 8 8 8

The Plouvins and Duponts are planning an evening to go on tract distribution.

M. Dupont: On va distribuer des traités ce soir?

M. Plouvin: Attends. (Il regarde le journal.) Nous sommes bien mardi. Ah . . . non, pas ce soir, car selon la météo il va pleuvoir.

M. Dupont: Oui, elle a raison. Il pleut déjà. Quel temps est-ce qu'il va faire demain soir?

M. Plouvin: Il va faire beau demain.

M. Dupont: Bon. A demain.

maintenant en anglais . . .

Mr. Dupont: Are we going to pass out tracts this evening?

Mr. Plouvin: Wait. (He looks at the newspaper.) Today is Tuesday. Uh . . . no, not this evening, because, according to the forecast, it's going to rain.

Mr. Dupont: That's right. It's raining already. What will the weather be like tomorrow night?

Mr. Plouvin: It is going to be nice tomorrow.

Mr. Dupont: Good. Till tomorrow.

vocabulaire

Quel temps fait-il?

Il fait du soleil.　　Il fait du brouillard.　　Il pleut.　　Il neige.

Il gèle. _____　　　　　　　　　　　　　Il fait du vent.

Il fait chaud.　　　　　　　　Il fait froid.
Il fait 30°C.　　　　　　　　Il fait 2° de température.

Il fait frais.
Il fait 10°C.

Il fait beau.

Il fait mauvais.

les saisons

Quelle saison est-ce? C'est l'automne.

le printemps
Il pleut beaucoup au printemps.

l'été
Il fait très chaud en été.

l'automne
Il fait un peu frais en automne.

l'hiver
Il neige souvent en hiver.

Notice that to say ''*in* spring,'' one uses *au* printemps; for the other seasons *en* is used.

les jours de la semaine

Quel jour sommes-nous? Nous sommes lundi.
Quel jour est-ce aujourd'hui? C'est aujourd'hui lundi.

lundi *Monday*
mardi *Tuesday*
mercredi *Wednesday*
jeudi *Thursday*
vendredi *Friday*
samedi *Saturday*
dimanche *Sunday*

lundi	mardi	mercredi	jeudi	vendredi	samedi	dimanche
	1	2	3	4	5	6
7	8	9	10	11	12	13
14	15	16	17	18	19	20
21	22	23	24	25	26	27
28	29	30	31			

A. Quel jour sommes-nous?
   modèle: Nous n'avons pas de cours *(classes)*. *Nous sommes samedi.*
   1. Nous allons à l'église.
   2. On fait la lessive.
   3. En France, c'est le deuxième jour de la semaine.
   4. En France, c'est le premier jour de la semaine.
   5. Après ce jour, le weekend commence.
   6. C'est le jour après mercredi.

B. Répondez.
   1. Quel jour sommes-nous aujourd'hui?
   2. Quel temps fait-il aujourd'hui?
   3. Quelle est la température chez toi en été?
   4. Fait-il froid chez toi en hiver?
   5. C'est quelle saison quand *(when)* . . .
           il pleut souvent?
           il neige?
           il fait beaucoup de soleil?
           on rentre à l'école?
           c'est Noël?
           nous allons en vacances?
           il fait 1°C?

prepositions of geography

Use the preposition *à* to mean *at, to,* or *in* with the name of a city.
   Nous allons à Paris en été.
   L'Echalotte est à Toulouse.

C. Tell where each of these people is going.
      modèle: je (the capital of France) *Je vais à Paris.*
      1. nous (the capital of the USA)
      2. Adèle (the capital of the USSR)
      3. je (the capital of Italy)
      4. tu (the hometown of the Yankees)
      5. Diane et Etienne (the home of the Plouvins)
      6. vous (the capital of Spain)

D. Quel temps fait-il?
      1. Quel temps fait-il en hiver à Québec?
      2. Quel temps fait-il en été à Washington?
      3. Quel temps fait-il en automne à Boston?
      4. Quel temps fait-il toujours à Honolulu?
      5. Quel temps fait-il en été à Anchorage?
      6. Quel temps fait-il en hiver à Miami?

faire (to do, to make)

je fais	nous faisons
tu fais	vous faites
il, elle, on fait	ils, elles font

Faire is the most common verb in the French language. The main meanings of *faire* are *to do* or *to make,* but *faire* is also used in many idiomatic expressions such as those referring to the weather. Here are some other *faire* idioms:

On fait des courses.	*We are doing some errands.*
Je fais la queue.	*I stand in line.*
Deux et trois font cinq.	*Two and three make five.*
Pierre fait des achats.	*Peter does some shopping.*
Elle fait la grasse matinée.	*She sleeps in.*
Les filles font du jogging.	*The girls are jogging.*
Mon frère fait la lessive.	*My brother is doing the laundry.*
Elle fait du français.	*She is studying French.*
On fait attention au professeur.	*One pays attention to the teacher.*
Nous faisons la vaisselle.	*We do the dishes.*

E. Change the verb to agree with the new subject given.
 1. Je fais la grasse matinée. (nous)
 2. Elle fait des achats. (tu)
 3. Nous ne faisons pas de courses. (ils)
 4. Elles font du français. (je)
 5. Tu fais la queue. (vous)
 6. Vous faites la lessive. (Maman)

chapitre huit

F. Use the verb *faire* to describe what each person is doing.
   modèle:

Florence fait la grasse matinée.   David

M. Fisel   Mme Leclerc

Jean-Pierre   Lise et Germaine

G. Use the verb *faire* to describing each of these situations.
   1. Your sister has her French book open before her as she listens to a cassette of French grammar drills.
   2. We are at a shopping mall buying Christmas gifts.
   3. Your mother is mixing ingredients for a cake.
   4. Tell that the sum of 30 and 45 is 75.
   5. I am waiting in line to buy a ticket to a football game.
   6. Your brother sleeps until 10:30.
   7. It is a beautiful day.
   8. It's 15°C.

demonstrative adjectives

Il va pleuvoir ce soir.   *It is going to rain this evening.*

In this sentence from the dialogue the word for *this* is *ce*. *Ce* is a demonstrative adjective since it "points out" a specific evening. The French demonstrative adjectives take four different forms in order to show number and gender agreement:

masculine	feminine	plural
ce garçon	cette fille	ces traités
cet enfant		

Two different masculine forms are used, depending on whether the noun begins with a consonant or vowel sound. The demonstrative adjectives are translated as either *this* or *that* in the singular and either *these* or *those* in the plural. The distinction of closeness or distance cannot be made with just a demonstrative adjective in French. *J'aime ce livre* can mean either *I like this book* or *I like that book*.

H. Change the italicized articles to demonstrative adjectives.
   modèle: Le chat est sur la table. *Ce chat est sur la table.*
   1. *Le* chat regarde *un* oiseau dans une cage.
   2. Mlle Roselle cherche *une* boîte de sardines.
   3. Elle donne *les* sardines au chat.
   4. *Le* chat ne mange jamais de sardines.
   5. Il n'aime pas *les* petits poissons dans une boîte.
   6. Il préfère *un* animal dans une cage.
   7. Le chat entre dans *la* cage.
   8. *Le* repas est délicieux.

I. Tell which item you prefer for each category as you point to your preference. Use a demonstrative adjective in your statement.
   modèle:

   Je préfère ces fruits. (point to your preference)

   1.

lundi	mardi	mercredi	jeudi	vendredi	samedi	dimanche

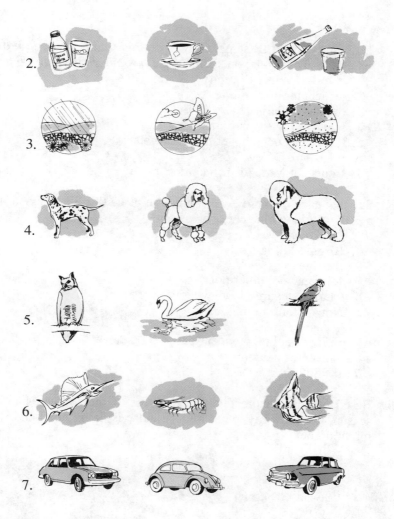

2.
3.
4.
5.
6.
7.

futur proche

The near future is expressed in French much as it is in English–with a form of the verb *to go* and an infinitive:

> Il va neiger demain.
> *It is going to snow tomorrow.*
> Vous allez manger au café.
> *You are going to eat at the café.*

In the negative *futur proche* structure, the *ne* and the *pas* surround the form of the verb *aller*. The infinitive follows *pas*.

> Je ne vais pas prendre l'autobus.
> *I am not going to take the autobus.*

J. Tell what each of these people will do this summer based on the cue.
   modèle: Isabelle–faire du ski nautique *Isabelle va faire du ski nautique.*
   1. Yves–traverser l'océan
   2. je–acheter une voiture
   3. tu–aller à Paris
   4. nous–faire la grasse matinée
   5. Hervé et Luc–manger des escargots
   6. vous–être à New York
   7. Louise et Marc–distribuer des traités

K. Say that each of these events will take place this Saturday.
   modèle: Roland dîne chez ses parents.
        Roland va dîner chez ses parents ce samedi.
   1. Brigitte fait la lessive.
   2. Il neige.
   3. Je prépare le dîner pour ma famille.
   4. Clarisse regarde la télévision.
   5. Nous allons au musée.
   6. Tu as sommeil.
   7. Eric et Paul ne prennent pas le train.
   8. Vous êtes heureux.
   9. Il fait 25°.

L. Based on this picture give at least five of the following facts–date,
   season, weather, city, what Mme Baudry is doing now, and what she
   might do next.

M. Using the *futur proche,* write or tell the class about five things you are
going to do this weekend.

French oral vowel sounds (part III)

The mid vowel sounds produced in the back of the mouth are /ɔ/ and /o/.
The lips are rounded in the articulation of both of these sounds. Here are
some words containing them:

/ɔ/	/o/
éc*o*le	vél*o*
s*o*mmes	gig*o*t
fér*o*ce	s*o*leil
v*o*tre	h*ô*tel
m*o*nnaie	c*ô*té
b*o*nne	cha*u*d
Nic*o*le	Ma*u*rice

The /ɔ/ sound is always found in a syllable ending in a consonant sound. In
fact, all the lower mid vowels (/ɛ/, /o/, /ɔ/) are generally found in syllables
ending in a consonant sound. On the other hand, the higher mid vowels
(/e/, /ø/, /o/) are generally found in open syllables, that is, those syllables
ending in the vowel sound itself.

lower mid vowels	**higher mid vowels**
/ɛ/ + consonant sound	/e/ at end of syllable
*e*lle	mang*e*r
pèr*e*	vél*o*
/œ/ + consonant sound	/ø/ at end of syllable
j*eu*ne	j*e*
*œu*f	p*eu*
/ɔ/ + consonant sound	/o/ at end of syllable
Christ*o*phe	Lé*o*
n*o*tre	h*ô*pital

There are a few exceptions to this principle. Notably, the letters *au* and *ô*
are always pronounced /o/, regardless of where they are found:

cha*u*d	cha*u*de
h*ô*tel	h*ô*te (*host*)

All four of the above are pronounced with /o/.

France has a wide variety of climates which are all, generally speaking, quite mild. For example, the average temperature in Paris in the winter is 35°F and in the summer 70°F. This often surprises people when they see on a map that Paris is farther north than Québec City or even that Nice on the coast of the Mediterranean is farther north than Boston. The three main influences on the climate of France are the Gulf Stream in the Atlantic Ocean, the mountain ranges, and the Mediterranean Sea. Because of the Gulf Stream, the western part of France has a temperate climate similar to the coastal region in the western United States (Northern California, Oregon, and Washington). Except in the high mountainous regions of the Pyrenees and the Massif Central, western France has mild winters with very little snow and mild, rainy summers which are cool in the north and hot in the south. Eastern France has cold, dry winters because of its distance from the ocean and its three mountain ranges–the Vosges, the Jura, and the Alps. Summers in the eastern part of France are hot, humid, and rainy. The climate of the southeastern section of France is influenced by the Mediterranean Sea. The winters are moderately mild, and the summers are dry and hot. In the spring and fall, the southeast receives heavy rains, but the rest of France receives ample rain all year, with some sections getting rain or drizzle two days out of three. Because of the adequate rains and the mild climate, the farmland of France is highly productive and the crops are varied.

une journée typique

Romains 6, 23 Car le salaire du péché, c'est la mort, mais le don gratuit de Dieu, c'est la vie éternelle en Jésus-Christ notre Seigneur.

9 9 9 9 9 9 9 9 9 9

in the morning	*Le matin*, Mme Plouvin fait sa toilette, met des chaussures con-
the kitchen	fortables et fait son lit. Puis dans *la cuisine* elle prépare du café
	au lait pour sa famille. Son mari étudie la Bible et les enfants
leave	mettent la table. Après le petit déjeuner Jean-Luc et Denis *partent*
	pour l'école. M. Plouvin vide la corbeille, donne à manger au
leave/office	chien et *quitte* la maison pour aller à son *bureau* à l'église. Mme
to do the housework	Plouvin commence alors à *faire le ménage*. Elle fait la vaisselle
food	et passe l'aspirateur. Elle va au marché pour acheter *de la nour-*
	riture pour le déjeuner et le dîner. Quand elle rentre, elle repasse
in the afternoon	les vêtements. *L'après-midi* elle fait une étude biblique avec sa
in the evening/serves	voisine. *Le soir* elle prépare et *sert* le dîner pour sa famille. La
full	journée typique de Mme Plouvin est *pleine* d'activités.

vocabulaire

Qu'est-ce qu'on fait?

Elle fait sa toilette.

Elle met des chaussures.

Elle fait son lit.

Il étudie sa Bible.

Les enfants mettent la table.

Il vide la corbeille.

Il donne à manger au chien.

Elle fait la vaisselle.

Elle passe l'aspirateur.

Elle fait la cuisine.

Elle repasse des vêtements.

Elle sert le dîner.

une journée typique

A. Qu'est-ce que tu fais quand . . . ? Describe what you do in the following situations.

modèle: The dog is hungry. *Je donne à manger au chien.*

1. The dishes are dirty.
2. The bedclothes are in a pile.
3. You need to prepare for your Sunday school class.
4. Your shirt (*chemise*, f.) is wrinkled.
5. There are crumbs on the floor.
6. You are in your stocking feet and want to go outside.
7. You need to prepare dinner.
8. Your food is ready to be served.
9. The wastebasket is overflowing.

Qu'est-ce qu'on utilise?

B. Qu'est-ce qu'on utilise pour . . . ? Refer to the picture above.

modèle: couper *(cut)* la viande   *un couteau*

1. manger de la soupe
2. manger de la viande
3. prendre du café
4. prendre de l'eau
5. couvrir *(cover)* la table
6. mettre les aliments sur la table

Qu'est-ce qu'on porte? (porter *to wear*)

les vêtements pour hommes

les vêtements pour femmes

une chemise

un tee-shirt

un pantalon

des chaussettes

des chaussures

un chapeau

un chemisier

une jupe

un sac

des bas de nylon

des chaussures

un blue-jean (blue jeans)
une veste (a jacket)
un complet (a suit)
une cravate (a tie)
un imperméable (a raincoat)
un parapluie (an umbrella)

une robe (a dress)
un tailleur (a suit)
un manteau (a winter coat)
un pull-over (a sweater)
un foulard (a scarf)

C. Répondez en français.
1. Qu'est-ce que tu portes maintenant?
2. Et ton ami(e), qu'est-ce qu'il (elle) porte?
3. Qu'est-ce que tu portes le dimanche pour aller à l'église?
4. Qu'est-ce que le professeur porte aujourd'hui?
5. Qu'est-ce que tu vas porter demain?

une journée typique

mettre (to put, to put on)

je mets	nous mettons
tu mets	vous mettez
il, elle, on met	ils, elles mettent

Mettre has several meanings, according to its context. The basic meaning is "to put" or "to place."

Elle met la Bible sur l'étagère.

It can also mean "to set" when referring to the table:

Les fils mettent la table.

Another meaning is "to put on" when referring to clothing:

Je mets mon pyjama.

D. You are going on vacation. Tell what everyone puts in the car as you pack.

modèle: mon frère/le chien   *Mon frère met le chien dans la voiture.*
1. nous/nos Bibles
2. mes sœurs/des parapluies
3. ma mère/des sandwichs
4. mon frère/des bouteilles d'orangeade
5. je/mon pyjama

E. Tell what each person is putting on according to the drawing.

modèle:

Martine met sa jupe.

1.

vous

2.   Brigitte

3.   M. Henry

4.   tu

5.   nous

6.   les femmes

7.   je

8.   Georges et Paul

-ir verbs like *dormir* (to sleep)

je dors	nous dormons
tu dors	vous dormez
il, elle, on dort	ils, elles dorment

You have already studied the verbs ending in -er *(regarder,* etc.) The -ir verbs like *dormir* are a group of verbs conjugated in a slightly different manner. The main characteristic of all these verbs is a consonant that is pronounced in the infinitive and plural forms, but not in the singular forms. This difference is reflected in the spelling. For example, in the verb *dormir,* there is an *m* in the infinitive and plural forms that does not appear at all in the singular forms. Another common characteristic of these verbs is the endings of the singular forms: *-s, -s, -t.* Other *-ir* verbs like *dormir* are *partir* (to leave), *sortir* (to go out), *servir* (to serve), and *mentir* (to lie). Notice the difference between the second-person singular and plural forms of these verbs. What consonant sound is heard in the plural but not the singular for each verb?

tu pars	but	vous partez
tu sors	but	vous sortez
tu sers	but	vous servez
tu mens	but	vous mentez

F. Answer the questions using the cues provided.
    modèle: Qui dort dans mon lit? (le chat) *Le chat dort dans ton lit.*
    1. Qui sort avec ma sœur? (Didier)
    2. Qui part après le petit déjeuner? (les enfants)
    3. Qui ment à Paul? (le petit garçon)
    4. Qui part pour Toulouse? (nous)
    5. Qui dort tous les matins? (vous)
    6. Qui sort du restaurant? (je)
    7. Qui sert le repas? (le garçon)
    8. Qui ment au professeur? (Natacha)
    9. Qui dort chez nous? (nos amis)
   10. Qui sert le Seigneur? (nous)

Partir, sortir, and *quitter* are similar in meaning, but are used in different grammatical contexts. *Partir,* meaning "to leave," is intransitive. It may be followed by a prepositional phrase, but never a direct object:

Je pars de la maison.   *I am leaving the house.*
Nous partons pour Paris.   *We are leaving for Paris.*

Sortir means "to go out" or "to exit" and may also be followed by a prepositional phrase.

Je sors avec ma petite amie.   *I am going out with my girlfriend.*
Il sort de la maison.   *He is going out of the house.*

Quitter can take a direct object:

Ils quittent leurs amis.   *They are leaving their friends.*
Tu quittes la maison.   *You are leaving the house.*

G. Give the correct form of *partir, sortir,* or *quitter* to complete each of these sentences.

    modèle: Je _____ la gare. *Je quitte la gare.*
    1. Vous _____ pour Nice.
    2. Les filles _____ avec leurs amis.
    3. Tu _____ de l'église.
    4. Nous _____ nos cousins.
    5. Christophe _____ en autobus.
    6. Pascale et Ida _____ le salon.

H. Answer according to your situation?

    1. Tu pars pour la France cet été?
    2. Tu sors souvent avec tes amis?
    3. Est-ce que ta mère sert du bifteck ce dimanche?
    4. Tu mets des chaussures confortables après l'école?
    5. Tu pars pour aller à une étude biblique ce soir?
    6. Tu dors dans un sac de couchage ce weekend?
    7. Tu mets un complet (un tailleur) pour aller à l'église?
    8. Tu pars pour aller chez tes grands-parents pour Noël?
    9. Est-ce que ton chien (chat) dort avec toi?
   10. Tu sors de l'école pour déjeuner?
   11. Est-ce que ta mère sert des spaghetti cette semaine?

adjective placement

Until now you have seen adjectives used only as predicate adjectives:

> La fille est amusante.
> Les enfants sont bavards.
> Ses chaussures sont confortables.

When adjectives come within a noun phrase, most follow the noun they describe:

> La fille amusante va à mon école.
> Les enfants bavards ont beaucoup d'amis.
> Elle met ses chaussures confortables.

Among the adjectives that follow the noun are those denoting color:

> Je mange du fromage bleu.
> Elle porte une jupe verte.

De quelle couleur sont ces vêtements? What color are these clothes?

Voici une jupe rouge.

Voici une chemise jaune.

Voici une robe verte (m. vert).

Voici un pantalon bleu (f. bleue).

Voici un foulard violet (f. violette).

Voici des chaussures brunes (m. brun).

Voici un sac noir (f. noire).

Voici un chemisier blanc (f. blanche).

I. Describe what each person is wearing.
modèle:

Simone

Simone porte une robe rouge.

Jacques

1.

Renée

2.

je

3.

Edouard

4.

Christel

5.

une journée typique

J. Tell what you are wearing, including colors.

K. Answer the questions, rewording the sentences so that the predicate adjective becomes part of a noun phrase.
   modèle: Ce livre est ennuyeux? *Oui, c'est un livre ennuyeux.*
   Ces enfants sont bavards? *Oui, ce sont des enfants bavards.*
   1. Cette femme est heureuse?
   2. Ces oiseaux sont rouges?
   3. Cet homme est pauvre?
   4. Ce fauteuil est confortable?
   5. Cette pomme est délicieuse?
   6. Ces chaussettes sont vertes?
   7. Ces chiens sont méchants?
   8. Cet imperméable est brun?

A small number of adjectives precede the noun that they modify. You have already seen several of these:

   Nous prenons le petit déjeuner.
   Il parle à la jeune fille.
   Faites-le de bon cœur.
   Elle va à la grande surface.

Here is a list of the most common adjectives that come before nouns along with a helpful way to remember them–the acronym **bags**:

beauty	age	goodness	size
beau (belle)	vieux (vieille)	bon(ne)	grand(e)
joli(e)	nouveau (nouvelle)	mauvais(e)	gros(se)
	jeune		petit(e)

L. Answer the questions affirmatively, rewording the sentences so that the predicate adjective becomes part of the noun phrase.
   modèle: Cette cathédrale est belle? *Oui, c'est une belle cathédrale.*
   1. Ce livre est mauvais?
   2. Cette tomate est bonne?
   3. Cet homme est jeune?
   4. Cette maison est nouvelle?
   5. Ce garçon est grand?
   6. Cette voiture est grosse?
   7. Cette robe est jolie?

chapitre neuf

M. Add the adjectives in parentheses to the sentence to describe the nouns in italics. Be sure to use correct adjective agreement and placement.

modèle: Ma *sœur* fait la vaisselle. (têtu, petit)

Ma petite sœur têtue fait la vaisselle.

1. Le *professeur* va au musée. (bavard, vieux)
2. Les *jeunes filles* dorment bien. (blond, petit)
3. Il porte un *pantalon*. (noir, nouveau)
4. Je porte mes *chaussures*. (confortable, vieux)
5. Le *chien* mange derrière la maison. (brun, gros)

For the most part, when a masculine singular adjective comes before a vowel sound, it sounds like the feminine adjective. This is the result of liaison.

Le petit garçon va avec nous.   Le petit₍ₜ₎enfant va avec nous.
C'est un mauvais livre.   C'est un mauvais₍z₎exemple.

In liaison contexts, the adjectives *beau, vieux,* and *nouveau* also have forms that sound like their feminine counterparts. With these words, however, this change is reflected in the spelling. Thus a separate written form exists for each of these adjectives–a form that occurs only before a masculine word beginning with a vowel.

masculine	masculine before a vowel	feminine
le beau garçon	le bel homme	la belle femme
le nouveau complet	le nouvel ami	la nouvelle robe
le vieux musée	le vieil autobus	la vieille église

N. Answer these questions using the noun in parentheses. Make any necessary changes in the adjective.

modèle: Elle porte un nouveau manteau? (imperméable)

Non, elle porte un nouvel imperméable.

1. Elle achète une belle tomate? (oignon)
2. Il cherche la nouvelle poste? (restaurant)
3. M. Lafond est le vieux boulanger? (épicier)
4. Il déjeune avec sa nouvelle amie? (ami)
5. Marie parle à son vieux voisin? (voisine)
6. C'est le nouveau musée? (hôpital)
7. Philippe a une belle chatte? (chat)

une journée typique

O. Tell about each drawing, describing the nouns based on the sentence cue.

modèle:

Le garçon est petit.
Le petit garçon fait son lit.

1. Cet homme est vieux.

2. La Bible est nouvelle.

3. L'imperméable est nouveau.

4. Cette église est belle.

Suzette dîne avec son ami.
5. Il est beau.

6. Ces garçons sont grands.

P. Today is Saturday. Tell what each member of the family is doing in this picture. Make up names.

Q. You are going to have a yard sale. Describe five articles of clothing that will be on sale there. Include colors, quality, age, and size.

une journée typique

French nasal vowel sounds

There are three nasal vowel sounds in French.

	front	back
unrounded	/ɛ̃/	/ɑ̃/
rounded		/ɔ̃/

These sounds are written as a vowel followed by an *n* or an *m*. Some of the most common spellings are listed below.

/ɛ̃/	/ɑ̃/	/ɔ̃/
in, im	an, am	on, om
en (-ien)	en, em	
ain		
un, um		

Here are some words containing each of these sounds. Remember that in these words the *n* or *m* is not pronounced–it indicates only that the vowel preceding it is nasal. (See Chapter 3.)

/ɛ̃/	/ɑ̃/	/ɔ̃/
cous*in*	bl*an*c	b*on*
c*in*q	amus*ant*	bl*on*d
*im*perméable	gr*an*d	mett*on*s
b*ien*	*jam*bon	c*om*plet
p*ain*	*en*f*an*t	b*om*be
un	*en*s*em*ble	
parf*um*		

General principles for the pronunciation of the *n* or *m:*

- If the *n* or *m* is double or followed by a vowel, pronounce it. Remember that the vowel is not nasal here.

  Etienne /etjɛn/   Anne /an/   bonne /bɔn/
  cousine /kuzin/   ami /ami/   téléphone /telefɔn/

- If the *n* or *m* is at the end of a word or followed by a consonant sound, do not pronounce it.

  cousin /kuzɛ̃/   an /ã/   maison /mɛzɔ̃/
  simple /sɛ̃plø/   tante /tãt/   onze /ɔ̃z/

culture

The role of women in France is undergoing change. While more women in France than in America choose to be full-time homemakers, over half of all French women now hold jobs. This trend has begun to bring about some changes in the traditional French lifestyle. If both the husband and the wife work, neither is available to go to the market during the day. This has made the *supermarchés* and the *grandes surfaces* more and more popular. The husband and other family members have now started to help with tasks that were always considered part of the wife's duties–cleaning, dishwashing, child care, etc.

No matter who does them, though, the household chores are basically the same in France as in America–cooking, cleaning, laundry, ironing, mending, making beds, etc. In recent years household appliances and gadgets that make all of these chores faster and easier are readily available everywhere in France. In fact French homemakers have a choice of some conveniences that are rare in America, such as kitchen ranges with two gas burners and two electric burners. Since France is extremely energy-conscious, appliances do not have pilot lights that burn constantly, using up precious gas. Instead these appliances have electronic ignitions. Water heaters are quite small and heat water only if someone has turned the hot water on. As soon as the faucet is turned off, the flame goes out. French dishwashers and washing machines all have built-in water heaters for generating their own hot water.

chapitre neuf

écrire une lettre

Romains 3, 10 Selon qu'il est écrit: Il n'y a point de juste, Pas même un seul.

lecture

<table>
<tr><td>several/writes</td><td>Après *plusieurs* semaines, Mme Dupont *écrit* une lettre à son</td></tr>
<tr><td>former</td><td>*ancien* professeur de français à l'université. Voici sa lettre:</td></tr>
</table>

Toulouse, le 19 janvier 19–

Chère Madame,

finally	Nous sommes *enfin* à Toulouse. La famille va bien. Nos enfants
are beginning/already	aiment beaucoup la France et *commencent déjà* à parler un peu
hear French spoken	le français. Quand j'*entends parler français,* je suis surprise de
	bien comprendre. Et je parle assez bien! Les Français parlent vite.
	Mon mari va commencer ses études en automne à l'université de
	Toulouse.

nice	La famille Plouvin, une famille française, est très *sympathique.*
	Nous faisons la connaissance de nos voisins et des membres de
worship service/	l'église. Au *culte* du dimanche *matin il y a environ* 100 per-
morning there are about	sonnes—c'est une grande église pour la France. Il y a des églises
only	protestantes qui n' ont *que* 10 ou 15 personnes. Nous participons
help	à la distribution de traités et nous *aidons* le ministère de la jeu-
pray/salvation/people	nesse. *Priez* avec nous pour le *salut* de deux jeunes *gens* de
student/take part	l'université—Christel et Hassan, un *étudiant* arabe. Ils *font partie*
meetings/are reading	des *réunions* de jeunes. Ils *lisent* la Bible et posent beaucoup de
	questions. Cet été nous allons avoir un camp pour les jeunes. Les
	Français aiment le camping.

other	Dites bonjour de ma part à votre famille et aux *autres* professeurs
	de français. Continuez à prier pour nous.

friendship (kind regards)	Mes *amitiés sincères,*

Alice Dupont

stamp	Mme Dupont écrit l'adresse sur l'enveloppe. Elle y met un *timbre*
label/by airmail/mailbox	et une *étiquette « par avion ».* Elle met la lettre dans la *boîte aux*
mail carrier	*lettres,* et quand le *facteur* passe, il prend la lettre.

A. Répondez.
1. Qui écrit cette lettre?
2. A qui écrit-elle?
3. Est-ce que les enfants parlent beaucoup le français?
4. Où est-ce que M. Dupont va étudier?
5. Comment est la famille Plouvin?
6. Est-ce que l'église de Toulouse est petite?
7. Qui sont Christel et Hassan?
8. Est-ce qu'ils sont sauvés?
9. Qu'est-ce que Mme Dupont met sur l'enveloppe?
10. Qui prend sa lettre?

vocabulaire

Quels sont les mois de l'année?

What are the months of the year?

janvier	juillet
février	août
mars	septembre
avril	octobre
mai	novembre
juin	décembre

Quelle est la date aujourd'hui?

C'est le 23 juin.

Cardinal numbers are used in giving dates in French with the exception of the first day of the month:

le premier janvier = le 1er janvier
le deux mars = le 2 mars
le trois septembre = le 3 septembre

A definite article always precedes the number, and there is no preposition *of* as in English:

le 4 juillet   *the fourth of July*

B. Répondez.
   1. Quelle est la date aujourd'hui?
   2. Quelle est la date de ton anniversaire *(birthday)*?
   3. Quelle est la date de la fête *(holiday)* nationale américaine?
   4. Quelle est la date de la fête nationale française?
   5. Quelle est la date de Noël?

French people can choose one of two ways to express the year.
   1992   dix-neuf cent quatre-vingt-douze
   1992   mil neuf cent quatre-vingt-douze

C. Read these years aloud.
   1. 1985
   2. 1947
   3. 1840
   4. 1789
   5. 1621
   6. 1979
   7. 2002
   8. 1968

D. Répondez.
   modèle: Quelle est l'année de la mort du Président Kennedy? (1963)
           C'est mil neuf cent soixante-trois.
           C'est dix-neuf cent soixante-trois.
   1. Quelle est l'année de ta naissance?
   2. Quelle est l'année de la découverte de l'Amérique? (1492)
   3. Quelle est l'année de la dédicace de la Tour Eiffel? (1889)
   4. Quelle est l'année de la mort de Napoléon? (1821)
   5. Quelle est l'année de l'atterrissage sur la lune? (1969)
   6. Quelle est l'année du commencement de la 5e République? (1958)
   7. Quelle est l'année de la naissance de Blaise Pascal? (1623)
   8. Quelle est l'année de la mort de Voltaire? (1778)

Quel est ton numéro de téléphone?

Mon numéro de téléphone est le 04.62.37.89.16.

French phone numbers contain 10 digits arranged in pairs separated by decimal points.

If you wanted to telephone someone in France from the United States, you would dial 011-33 and the number. The first three digits (011) are the international access, and 33 is the number code for France. Leave out the initial zero (0), dialing the other nine digits of the phone number.

E. Read the following telephone numbers.

modèle: Quel est le numéro des Plouvin? (05.61.84.48.02)
C'est le 05.61.84.48.02.

1. Quel est le numéro de l'Echalotte? (05.36.79.11.06)
2. Quel est le numéro de la gare? (05.84.23.17.42)
3. Quel est le numéro de l'hôpital? (05.95.14.41.70)
4. Quel est le numéro de la banque? (05.64.16.38.57)
5. Quel est le numéro des Dupont? (011.33.5.61.99.46.26)

Quelle est ton adresse?

M. et Mme Robert DUPONT
23, rue des Acacias
31100 Toulouse
FRANCE

By AIR MAIL
PAR AVION
MIT LUFTPOST

You have already learned that the French either put their return address on the back of the envelope or do not write one at all. They will usually write the family name of the recipient in all capital letters. They usually put a comma after the house number. The French word for street *(rue)* is not capitalized. The Zip Code *(le code postal)* precedes the name of the town. The first two digits of the Zip Code are the number of the department in which the town is located. (For more about departments, see p. 236.)

F. You want to send some letters to France. You need to convert the English information to a French format. How would these addresses read in French?

1. Mr. and Mrs. Philip Plouvin
   48 Molière St.
   Toulouse 31170

2. Miss Suzanne Delacroix
   17 de la Langue St.
   Paris 75020

3. Mrs. Lucienne Benoît
   56 La Fayette Street
   Calais 62100

grammaire

regular *-re* verbs

Here is the conjugation of the verb *répondre* "to answer":

je réponds	nous répondons
tu réponds	vous répondez
il, elle, on répond	ils, elles répondent

This verb represents a third group of regularly conjugated verbs. Other verbs in this group include:

attendre	*to wait*
entendre	*to hear*
perdre	*to lose*
vendre	*to sell*
descendre	*to go down*

G. Follow the model in making these substitutions.

modèle: Thomas répond toujours au professeur. (Je . . . quelquefois.)
Je réponds quelquefois au professeur.

1. Nous attendons le bus. (Rosalie . . . le train)
2. Je descends la première rue. (tu . . . la deuxième)
3. L'épicier vend le camembert à 15 F. (vous . . . à 20 F)
4. Antoine perd souvent son parapluie. (les étudiants . . . leurs livres)
5. Tu entends la pendule. (nous . . . la musique)
6. Vous répondez à vos lettres. (je . . . à mes lettres aussi)

H. Write the correct form of the verb. Choose the verb that makes sense–*répondre, attendre, entendre, vendre, perdre, descendre.* Use each verb only once.

modèle: Il _____ sa voiture à son ami.
Il vend sa voiture à son ami.

1. Vous montez la rue? Non, nous _____ la rue.
2. Mon frère _____ toujours son argent.
3. Je _____ à la question du professeur.
4. Vous _____ la météo à la radio?
5. Natalie et Yvette _____ un taxi.
6. Tu _____ ton vélo à ton cousin?

I. Répondez aux questions suivantes. Utilisez des phrases complètes.

1. Qui répond d'habitude *(usually)* au téléphone chez toi?
2. Est-ce que tu perds souvent tes livres?
3. Tu attends l'autobus le matin pour aller à l'école?
4. Est-ce que ta grand-mère entend bien?
5. Tu descends en ville *(to town)* ce weekend?

three irregular *-re* verbs

écrire *(to write)*

j'écris	nous écrivons
tu écris	vous écrivez
il, elle, on écrit	ils, elles écrivent

lire *(to read)*

je lis	nous lisons
tu lis	vous lisez
il, elle, on lit	ils, elles lisent

dire *(to say, to tell)*

je dis	nous disons
tu dis	vous dites
il, elle, on dit	ils, elles disent

All three of these verbs have the endings *-s, -s,* and *-t* in the singular forms, like those you have already seen in the *-ir* verbs like *dormir.* Before each of the plural endings, there is a consonant sound not found in the infinitive. In *écrire* it is /v/, and for *lire* it is /z/. *Dire* also has a /z/ sound in the *nous* and *ils/elles* forms, but the *vous* form is irregular. Only three verbs in French have *vous* forms that do not end in *-ez.* You have learned all three; *vous êtes, vous faites,* and *vous dites.*

J. Write the correct form of the verb in parentheses.
1. Olivier _____ une lettre à ses parents. (écrire)
2. Nous _____ la réponse correcte. (écrire)
3. Quel livre est-ce que vous _____? (lire)
4. Je _____ dans ma Bible chaque matin. (lire)
5. Elles _____ bonjour à leurs amies. (dire)
6. Vous _____ la vérité? (dire)
7. Je _____ une carte postale à mon ancien professeur. (écrire)
8. Ils _____ des magazines de sport? (lire)
9. Tu _____ au revoir. (dire)
10. On _____ qu'il va neiger. (dire)

K. Construct complete sentences from the words supplied.

modèle: nous/dire/vérité/à/parents

Nous disons la vérité à nos parents.

1. je/écrire/souvent/à/frère
2. elles/lire/lettre/de/mère
3. nous/dire/bonjour/à/nouveau/étudiant
4. Patrick/lire/livre de français
5. tu/écrire/lettre/à/oncle
6. vous/ne . . . pas/dire/vérité

L. Using *écrire*, *lire*, and *dire*, make up a sentence to explain what is happening in each drawing.

il y a and voilà

The expression *il y a,* which means "there is" or "there are," denotes the existence of a particular noun.

Il y a un garçon français dans ma classe.
There is a French boy in my class.

Il y a peu d'églises protestantes en France.
There are few Protestant churches in France.

Voilà denotes the actual presence of a particular noun somewhere within sight.

> Voilà le garçon français qui est dans ma classe.
> *There is the French boy who is in my class. (pointing to the boy)*
> Voilà une église protestante, là-bas en face du musée.
> *There is a Protestant church, over there across from the museum. (pointing to the church building)*

M. Tell what is in each place.

> *modèle:* dans la rue . . . une auto   *Il y a une auto dans la rue.*
> 1. sur l'étagère . . . un livre
> 2. dans la cage . . . deux oiseaux
> 3. à Toulouse . . . beaucoup de bons restaurants
> 4. à la pâtisserie . . . une belle tarte aux pommes
> 5. sous la table . . . un gros chien féroce

N. Choose between *voilà* and *il y a*.

> 1. _____ mon frère.
> 2. En face de la poste _____ une banque.
> 3. _____ trois garçons dans ma classe.
> 4. _____ notre professeur.
> 5. _____ un bon restaurant dans ma ville.
> 6. « Où est le musée? » « _____ le musée.»

français, le français, le Français

In Mme Dupont's letter you saw various forms of the word *français* in these contexts:

> Les enfants . . . commencent déjà à parler un peu le français.
> . . . quand j'entends le français.
> Les Français parlent vite.
> . . . une famille française.

The word *français* is capitalized only when it is a noun referring to a French person:

> Philippe est un Français, et Sophie est une Française.

When the noun refers to the French language, it is not capitalized, and it is usually preceded by the article *le*. The article is not used immediately after the verb *parler* or after the preposition *en:*

J'étudie le français.	Parlez-vous français?
Elle comprend le français.	Ecrivez cette lettre en français.

As an adjective, *français* shows agreement, follows the noun it modifies, and is not capitalized:

un livre français   *a French book*
une voiture française   *a French car*

O. What is the correct written form of *français* in each of these sentences? Tell whether it should include an article and if it should be capitalized or not. Make it agree if it is an adjective.
  1. Ma mère parle _____.
  2. J'aime la cuisine _____.
  3. Oui, _____ mangent les escargots.
  4. Tu comprends _____?
  5. La femme de mon cousin est _____.
  6. Ils écrivent une lettre en _____.
  7. Est-ce que tu parles _____?

ne . . . que

Ne . . . que follows the same pattern as the other negatives you have learned—*ne* precedes the verb and *que* follows it. It means *only*.

Je n'ai que cent francs.   *I have only a hundred francs.*

Compare with the following sentences:

Je n'ai pas cent francs.   *I do not have a hundred francs.*
Je n'ai jamais cent francs.   *I never have a hundred francs.*

P. Answer the question with the indicated limitation.
   modèle: Combien de frères est-ce que tu as? (un)
            Je n'ai qu'un frère.
            Est-ce que tu parles français et japonais? (français)
            Je ne parle que le français.
  1. Combien d'argent est-ce que tu as? (trois francs)
  2. Combien de cousins est-ce que tu as? (deux)
  3. Est-ce que tu manges beaucoup de bananes? (une)
  4. Est-ce que tu aimes les crevettes et les escargots? (les crevettes)
  5. Combien de lettres est-ce que tu écris chaque semaine? (trois)
  6. Est-ce que tu aimes l'été et l'hiver? (l'été)

Q. State what is true in your case for each of these items. Begin your sentence with one of these: *J'ai, Je n'ai que, Je n'ai pas, Je n'ai jamais*. *modèle:* deux frères   *Je n'ai pas deux frères.*

1. deux dollars
2. deux amis
3. deux sœurs
4. deux chats

5. deux chapeaux
6. deux Bibles
7. deux voitures
8. deux parapluies

R. You have just received the name and address of a pen pal in France. Write a letter in French telling him about yourself and your family. Include some descriptions, likes, dislikes, and plans for the future. Limit yourself to structures that you have learned.

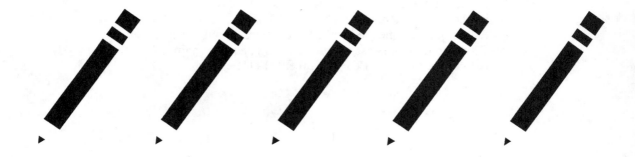

French consonant sounds (part I)

sound	letter(s)	representative words
/p/	p	père
/t/	t, th	table, théâtre
/k/	c, k, ch, q	cage, kilo, Christ, cinq
/b/	b	beau
/d/	d	deux
/g/	g	gare
/f/	f, ph	fenêtre, Philippe
/v/	v, w	vous, wagon
/s/	s, ç, ss, t, x	sœur, ça, croissant, station, dix
/z/	z, s	zéro, lisons
/š/	ch	chaise
/ž/	j, g	je, Georges
/r/	r	rouge
/l/	l	le, il
/m/	m	mardi
/n/	n	nous
/ñ/	gn	oignon
/ŋ/	ng	camping

culture

The post office in France has more functions than just mail service. A person can buy a *mandat* (money order), cash a check, send a *télégramme* (telegram), or make a phone call from a *cabine téléphonique* (telephone booth). Formerly, many people had to make all of their phone calls from the post office since very few people had telephones in their homes. However, the French phone system changed radically in the 1980s. Until then, phone service in France was very poor, and a phone conversation often consisted of, «Allô! Allô! Ne quittez pas . . . Allô?» Usually, a normal telephone conversation was cut off at least once by the system itself. A popular French joke in the 1970s was that "half of France is waiting to have a phone installed, and the other half is waiting for a dial tone." The *Direction Générale des Télécommunications (DGT)* went through a long process of upgrading the telephone system in the 1980s, which reached its climax at 11:00 P.M., October 25, 1985. At that time, all the phone numbers in France were changed from seven to eight digits. An eighth digit was necessary because eventually there would not have been enough phone numbers. Since the phone system in France improved, the waiting period for telephone installation has gone from six months to one or two days. Fiber optics have made service reliable and phone calls clear.

écrire une lettre

Today, France is a world leader in the field of telecommunications. Not only has the quality of the nation's telephone service improved, but the types of service have also become quite varied. About half of the phone booths still require coins, but the other half allow the user to insert a phone card equipped with a microchip which has a certain number of units programmed into it. The computerized phones subtract units from the chip, based on the time of day and distance of the call. These cards are on sale at the post office and many different stores, such as the *tabac,* a shop that sells a variety of things–tobacco products, postcards, postage stamps, and reading materials. Another telephone service available in France is Minitel. This is a small computer terminal which can be hooked up to a phone. For most people the Minitel serves as a telephone directory for the address and phone number of everyone in France, except those whose numbers are unlisted. Users are able to make travel arrangements and reservations, find out arrival and departure times of trains and planes, check their bank balance, and even play chess with someone else at another Minitel. Through Minitel over 4,000 different services are available from small businesses or large corporations. Although the rates for using Minitel are high, telephone customers receive the first three minutes of every transmission free, and the terminals are available at no charge.

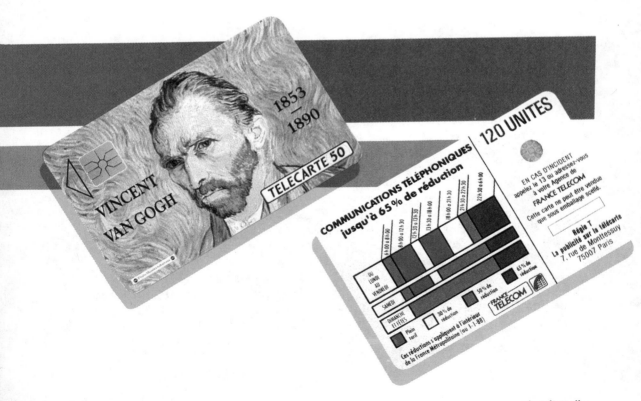

chapitre dix

chapitre onze

chez le médecin

Jean 3, 16 Car Dieu a tant aimé le monde qu'il a donné son Fils unique, afin que quiconque croit en lui ne périsse point, mais qu'il ait la vie éternelle.

11 11 11 11 11 11 11 11

yesterday/spent a night		*Hier* M. Dupont *a passé une nuit* terrible. Il a beaucoup toussé
eight thirty		et il n'a pas bien dormi. Il téléphone à M. Plouvin à *huit heures et demie* du matin.

sick	M. Dupont:	Philippe, je suis *malade*.
	M. Plouvin:	Qu'est-ce que tu as?
headache/all night	M. Dupont:	J'ai *mal à la tête* et j'ai toussé *toute la nuit*.
fever	M. Plouvin:	Tu as de *la fièvre?*
	M. Dupont:	Oui, j'ai pris ma température. J'ai 39° de température.
thinking about going	M. Plouvin:	Tu *penses aller* chez le médecin?
why	M. Dupont:	C'est *pourquoi* je t'appelle. Comment s'appelle
make an appointment		ton médecin? Je voudrais *fixer un rendez-vous* aujourd'hui.
	M. Plouvin:	Ecoute, je vais téléphoner pour toi. Tu voudrais y aller ce matin?
	M. Dupont:	Oui, si c'est possible.
	M. Plouvin:	Quelle heure est-il maintenant?
about	M. Dupont:	Il est huit heures et demie. Est-ce possible *vers* dix heures?
okay	M. Plouvin:	*D'accord*. Je téléphone au médecin.
	M. Dupont:	Merci beaucoup. A tout à l'heure.

A. Répondez.
1. Quelle sorte de nuit est-ce que M. Dupont a passé hier?
2. Pourquoi est-ce qu'il n'a pas bien dormi?
3. Quelle est sa température?
4. Qui va téléphoner au médecin?
5. Quand est-ce que M. Dupont préfère aller chez le médecin?

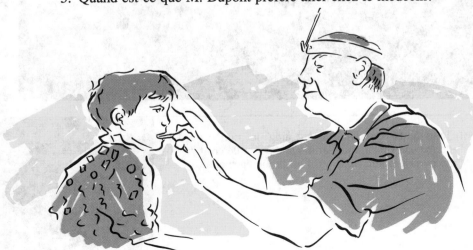

la tête

le corps

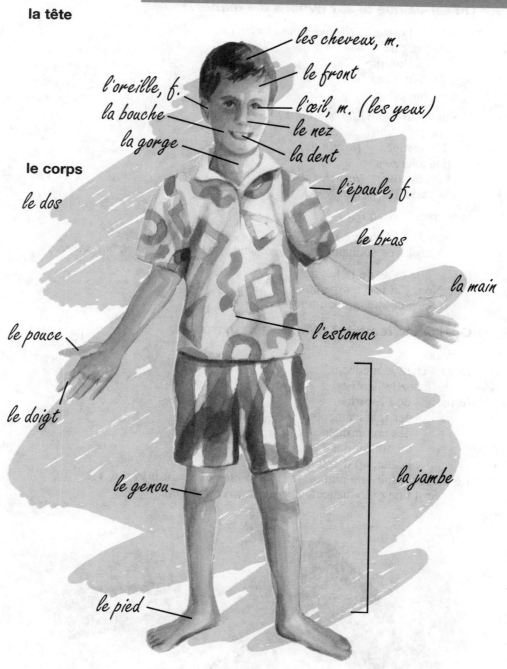

les cheveux, m.

le front

l'oreille, f.

la bouche

la gorge

l'œil, m. (les yeux)

le nez

la dent

l'épaule, f.

le bras

la main

le dos

l'estomac

le pouce

le doigt

le genou

la jambe

le pied

chez le médecin

153

Qu'est-ce que tu as? *(What's the matter?)*

J'ai mal à la tête.   *(I have a headache.)*
       au dos
       à l'oreille
       aux yeux
       aux dents

J'ai un rhume.   *(I have a cold.)*
    une infection
    des vertiges   *(dizziness)*
    des allergies
    la rougeole   *(measles)*
    la varicelle   *(chicken pox)*

Je tousse.   *(I cough.)*

J'éternue.   *(I sneeze.)*
    à tes/à vos souhaits   *(to your wishes, said when someone sneezes)*

Est-ce que tu as de la fièvre?
    Non, j'ai une température de 37°.
    Oui, j'ai une température de 39°.

Quel est le remède? *(What is the remedy?)*

Je dors.
Je vais chez le médecin.
      chez le dentiste
Je prends de l'aspirine.
      des médicaments   *(medicine)*
      des comprimés   *(pills)*
      un antibiotique
      beaucoup d'eau
Le médecin fait une piqûre.   *(The doctor gives an injection.)*
    écrit une ordonnance   *(writes a prescription)*

B. Qu'est-ce que tu as?
modèle:

J'ai mal aux dents.

C. Tu es en France et tu ne vas pas bien du tout. Tu vas chez le médecin.
Il demande, «Quels sont tes symptômes?»
modèle: Tell him that you are dizzy. *J'ai des vertiges.*
1. Tell him that you coughed all night.
2. Tell him that you sneeze a lot.
3. Tell him that you have a fever.
4. Tell him that you have a stomachache.
5. Tell him that your leg hurts.
6. Tell him that your eyes hurt.

D. Qu'est-ce que tu fais quand . . .
1. tu as mal à la tête?
2. tu as une infection?
3. tu as la varicelle?
4. tu tousses beaucoup?
5. tu as mal aux dents?
6. tu as de la fièvre?
7. tu es très fatigué(e)?

E. With a partner, construct a brief conversation between a patient and a doctor. The patient should describe symptoms, and the doctor should diagnose and prescribe.

grammaire

Quelle heure est-il?

Il est huit heures.

Il est huit heures et quart.

Il est huit heures et demie.

Il est neuf heures moins le quart.

Il est quatre heures dix.

Il est une heure moins vingt.

Il est midi.

Il est minuit.

F. Quelle heure est-il?

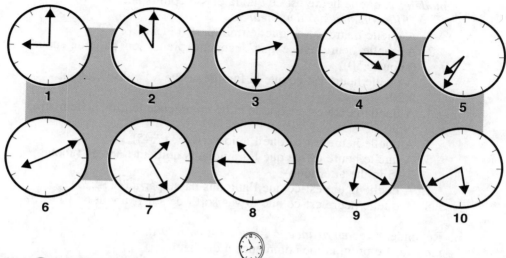

1   2   3   4   5

6   7   8   9   10

Martin prend son petit déjeuner vers sept heures du matin.

Son premier cours commence à huit heures. Martin arrive en avance.

Martin a un rendez-vous avec Christine à midi. Il arrive à midi juste. Il est à l'heure.

Martin est en retard. Son dernier cours commence à quatre heures de l'après-midi.

Qu'est-ce qu'il fait à huit heures du soir?

chez le médecin

G. Répondez.

    modèle: A quelle heure est-ce que la classe commence? (9:00)

        Elle commence à neuf heures.

1. A quelle heure est-ce que le train part? (11:22)
2. A quelle heure est-ce que Jeannette prend son petit déjeuner? (about 6:50)
3. A quelle heure est-ce que la famille arrive à l'église? (about 9:20)
4. A quelle heure est-ce que le culte commence le dimanche matin? (9:30)
5. A quelle heure est-ce que l'avion arrive? (7:45)
6. A quelle heure est-ce que les étudiants quittent l'école? (about 5:15 in the afternoon)
7. A quelle heure est-ce que l'autobus passe par ici? (12:25)
8. A quelle heure est-ce que tu vas sortir ce soir? (about 6:30)

H. Répondez avec *en avance, à l'heure* ou *en retard.*

    modèle: Le programme commence à dix heures.

        Tu arrives à dix heures moins dix.

        J'arrive en avance.

1. Le culte commence à neuf heures trente. Les Dupont arrivent à neuf heures et quart.
2. Ton rendez-vous chez le médecin est fixé à quatre heures moins le quart. Tu arrives à quatre heures.
3. L'avion part à minuit. Tu arrives à douze heures.
4. Ton cours de français commence à une heure. Tu arrives à une heure juste.
5. Le train part à six heures dix. Tu arrives à six heures moins dix.

I. Questions personnelles.

1. Quand est-ce que tu prends le petit déjeuner?
2. Quand est-ce que tu pars pour l'église le dimanche matin?
3. Quand est-ce que tu arrives à l'école le matin?
4. Quand est-ce que tu prends le déjeuner?
5. Quand est-ce que tu fais la vaisselle?
6. Quand est-ce que tu regardes la télévision?
7. Quand est-ce que tu quittes l'école?
8. Quand est-ce que tu prends le dîner?

le *passé composé* (compound past tense)

Observe the verbs in these sentences:

J'ai toussé toute la nuit.
J'ai pris ma température.
M. Dupont n'a pas bien dormi.
Il a téléphoné à M. Plouvin.
Ils ont fixé un rendez-vous chez le médecin.

formation of *passé composé*

The *passé composé* is the third and final verb tense to be presented in this text. With the *passé composé* you will be able to talk about past events. As its name suggests, the *passé composé* is "composed" of two parts: an auxiliary verb and a past participle. The auxiliary for most verbs is the present tense of the verb *avoir*:

j'ai	nous avons
tu as	vous avez
il, elle, on a	ils, elles ont

The past participle is formed from the infinitive.

- To form the past participle of regular -*er* verbs, drop the -*er* ending and add -*é*.

donner	→	donné
parler	→	parlé
téléphoner	→	téléphoné

  The infinitive and the past participle of regular -*er* verbs are pronounced identically.

Therefore, to change the verb from the present to the *passé composé* in this sentence, *Elle donne un traité à la femme,* select the form of *avoir* that corresponds to the subject *elle,* and add the past participle of the verb *donner*.

subject	auxiliary	past participle	rest of sentence
Elle	*a*	*donné*	*un traité à la femme.*

J. Tell that each of these events took place yesterday *(hier)* by changing the verbs from the *présent* to the *passé composé*.
1. Ma mère cherche du sucre vanillé.
2. Nous mangeons du poulet.
3. Je trouve une jolie chemise.
4. Tu achètes de l'aspirine.
5. Les enfants parlent avec leurs grands-parents.
6. Vous montrez vos photos à la famille.
7. M. Dupont tousse toute la nuit.
8. Je téléphone au médecin.

K. Your friend is asking you whether different people are doing a variety of tasks today. You tell him that they have already done those things at the time given in parentheses.
modèle: Jean-Pierre téléphone à sa mère aujourd'hui? (hier)
Non, il a téléphoné à sa mère hier.
1. Tu parles à ton professeur aujourd'hui? (je . . . hier)
2. Geneviève dîne au restaurant ce soir? (lundi passé)
3. Vous visitez le musée d'art moderne cet après-midi? (nous . . .hier après-midi)
4. Les enfants vident la corbeille ce matin? (hier matin)
5. Nous achetons des pâtisseries aujourd'hui? (vous . . . mardi)
6. Raoul étudie pour son examen ce matin? (hier soir)

- To form the past participle of *-ir* verbs like *dormir,* drop the *-r.*

dormir	→	dormi
mentir	→	menti
servir	→	servi

- To form the past participle of regular *-re* verbs, drop the *-re* and add *-u.*

répondre	→	répondu
attendre	→	attendu
perdre	→	perdu

- Memorize the past participles of these irregular verbs.

avoir	→	eu
être	→	été
faire	→	fait
prendre	→	pris
mettre	→	mis
dire	→	dit
écrire	→	écrit
lire	→	lu

L. Tell that the following events, which are happening today, also happened yesterday at the designated times.

modèle: Paul prend le train. (9 h 00)

Paul a pris le train à 9 heures hier.

1. Je fais la vaisselle. (6 h 30)
2. Nous répondons à la lettre. (10 h 15)
3. Renée met la table. (12 h 00)
4. Vous lisez la Bible. (7 h 10)
5. Tu dors. (toute la nuit)
6. Ma sœur a un accident. (après le dîner)
7. Je dis au revoir aux enfants. (7 h 45)
8. Marc et Ferdinand attendent le bus. (4 h 35)
9. Tu prends le petit déjeuner. (8 h 30)
10. On sert le repas. (8 h 00)

meaning of *passé composé*

Passé composé corresponds to either the past tense or the present perfect tense in English. For example, the sentence

J'ai toussé toute la nuit.

may be translated either

I coughed all night, *or*
I have coughed all night.

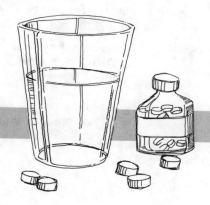

chez le médecin

In negation or in questions the passé composé may be translated with forms of *do* or *have* as helping verbs:

> Il n'a pas téléphoné au médecin.
> *He did not call the doctor.*
> *He has not called the doctor.*

> Est-ce qu'elle a pris le bus?
> *Did she take the bus?*
> *Has she taken the bus?*

The context of the *passé composé* will determine the appropriate translation. The following exercise will help to illustrate the different meanings in English that *passé composé* can express.

M. Mettez ces verbes au passé composé.
  1. Yesterday Mr. Dupont ate at a restaurant.
     Hier M. Dupont _____ au restaurant. (dîner)
  2. He did not read the menu.
     Il n'_____ pas _____ la carte. (lire)
  3. He ordered the dinner special.
     Il _____ le menu. (commander)
  4. The waiter served the meal to Mr. Dupont.
     Le garçon _____ le repas à M. Dupont. (servir)
  5. He did not like his meal.
     Il n'_____ pas _____ son repas. (aimer)
  6. Have you ever eaten raw meat?
     Est-ce que tu _____ déjà _____ de la viande crue? (manger)

adverb and pronoun placement in *passé composé*

- Short adverbs (one or two syllables) are generally placed between the auxiliary and the past participle:

> Il a *beaucoup* toussé.
> Car Dieu a *tant* aimé le monde.

- In negation, *ne* precedes the auxiliary and *pas* follows it:

> Il *n'a pas* dormi
> Je *n'ai pas* pris ma température.

- The object pronouns *y* and *en* always precede the auxiliary verb:

Ils ont étudié la Bible à l'église. → Ils **y** ont étudié la Bible.
Elle a pris du beurre. → Elle **en** a pris.
Je n'ai pas mis la tasse sur la table. → Je n'**y** ai pas mis la tasse.

N. Mettez ces phrases au passé composé.
   modèle: Je mange beaucoup au restaurant.
       J'ai beaucoup mangé au restaurant.
   1. Les enfants répondent bien.
   2. Elle y met l'assiette.
   3. Mon frère mange trop.
   4. J'en prends pour le petit déjeuner.
   5. Tu lis souvent la Bible?
   6. Vous dormez assez, mes enfants?
   7. Raymond y trouve son parapluie.
   8. Nous en achetons un kilo au marché.

O. Répondez à la forme négative.
   modèle: Vous avez compris le professeur?
       Non, nous n'avons pas compris le professeur.
   1. Tu as bien dormi?
   2. On a fait un voyage?
   3. Vous avez parlé au pasteur?
   4. Guillaume a été en France?
   5. August et Sylvie ont écrit à leurs parents?
   6. Tu as servi le repas?
   7. Nous avons perdu nos cahiers?
   8. Vous avez lu ce livre?

P. You read about Mrs. Plouvin's typical day in Chapter 9. Tell what she did yesterday by putting the following paragraph in *passé composé*.

Mme Plouvin fait sa toilette, met des chaussures confortables et fait son lit. Puis elle prépare du café au lait pour sa famille. Son mari étudie la Bible et les enfants mettent la table. Après le petit déjeuner M. Plouvin vide la corbeille, donne à manger au chien et quitte la maison enfin pour aller à son bureau à l'église. Mme Plouvin commence à faire le ménage. Ensuite elle fait la vaisselle et passe l'aspirateur. Plus tard elle repasse les vêtements. Après le déjeuner elle a une étude biblique avec sa voisine.

chez le médecin

Q. Write at least five sentences to tell some of the things that you did yesterday. Include the times at which you did them.
modèle: J'ai pris le petit déjeuner avec ma famille à 7 h 00.

dialogue

Chez le médecin M. Dupont apprend qu'il a une infection. Le médecin fait une piqûre à M. Dupont et écrit une ordonnance. Plus tard M. Dupont va à la droguerie.

la vendeuse:	Bonjour, monsieur. Que désirez-vous?
M. Dupont:	Voilà, mademoiselle. Le médecin a écrit cette ordonnance.
la vendeuse:	Je regrette, monsieur. C'est ici une droguerie. Vous *avez besoin d*'aller à la pharmacie pour acheter vos médicaments.
M. Dupont:	Oh, pardon, mademoiselle. Merci bien et au revoir.

need

R. Répondez.
1. Qu'est-ce que M. Dupont a?
2. Qu'est-ce que le médecin fait?
3. M. Dupont va à la droguerie pour acheter ses médicaments. Est-ce qu'il a raison?
4. Où est-ce qu'il va enfin?

grammaire

avoir idioms (review)

S. Translate the following sentences into French.
1. He is cold.
2. You look sick.
3. I need to sleep.
4. We are right.
5. Tom is afraid of dogs.
6. She's wrong.
7. They are thirsty.
8. The child is sleepy.
9. My father has a headache.
10. Are you hungry?

chapitre onze

French consonant sounds (part II)

Differences between the articulation of French consonant sounds and their English counterparts compose part of what speakers of English call a "French accent." Here are three differences that you should recognize as you try to improve your French pronunciation.

- the /r/ sound

  In French the /r/ sound is articulated as a slight fricative produced in approximately the same location as the /g/ in the word *ugh* using the back part of the tongue. The tip of the tongue remains down, behind the lower front teeth.

initial	medial	final
rue	Paris	cher
Régis	arrêt	par
Roland	Arnaud	sur
rideau	périsse	lire
roux	merci	cœur

- the /l/ sound

  In English there are two different /l/ sounds. One is found at the beginning of words, as in *light*. The other is found at the end of words as in *bell*. In French there is only one /l/ sound–the one that is found at the beginning of words in English. Therefore, *belle* is not pronounced like the English word *bell*, since the *l* in *belle* sounds like the initial *l* of *light*. Compare these English and French words:

eel	il
bowl	bol
mall	mal
fool	foule
tell	telle

Now practice pronouncing the /l/ sound in these positions.

initial	medial	final
lire	allez	elle
lundi	salon	s'appelle
Louis	Toulouse	école
le	malade	cheval
l'eau	il est	nouvel

- the /ñ/ sound

  As the French make it, this sound does not exist in English. The closest sound to it is the combined /n/ and /j/ sounds in *canyon* or *onion*. In French, however, the nasal consonant is produced when the middle part of the tongue hits the top of the mouth. The tip of the tongue is down against the lower front teeth. The /j/ sound follows as it does in English. The sound is spelled *gn*.

medial	**final**
oignon	campagne
champignon	cologne
signal	ligne

The /ñ/ sound is never found in the initial position in French.

culture

Medical care in France is socialized. Most doctors participate in the *Sécurité Sociale* (Social Security system), but their participation is not obligatory. Since the fee schedule for doctors is set by the Social Security system, costs for services rendered are standardized. Patients are free to choose their own doctors. For convenience most people select a doctor in their own town; however, they sometimes go to another city or even another part of the country to consult a general practitioner or specialist who has a very good reputation. For less severe sicknesses some people will consult a pharmacist. French doctors still make house calls, though this is usually restricted to the aged, the bedridden, or very small children. Patients usually pay the doctor immediately for his services and fill out and submit the necessary forms to Social Security for reimbursement. Nonessential services, such as cosmetic surgery, are not covered by Social Security. However, for normal services Social Security usually reimburses up to 80 per cent. Medical expenses, especially scans and ultrasonic diagnoses, are extremely expensive in France, and the Social Security system is constantly in debt, even though taxes continue to rise to help meet the need. Most French people boast about their free medical care, but they also complain about some doctors' mediocre services and about the high taxes that are necessary in order to support the socialist system. Some French people lose 50 per cent of their income in taxes.

chapitre onze

à l'école

2 Timothée 2, 15 Efforce-toi de te présenter devant Dieu comme un homme éprouvé, un ouvrier qui n'a point à rougir, qui dispense droitement la parole de la vérité.

12   12   12   12   12   12   12   12

Denis et Jean-Luc Plouvin vont à l'école publique en France. Les Dupont *ont choisi de donner des cours particuliers* à leurs enfants chez eux. Anne et Paul *veulent* visiter les classes de Denis et de Jean-Luc. C'est *ainsi* que samedi matin ils prennent leurs stylos et leurs cahiers et vont à l'école avec *eux*. Anne va au lycée avec Denis, et Paul va à l'école primaire avec Jean-Luc. Le soir ils parlent de leurs expériences.

have chosen to teach
want
thus
them

M. Dupont:	Anne, tu as aimé les *cours* de Denis?
Anne:	Oui, Papa, son *lycée* est fort intéressant. Les élèves ne font pas attention à leurs profs, mais les études sont très très difficiles.
Mme Dupont:	Qu'est-ce que Denis a comme cours le samedi?
Anne:	*A huit heures* il a l'anglais, à neuf heures les maths et à onze heures le français. Le samedi ses cours *finissent* à midi.
Paul:	Moi, j'ai visité l'école de Jean-Luc ce matin.
M. Dupont:	Est-ce que son *institutrice* est gentille?
Paul:	Oui, elle est très sympa. Nous *avons chanté* en classe.

classes
a secondary school
at eight o'clock
finish
elementary school teacher
sang

A. Répondez.
1. Est-ce que Jean-Luc et Denis vont à l'école chrétienne?
2. Quand est-ce qu'Anne et Paul vont à l'école avec eux?
3. Comment sont les élèves dans les cours de Denis?
4. Combien de cours est-ce qu'il a le samedi matin?
5. Qu'est-ce qu'on a fait dans la classe de Jean-Luc?

vocabulaire

des activités scolaires

Charles écrit avec un crayon
à son pupitre.

Clément a du papier
dans son cahier.

Suzanne écrit avec une
craie au tableau noir.

Nicole achète un livre et une
règle à la librairie.

Thomas et Jérôme lisent
à la bibliothèque.

L'institutrice écrit avec
un stylo à son bureau.

B. Répondez.
1. Qu'est-ce qu'on utilise pour écrire une lettre?
2. Qu'est-ce qu'on utilise pour écrire un problème d'algèbre?
3. Qu'est-ce qu'on utilise pour écrire au tableau noir?
4. Où est-ce qu'on achète du papier pour son cahier?
5. Qui enseigne dans une école primaire?
6. Où est-ce qu'on emprunte *(borrow)* un livre?
7. Est-ce qu'un professeur enseigne dans une école primaire?
8. Nommez quelque chose qu'un élève met dans son pupitre.

Quels cours est-ce que tu fais à l'école?

Je fais de la Bible.
          du français
          des maths
          de la géographie
          de l'histoire
          de l'anglais
          de l'algèbre
          de la géométrie
          de la biologie
          de la chimie *(chemistry)*
          des arts ménagers *(home economics)*
          du dessin *(drawing)*
          de l'éducation physique

Another way to express what course you are taking is *J'ai un cours de Bible.*

C. You are an exchange student in France. You will be studying in a French school. Which courses would you be taking in order to learn the following information?
    modèle: the population of Togo   *Je fais de la géographie.*
    1. the area of a square
    2. the placement of grave and acute accent marks
    3. the conjugation of the verb *to be*
    4. recipes for snails
    5. $2H_2 + O_2 \rightarrow 2H_2O$
    6. perspective and the primary colors
    7. how to dissect a worm
    8. the date of the Battle of Hastings

grammaire

-*ir* verbs like *finir*

The verb *finir* represents a group of verbs that are conjugated as follows:

je fini**s**	nous fini**ssons**
tu fini**s**	vous fini**ssez**
il, elle, on fini**t**	ils, elles fini**ssent**

The main characteristic of this group is the -iss in the endings of the plural forms. The final letter of each of the singular forms (-s, -s, -t) is a pattern that you have seen before in other verbs. Some other verbs conjugated like *finir* include the following:

- verbs that end in *-ish* in English
  établir   *to establish*
  accomplir   *to accomplish*
  polir   *to polish*
  punir   *to punish*

- verbs formed from adjectives
  maigrir   *to lose weight*
  grossir   *to gain weight*
  rougir   *to blush, redden*
  vieillir   *to grow old*

- other verbs
  choisir   *to choose*
  obéir   *to obey*
  désobéir   *to disobey*
  réussir (à)   *to succeed (at)*

D. Substitute the subjects given in parentheses.
   modèle: Gauthier réussit à l'examen. (je) *Je réussis à l'examen aussi.*
   1. Le pasteur établit une église à Lyon. (les missionnaires)
   2. J'obéis à mes parents. (tu)
   3. Nous punissons notre chien. (notre voisin)
   4. Vous maigrissez. (nous)
   5. Il rougit en classe. (vous)
   6. Tu choisis une voiture. (je)

E. Choose an *-ir* verb from the lists above to fit the context of the sentence. Give the correct form of the verb.
   modèle: Tu manges trop, alors tu *grossis.*
   1. Bruno n'a pas préparé son examen, alors il ne _____ pas à l'examen.
   2. L'enfant désobéit à la règle, alors on _____ cet enfant.
   3. Je vais aller à l'église, alors je _____ mes chaussures.
   4. Ma tante a 96 ans et mon oncle a 97 ans. Ils _____, n'est-ce pas?
   5. Est-ce que tu _____ quand tu chantes devant la classe?
   6. Voici trois jolies cravates. Quelle cravate est-ce que tu vas _____?
   7. Nous _____ le projet que nous avons commencé.
   8. Olive mange très peu, alors elle va _____.

The past participle of -ir verbs like *finir* is formed by dropping the final *r* of the infinitive (similar to -ir verbs like *dormir*–see Chapter 9):

finir   →   fini
choisir   →   choisi

Used in passé composé it would look like this:

Denis a fini à midi.   *Dennis finished at noon.*

F. Mettez les verbes au passé composé.
1. Dieu établit un jardin en Éden.
2. Adam et Eve désobéissent.
3. Adam rougit devant son Dieu.
4. Il ne réussit pas à cacher son péché.
5. « Vous choisissez la mort, » a dit Dieu.
6. Dieu punit nos premiers parents.

G. Répondez.
1. Est-ce que tu as maigri l'été passé?
2. Quel dessert est-ce que tu as choisi hier?
3. Est-ce que tu obéis à tes parents?
4. Est-ce que tu vas réussir à ton cours de français?
5. Est-ce que tu rougis souvent?
6. Est-ce que tu vas finir cet exercice sans faire une faute *(without making a mistake)*?
7. Est-ce que tu as accompli des projets cette année?

le passé composé (révision)

H. Tell this story in the past tense.

Paul visite l'école de Jean-Luc. L'institutrice donne du papier et un crayon à chaque *(each)* enfant. Les écoliers *(elementary students)* dessinent leurs familles. Ils finissent leurs dessins et après ils chantent. Ils choisissent la chanson «En passant par la Lorraine.» Ensuite les enfants font des maths et lisent un poème. L'institutrice pose des questions et les écoliers y répondent. Elle demande à Paul de parler de sa famille en Amérique. Paul rougit un peu, mais il en parle très bien. A midi les enfants disent ''au revoir'' à leur nouvel ami américain et tout le monde *(everyone)* quitte l'école. Paul apprécie beaucoup sa visite dans une école française.

M. Dupont: Qu'est-ce que Denis veut devenir?

Anne: Il veut devenir pasteur comme son père.

Mme Dupont: Lui, il peut être un bon pasteur. Il parle très bien devant l'église.

Paul: Anne, qu'est-ce que tu veux devenir?

Anne: J'ai toujours voulu devenir professeur, moi. Tante Julie est professeur et j'aime bien travailler avec les petits.

Paul: Moi, je veux devenir missionnaire.

M. Dupont: J'en suis très content, Paul.

à l'école

two irregular verbs: *pouvoir* and *vouloir*

pouvoir *(to be able)*

je peux	nous pouvons
tu peux	vous pouvez
il, elle, on peut	ils, elles peuvent

past participle: pu   Paul a pu comprendre l'institutrice.
Paul was able to understand the teacher.

vouloir *(to want)*

je veux	nous voulons
tu veux	vous voulez
il, elle, on veut	ils, elles veulent

past participle: voulu   J'ai toujours voulu devenir professeur.
I have always wanted to become a teacher.

A common French proverb is « Vouloir, c'est pouvoir. »
Where there's a will, there's a way.

Notez bien:
- The three plural forms contain the *v* of the *pouvoir* and the *l* of *vouloir* which are missing in the singular forms.

- The three singular forms and the third person plural form all contain a vowel sound not in the infinitive or in the first and second plural forms. This vowel sound is pronounced /ø/ in the singular forms and /œ/ in the closed syllable of the third person plural form. (See Chapter 8.)

- The endings on the first and second person singular forms are *-x* instead of *-s*.

- If the verbs *pouvoir* and *vouloir* are used with another verb, that verb will be in the infinitive form.

  > Denis peut devenir pasteur.
  > > *Dennis can become a pastor.*
  > Anne et Paul veulent visiter les classes.
  > > *Anne and Paul want to visit the classes.*

- *Voudrais* is a special form of *veux* that renders the verb somewhat more polite.

  > Je voudrais une chambre.
  > > *I would like a room.*

I. Répondez.
  modèle: Qui peut conjuguer ce verbe? (nous)
  > *Nous pouvons conjuguer ce verbe.*
  1. Qui peut chanter devant la classe? (Maurice)
  2. Qui peut répondre à cette question? (nous)
  3. Qui peut repasser une chemise? (mes sœurs)
  4. Qui peut compter à 1.000 en français? (tu)
  5. Qui veut de la glace? (je)
  6. Qui veut dîner au restaurant ce soir? (les Dupont)
  7. Qui veut étudier à la bibliothèque? (vous)
  8. Qui veut ce livre? (Madeleine)

J. Répondez à ces questions personnelles.
  1. Est-ce que tu veux manger des escargots?
  2. Est-ce que tu veux dîner avec le Président?
  3. Est-ce que tu veux faire de la chimie?
  4. Est-ce que tu veux réussir à ce cours?
  5. Est-ce que tu peux parler japonais?
  6. Est-ce que tu peux aller à Paris cet été?
  7. Est-ce que tu peux comprendre le professeur?
  8. Est-ce que tu peux faire la cuisine?

à l'école

Qu'est-ce que tu veux devenir?

What do you want to become?

Je veux devenir professeur.
I want to become a teacher.

In this construction the profession is used without an indefinite article.

un pasteur *

un comptable/
une comptable

un dentiste/
une dentiste

un agent de police/
une femme-agent
de police

un mécanicien/
une mécanicienne

un journaliste/une journaliste (journalist)
un/une secrétaire (secretary)
un avocat/une avocate (lawyer)
un instituteur/une institutrice
(elementary teacher)
un ingénieur * (engineer)

une missionnaire/
un missionnaire

une pharmacienne/
un pharmacien

une infirmière / un infirmier

une coiffeuse/un coiffeur

une ménagère *

une doctoresse/un médecin

un professeur * (teacher)
une programmeuse/un programmeur
(computer programmer)

* There is no word for a person
of the opposite gender in this
profession.

177

K. Répondez.

    modèle: Qui travaille (works) dans un hôpital?
          Un médecin travaille dans un hôpital.
          Une infirmière travaille dans un hôpital.

1. Qui travaille dans une pharmacie?
2. Qui travaille dans un bureau (office)?
3. Qui travaille avec les nombres?
4. Qui travaille à la maison?
5. Qui travaille à l'église?
6. Qui travaille dans un lycée?
7. Qui travaille avec les ordinateurs (computers)?
8. Qui travaille dans un restaurant?

grammaire

c'est vs. il est and elle est

Quelle est la profession de M. Plouvin?
    C'est un pasteur.   *ou*   Il est pasteur.
Quelle est la profession de Mme Bernard?
    C'est une infirmière.   *ou*   Elle est infirmière.

Either of the two answers shown is correct. However, when the name of a
profession is preceded by *il est* or *elle est,* the article is dropped.

L. Answer these questions according to the models.

modèle: Elle est avocate?   *Oui, c'est une avocate.*
　　　　C'est un professeur?   *Oui, il est professeur.*

1. Il est dentiste?
2. Elle est mécanicienne?
3. Elle est institutrice?
4. Il est pasteur?
5. C'est un agent de police?
6. C'est une infirmière?
7. C'est un programmeur?
8. C'est une comptable?

stress pronouns

moi	*me*	nous	*we*
toi	*you*	vous	*you*
lui	*him*	eux	*them*
elle	*her*	elles	*them*

Stress pronouns *(pronoms toniques)* refer to people and are used only in certain grammatical contexts. Here are three contexts:

- to emphasize the subject
    Moi, j'ai visité l'école de Jean-Luc.
    I visited Jean-Luc's school.

- as the object of a preposition
    Ils vont à l'école avec *eux.*
    They go to school with them.
    Nous allons *chez lui.*
    We are going to his place.

- when used without a verb
    Qui est là?   *Moi.*
    Suzanne donne cinq francs à son frère. Et *toi?*

M. Answer the question using stress pronouns.

    modèle: Tu vas avec Jean? *Oui, je vais avec lui.*

1. Est-ce que ce livre est pour moi? (Oui, c'est . . .)
2. Jean va chez nous? (Oui, . . .)
3. Qui est à côté de Pierrick en classe? (Suzette . . .)
4. Qui parle avec les enfants? (Mme Dupont . . .)
5. Est-ce que le pasteur peut compter sur toi?
6. Qui est devant Nicole? (sa sœur)
7. Est-ce que vos amis partent sans *(without)* vous? (Non, . . .)

N. Answer these personalized questions about you and your classmates using stress pronouns, not names.

    modèle: Qui a déjà mangé des escargots? *Moi.*

          ou *Moi, j'en ai mangé.*

1. Qui a déjà fait un voyage en France?
2. Qui est à côté de la fenêtre?
3. Qui porte une jupe bleue?
4. Qui fait toujours ses devoirs *(homework)*?
5. Qui a déjà mangé de la glace au café?
6. Qui parle très bien le français?
7. Qui regarde le professeur?
8. Qui pose ces questions?

O. Tell what you want to do when you finish your studies, some courses that you are now taking, what your favorite course is, and why. Include some of the following expressions, making verbs agree with their subjects:

vouloir devenir . . . ; finir mes études . . . ; faire de . . . *(some course)*; moi, je préférer, aimer, détester . . . ; mon professeur . . . ; dans ce cours nous . . .

prononciation

French consonant sounds (part III)

When a /p/, /t/, or /k/ sound comes at the beginning of a word in English, it is followed immediately by a slight puff of air. If you hold a piece of paper close to your mouth and say "pony" or "table" or "cup," you can see the paper moving because of this *aspiration*. In French these initial sounds are unaspirated; that is, they are not followed by the puff of air. Compare the initial sounds in these English and French words:

post	poste
pop	père
table	table
too	tout
cat	cage
coin	cousin

Now pronounce these French words avoiding the English aspiration after the initial consonant.

page	télévision	coin
petit	tapis	qui
Pierre	temps	cœur
pauvre	théâtre	cahier
pendule	tu	coûter

à l'école

Many French children start school as soon as they are out of diapers, since children can go free of charge to *la maternelle* (nursery school) at that time. Even if mothers do not work outside the home, many of them send their children to nursery school several days a week. School attendance is compulsory for children from six to sixteen years of age. *L'école primaire* (elementary school) lasts for 5 years. After that, students begin *le collège* (secondary school). In secondary school the grade numbers count down instead of up; therefore, a student begins *en 6ᵉ* (in sixth grade), then *5ᵉ*, and so on through third. In *6ᵉ* students start to learn their first foreign language. For most of them this is English. Many students also study a second or even a third foreign language. The last three years of secondary school, *2ᵉ, 1ᵉʳᵉ,* and *classe terminale,* are in another school called *le lycée.* At the end of *terminale,* the students who hope to go on to the university must pass *le baccalauréat* (the final examination), in student slang *le bachot* or *le bac.* This exam covers all the courses the students have taken in secondary school. The exam contains two parts, an oral exam and a written exam. Only about 60 per cent of the students pass this examination on their first attempt. If a student fails, he may repeat the last year of the *lycée* and try the exam again the following June. The pressure that students feel from the exam is intense, and some teens even commit suicide if their plans for the future are changed by their not succeeding at the *baccalauréat.* Tuition at the universities of France is paid by the government; however, students must seek housing since dormitories, a common part of American college life, are almost nonexistent in France. Students must pay their living expenses with their own money.

chapitre treize

témoigner pour Jésus-Christ

Romains 3, 23 Car tous ont péché et sont privés de la gloire de Dieu.

13   13   13   13   13   13   13   13

Denis a fait la connaissance d'un jeune Français au lycée. Le jeune homme qui s'appelle François ne *connaît* pas le Seigneur. Ils ont souvent discuté après leurs cours et un jour ils *sont allés ensemble* dans un café. Pendant leur conversation Denis a commencé à parler des *choses spirituelles*.

knows
went
together
spiritual things

Denis:	Non, moi, je n'ai pas peur de *la mort*.
François:	Mais c'est *parce que* tu es jeune et quand on est jeune, on ne *pense* pas à la mort.
Denis:	Non, ce n'est pas ça. *Mon copain est mort* à l'âge de 17 ans l'été passé. Je suis *sûr* qu'il est maintenant *au ciel* avec le *Sauveur*. Moi, je connais le Seigneur Jésus personnellement et j'ai *confiance* en Lui et en sa *parole,* la Bible. Mon copain a accepté le Seigneur Jésus-Christ dans son cœur à l'âge de 15 ans.
François:	Le Seigneur Jésus-Christ? Qui est-ce?
Denis:	C'est le Fils de Dieu. Dieu a *révélé* son Fils et son *plan de salut* dans la Bible. Nous sommes *obligés* de confesser *que* nous sommes des *pécheurs* et que nous avons besoin d'être *lavé* par le *sang* de Christ pour le *pardon* de nos *péchés*. Si nous n'acceptons pas le salut de Dieu, nous allons *passer* l'éternité *en enfer*. Mais si nous acceptons *l'œuvre* de Christ sur la *croix* pour nous, nous allons passer l'éternité au ciel avec Lui.
François:	Tout cela est intéressant, mais je ne *crois* pas à la Bible.

death
because
thinks
My friend died
sure
in heaven/Saviour

confidence/word

revealed
plan of salvation
obligated/that
sinners/washed
blood/forgiveness/sins

to spend/in hell
work/cross

believe

Ils ont *longtemps discuté,* mais François n'a pas accepté l'*évangile* ce jour-là. Denis a donné une Bible à François et continue à *prier* pour lui. François *vient* souvent aux réunions de jeunes à l'église et il écoute attentivement les discussions.

discussed a long time/gospel
to pray
comes

A. Répondez.

1. Comment s'appelle le jeune Français?
2. Est-ce qu'il connaît le Seigneur?
3. Où est-ce que Denis et François sont allés?
4. De quoi est-ce qu'ils discutent?
5. Est-ce que Denis a peur de la mort? Pourquoi ou pourquoi pas?
6. Qui est Jésus-Christ?
7. Est-ce que nous avons besoin de faire de bonnes œuvres pour le pardon de nos péchés?
8. Où est-ce qu'on va aller après la mort si on accepte Jésus-Christ?
9. Est-ce que François a accepté l'évangile de Jésus-Christ?
10. Et toi, est-ce que tu as accepté Jésus-Christ comme ton Sauveur personnel?

vocabulaire

Qu'est-ce que tu crois?

Je crois en Dieu.
I believe in God.
Je crois à l'inspiration de la Bible.
I believe in the inspiration of the Bible.
Je crois que Dieu a créé le monde.
I believe that God created the world.
Je crois que Jésus-Christ est le Fils de Dieu.
I believe that Jesus Christ is the Son of God.
Je crois que Jésus-Christ est né de la vierge Marie.
I believe that Jesus Christ was born of the virgin Mary.
Je crois que Jésus-Christ est ressuscité des morts.
I believe that Jesus Christ is risen from the dead.
Je crois que le sang de Jésus-Christ lave les pécheurs de leurs péchés.
I believe that the blood of Jesus Christ washes sinners from their sins.

témoigner pour Jésus-Christ

la Bible

La Bible est composée de l'Ancien Testament et du Nouveau Testament.
  The Bible is composed of the Old Testament and the New Testament.
Le livre Philémon n'a qu'un chapitre.
  The book of Philemon has only one chapter.
Psaume 23, 1 est le verset favori de M. Dupont.
  Psalm 23:1 is Mr. Dupont's favorite verse.
Il a son culte personnel chaque jour.
  He has his devotions every day.

B. Répondez.
1. Qui a créé le monde?
2. Comment s'appelle le Fils de Dieu?
3. Combien de livres est-ce qu'il y a dans l'Ancien Testament?
4. Combien de livres est-ce qu'il y a dans le Nouveau Testament?
5. Combien de chapitres est-ce qu'il y a dans le livre de Proverbes?
6. Dis un verset pour témoigner de Jésus-Christ.
7. Quel est ton verset favori?
8. Est-ce que tu as ton culte personnel chaque jour?

le passé composé with *être*

In Chapter 11 you learned about the *passé composé* and its formation. You learned that the auxiliary verb of most verbs is *avoir:*

> J'ai parlé japonais.
> Ils ont pris le bus.
> Nous avons répondu à la lettre.

A small number of verbs use *être* as the auxiliary verb in *passé composé* One of these is *aller:*

je suis allé(e)	nous sommes allés(es)
tu es allé(e)	vous êtes allé(e, s, es)
il, on est allé	ils sont allés
elle est allée	elles sont allées

In the spelling system, the past participles of verbs conjugated with *être* have a variety of endings to show number and gender agreement with the subject of the verb. An *e* is added to reflect a feminine subject, an *s* for a plural subject, and *es* for feminine plural.

In writing about themselves, a boy and a girl would spell the past participle differently. Daniel would write, *Je suis allé à Paris,* but Monique would write, *Je suis allée à Dijon.*

None of the extra letters is pronounced. Thus the formation of past participles of verbs conjugated with *être* is essentially the same as that of verbs conjugated with *avoir,* at least as far as the spoken language is concerned. The only past participle of the verbs conjugated with *être* whose pronunciation reflects the agreement with the subject is *mort* (from the verb *mourir*–to die).

> Mon grand-père est mort. /mɔr/
> Ma grand-mère est morte. /mɔrt/

C. Tell where the following people went yesterday.

    modèle: Ma sœur . . . à l'école

        Ma sœur est allée à l'école.

1. Nous . . . en classe
2. Tu . . . à Marseille
3. Les Dupont . . . au marché
4. Joseph . . . à l'église
5. Je . . . chez moi
6. Vous . . . à la boulangerie
7. Elles . . . chez la coiffeuse
8. Henriette . . . à la poste

The picture of the house below may help you remember other frequently used verbs that are conjugated with *être*. Their past participles are given with them.

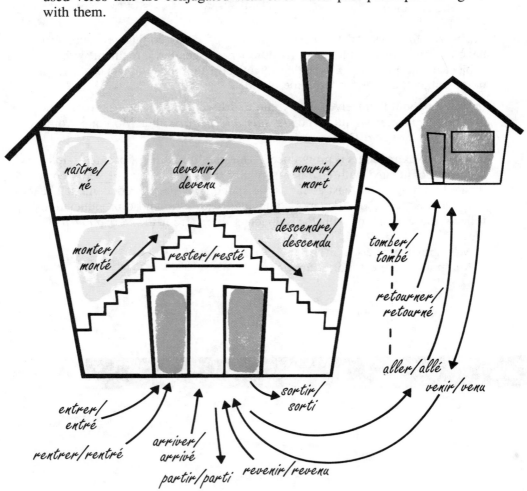

D. Make substitutions according to the model.

modèle: Mon père est parti à 7 h 30. (nous . . . 8 h 00)
Nous sommes partis à 8 h 00.

1. Ma tante et mes cousins sont partis lundi. (mon oncle . . . mercredi)
2. Ma sœur est née le 18 octobre. (je . . . le.)
3. Je suis arrivé à 11 h 15. (tu . . . à midi)
4. Mon ami est retourné à Paris en juillet. (tes amis . . . en août)
5. Ma petite sœur est tombée de la chaise. (je . . . par la fenêtre)
6. Tu es resté avec ton frère. (nous . . . avec notre grand-père)
7. Vous êtes entrés dans la maison. (Liliane et Annie . . . dans l'appartement)
8. Matthieu et Benoît sont sortis ensemble. (nous . . . sans eux)

E. Tell that these events happened yesterday.

modèle: Son train arrive à l'heure. *Hier son train est arrivé à l'heure.*

1. Gilbert part pour Paris.
2. Je descends en ville.
3. Nous rentrons vers minuit.
4. Elle sort avec ses amies.
5. Tu vas à l'église avec nous?
6. La photo tombe de l'étagère.
7. Les trois garçons montent ensemble au 3e.
8. On reste à la maison toute la journée.

venir (to come)

je viens	nous venons
tu viens	vous venez
il, elle, on vient	ils, elles viennent

The past participle is *venu,* which is conjugated with *être.*

The verbs *revenir* (to come back) and *devenir* (to become) are conjugated like *venir.*

Mon oncle vient de Bordeaux.
Christ revient un jour.
Mon frère devient très fatigué.

F. Tell that these events are happening again today, but at a different time.

    modèle: Je suis venu à 2 h 00 hier. (à 1 h 00)

        Je viens à 1 h 00 aujourd'hui.

1. Ma tante est venue chez nous hier soir. (cet après-midi)
2. Nous sommes venus par le train à 9 h 30. (à 9 h 00 juste)
3. André est venu après l'école. (avant l'école)
4. Tu es venue en retard. (en avance)
5. Vous êtes venu le matin. (le soir)
6. Je suis venu de mon bureau à 6 h 10. (à midi)
7. Mes enfants sont venus avec leurs amis à midi. (après l'école)
8. Vous êtes venues la semaine passée. (aujourd'hui)

G. Tell what Mme Plouvin did yesterday by changing the verbs in the following paragraph to the *passé composé*. Remember that some of the verbs are conjugated with *avoir* and some with *être*.

Mme Plouvin fait sa toilette, met des chaussures confortables et fait son lit. Puis elle va à la cuisine pour préparer du café au lait pour sa famille. Son mari étudie la Bible et les enfants mettent la table. Après le petit déjeuner Jean-Luc et Denis partent pour l'école. M. Plouvin vide la corbeille, donne à manger au chien et quitte la maison pour aller à son bureau à l'église. Ensuite Mme Plouvin commence à faire le ménage. Elle fait la vaisselle et passe l'aspirateur. Elle va au marché pour acheter de la nourriture pour le déjeuner et le dîner. Quand elle rentre, elle repasse les vêtements. Après le déjeuner elle a une étude biblique avec sa voisine.

H. Tell five things that you did yesterday, using at least two verbs that use *être* in the formation of *passé composé*.

connaître (to know, to be acquainted with)

je connais	nous connaissons
tu connais	vous connaissez
il, elle, on connaît	ils, elles connaissent

The past participle is *connu*.

The verb *connaître* is used with people or places, rather than with facts, to indicate familiarity:

    Est-ce que tu connais ma tante Julianne?
    Nous connaissons très bien la ville de Toulouse.

I. Tell who knows whom or what.
   modèle: mon frère/le Président
       Mon frère connaît le Président.
   1. nous/Toulouse
   2. elles/leurs cousines en Italie
   3. je/le dentiste de François Mitterand
   4. Tu/New York?
   5. Isabelle/M. Lenard
   6. Vous/mes parents?

J. Find out how many of these people or places your classmate knows.
   modèle: Paris   *Tu connais Paris?*
       Oui, je connais Paris.
       Non, je ne connais pas Paris.
   1. un homme riche
   2. un bon médecin
   3. Washington, D.C.
   4. ma grand-mère
   5. Toulouse
   6. un avocat
   7. une pharmacienne
   8. une ville en Afrique
   9. une actrice célèbre
   10. le Seigneur Jésus-Christ

lecture

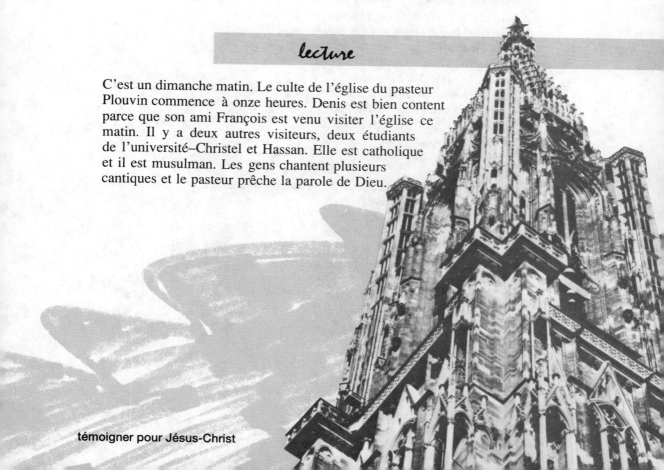

C'est un dimanche matin. Le culte de l'église du pasteur
Plouvin commence à onze heures. Denis est bien content
parce que son ami François est venu visiter l'église ce
matin. Il y a deux autres visiteurs, deux étudiants
de l'université–Christel et Hassan. Elle est catholique
et il est musulman. Les gens chantent plusieurs
cantiques et le pasteur prêche la parole de Dieu.

témoigner pour Jésus-Christ

K. Répondez.
1. Quel jour est-ce?
2. A quelle heure est-ce que le culte commence?
3. Qui visite l'église?
4. Christel est protestante?
5. Qu'est-ce que le pasteur prêche?

vocabulaire

quelques religions qu'on trouve en France

M. Plouvin est protestant? Oui, il est protestant.
M. Plouvin is Protestant? Yes, he is Protestant.
Denis est croyant et sa sœur est croyante.
Denis is a believer and his sister is a believer.
Hassan est musulman, et Christel?
Hassan is Muslim, and Christel?
C'est une catholique.
She's a Catholic.
Christel a une sœur qui est témoin de Jéhovah.
Christel has a sister who is a Jehovah's Witness.
Samuel est juif.
Samuel is Jewish.
Ses voisins sont des mormons.
His neighbors are Mormons.
Le professeur de Jean-Luc est athée.
Jean-Luc's professor is an athiest.
M. Dubois est occultiste.
M. Dubois is an occultist.

L. Answer these questions about the religions of the people listed above.
  modèle: Christel est juive?
        Non, elle est catholique.
        Non, c'est une catholique.
  1. Est-ce que la sœur de Christel est catholique aussi?
  2. Quelle est la religion de Samuel?
  3. Qui est mormon?
  4. Est-ce que M. Plouvin est catholique?
  5. Est-ce que Denis est athée?
  6. Qui est musulman?

M. Write in your own words a brief paragraph summarizing God's plan of salvation. Use structures you know.

prononciation

mute *e*

In Chapter 3 you saw that an *e* without an accent mark at the end of a word is silent.

laidé   jeuné   lavé

An exception is one-syllable words such as *je, ne, le,* where the *e* is pronounced as the sound /ø/. But there are times when the *e* in these words is silent. One such instance is illustrated in the following table:

le Fils de Dieu	plan dé salut
elle ne pense pas	on né pense pas
par le sang	connais lé Seigneur

The left column contains words whose *e* is pronounced. In the right column the *e* of the same word is silent. The principle that governs the pronunciation of the *e* in these contexts follows:

- If the *e* is immediately preceded by *two* consonant *sounds*, it is pronounced:

  elle ne pense pas   /ɛlnøpãspa/

- If the *e* is immediately preceded by only *one* consonant *sound*, it is silent:

  on ne pense pas   /ɔ̃npãspa/

This same principle applies for the pronunciation of *mute e* within single words:

vendredi	samédi
calmement	mainténant
probablement	madémoiselle
quatre-vingts	achéter

The religious situation in France is both disheartening and encouraging. It is disheartening because of the extreme lack of Christian heritage and Biblical knowledge. France is traditionally a Catholic nation, but even professing Catholics in France do not practice their religion. This tradition is visible everywhere–in place names, in the names of people, and in many of the laws of the land. However, the average Frenchman has no knowledge of the Bible and little realization that names familiar to him are names of Bible characters. French society is an almost totally secular and humanistic society. Because of the great void that exists in many people's lives, cults and "isms" of all sorts are finding acceptance by many Frenchmen who crave something that only the Lord is able to give them. Although it is saddening to learn of many who have become entangled in a cult or who are deeply involved in the occult, it is encouraging to realize that a hunger for spiritual things does exist in the hearts of some Frenchmen. Now is the time for Christians who know the truth of the gospel to spread the good news that Christ has paid the price for mankind's sins. The French need to be told that the heavy burden that religions of good works place upon people's shoulders can be removed if they will trust in Christ's finished work. Bible-believing pastors and missionaries are seeing people of all ages accept Christ's full pardon. Many people are skeptical and even antagonistic as a result of centuries of lifeless religion in their nation, but the Lord is touching hearts and melting resistance. Because of the French skepticism, evangelization is a slow process, and most fundamental churches are quite small. A church of 100 people is considered a large church in France. Pray for the people of France, and pray that the Lord would send more laborers into this harvest field.

chapitre quatorze

chercher du logement

Romains 5, 8 Mais Dieu prouve son amour envers nous, en ce que, lorsque nous étions encore des pécheurs, Christ est mort pour nous.

14   14   14   14   14   14   14   14

dialogue

leaders	Les Dupont sont les *responsables* du groupe de jeunes de leur église. Ils trouvent que leur appartement est trop petit, parce qu'il y a beaucoup de réunions chez eux. Ils ont besoin d'un autre
first/classified ads	appartement. M. Dupont regarde *d'abord* les *petites annonces*
newspaper	dans le *journal*. Il y trouve un appartement qui est près de l'église.
caretaker	Il téléphone au *concierge* et pose beaucoup de questions.

to know/still available, free	M. Dupont:	Je veux *savoir* si l'appartement est *toujours libre*.
	le concierge:	Oui, monsieur, il est libre.
bedrooms	M. Dupont:	Est-ce que l'appartement a trois *chambres?*
See culture section.	le concierge:	Non, monsieur, c'est un *F4*.
rooms	M. Dupont:	Bon, d'accord. Combien de *pièces* a l'appartement au total?
besides, in addition to	le concierge:	*En plus des* chambres, il y a aussi un salon, une
bathroom		salle à manger, une cuisine, une *salle de bains*,
toilet room		et les *W.C.*
floor	M. Dupont:	Il est à quel *étage?*
fifth floor (in this context)	le concierge:	Au *quatrième*, monsieur.
month's rent	M. Dupont:	Combien est le *loyer du mois?*
per	le concierge:	C'est 2 000 F *par* mois. Voulez-vous visiter l'appartement?
	M. Dupont:	Oui, cet après-midi ou ce soir, si c'est possible?
	le concierge:	Vers 3 h 00 cet après-midi?
	M. Dupont:	D'accord. Alors, à tout à l'heure.

A. Répondez.
1. Pourquoi est-ce que les Dupont trouvent que leur appartement est trop petit?
2. Où est-ce que M. Dupont cherche un autre appartement?
3. Est-ce ce que le nouvel appartement est loin de son église?
4. Combien de chambres a l'appartement?
5. Quelles sont les pièces de l'appartement?
6. A quel étage est l'appartement?
7. L'appartement est 2 000 F par année, n'est-ce pas?
8. Quand est-ce que M. Dupont va visiter l'appartement?

un appartement

Les Dupont habitent un appartement. Voici leur appartement:

le salon

la salle à manger

une porte

un couloir —— une télévision

une chaise

un divan

un buffet

une étagère une table

une table à café

un piano

un fauteuil

un escalier

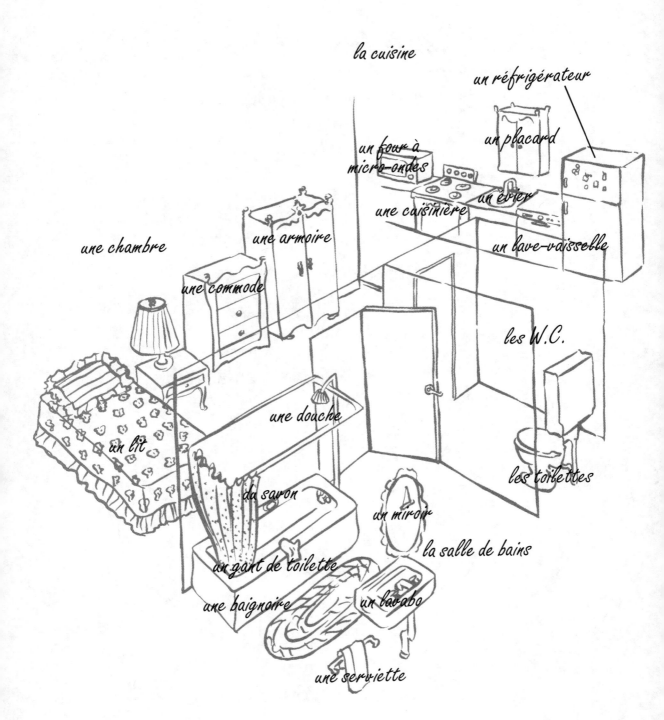

la cuisine

un réfrigérateur

un four à micro-ondes

un placard

une armoire

une cuisinière

un évier

une chambre

un lave-vaisselle

une commode

les W.C.

une douche

un lit

du savon

un miroir

les toilettes

la salle de bains

un gant de toilette

une baignoire

un lavabo

une serviette

A quel étage?

In general, Europeans do not count the ground floor (*rez-de-chaussée*) as a numbered floor. Thus, what Americans call the second floor, the French would call the first floor. Our third floor is their second floor, etc.

B. Répondez.
1. Est-ce que le nouvel appartement des Dupont est grand ou petit?
2. Leur appartement est au rez-de-chaussée?
3. Qu'est-ce qu'il y a dans la salle à manger?
4. Comment est-ce qu'on monte à l'appartement?
5. Est-ce que les toilettes sont dans la salle de bains?
6. Où sont les placards?
7. Est-ce que le four à micro-ondes est dans le salon?
8. Où est la télévision?
9. Pour prendre un bain qu'est-ce qu'on utilise?
10. Où est la commode?

le 4ᵉ étage

grammaire

le passé composé (révision)

C. Tell that the following events happened yesterday by putting the following paragraph in *passé composé*.

Aujourd'hui M. Dupont regarde les petites annonces dans le journal. Il y trouve un appartement et il téléphone au concierge. Cet après-midi les Dupont vont visiter l'appartement. Ils trouvent l'immeuble près de leur église, et ils montent au quatrième étage. Quand ils entrent dans ce joli appartement, ils regardent ses grandes pièces. Ils décident immédiatement de l'habiter.

le 1ᵉʳ étage

le rez-de-chaussée

chercher du logement

199

D. Tell what each of these people did with the listed items.

modèle: moi/le téléphone   *J'ai téléphoné à mon ami.*

lui/l'escalier   *Il est monté à son appartement.*

1. elle/la télévision
2. toi/l'appareil photographique
3. nous/le métro
4. moi/les œufs
5. eux/le papier, le stylo et l'adresse de leurs parents
6. vous/la Bible
7. lui/la librairie
8. elles/la bibliothèque
9. moi/la chanson
10. toi/le lave-vaisselle

question formation summary

A person asking a question desires one of two responses–a simple yes or no, or some sort of information.

yes/no questions

In yes/no questions the speaker's voice rises in pitch at the end of the question. There are four ways to ask yes/no questions.

- With intonation alone–This is an informal method of asking questions in conversation. Here are several examples from dialogues you have already seen:

  Anne, tu as aimé les cours de Denis?
  Alors, c'est tout?
  Tu as de la fièvre?

- With *n'est-ce pas?*–The words *n'est-ce pas?* can be added to the end of any statement to change it to a yes/no question.

  Il est jeune.
    Il est jeune, n'est-ce pas?
  Il va pleuvoir.
    Il va pleuvoir, n'est-ce pas?
  Je suis en retard.
    Je suis en retard, n'est-ce pas?

chapitre quatorze

- With *est-ce que*–The words *est-ce que* can be added to the beginning of any sentence to change it to a question.

    Joël va avec nous.
       Est-ce que Joël va avec nous?
    L'appartement a trois chambres.
       Est-ce que l'appartement a trois chambres?
    Vous voulez dîner au restaurant.
       Est-ce que vous voulez dîner au restaurant?

- With inversion–Inversion is switching the subject pronoun with the conjugated verb:

    Vous voulez voir l'appartement.
       Voulez-vous voir l'appartement?
    Ils ont un nouvel appartement.
       Ont-ils un nouvel appartement?
    Nous allons ensemble au concert.
       Allons-nous ensemble au concert?

As you learned in Chapter 5, you will not often hear inversion in informal conversation. However, you should gain a passive knowledge of its formation so that you will understand it when you encounter it in idioms, in writing, or in more formal conversation. Almost every French student has heard the phrase ''Parlez-vous français?'' sometime. This is a question that one might ask someone he does not know well. In this text we will usually use the less formal methods.

   E. Posez des questions.
      Change each of these statements into questions using *est-ce que*.

      1. Tu as pris sa température.
      2. Il va pleuvoir demain.
      3. Ses cours finissent à 5 h 30.
      4. Vous avez chanté en classe.
      5. Monique veut devenir avocate.
      6. Elle est catholique.
      7. Suzanne et Florence habitent près de la poste.
      8. Vous connaissez le Seigneur Jésus-Christ.

information questions

When asking information questions, the speaker's voice falls steadily to the end of the question. Information questions always begin with a question word. There are three categories of question words: adverbs, pronouns, and adjectives.

- interrogative adverbs

  In conversational French questions with interrogative adverbs are often formed with the words in the following order:

  > question word + *(est-ce que)* + subject + verb + (complement, if any)
  > (The use of est-ce que is optional; its omission is considered informal.)

  Comment est-ce que tu vas à l'école?
  > *How do you go to school?*

  Combien est-ce que cela coûte?
  > *How much does that cost?*

  Combien de livres est-ce que tu achètes?
  > *How many books are you buying?*

  Où est-ce que tu habites?
  > *Where do you live?*

  Quand est-ce que le train part?
  > *When does the train leave?*

  Pourquoi est-ce que M. Dupont cherche un appartement?
  > *Why is Mr. Dupont looking for an apartment?*

F. Qu'est-ce qu'il a dit?

Suppose that someone is talking to you, but you cannot hear part of what he is saying. Ask an appropriate question to elicit the information italicized in the sentences.

modèle: Pour aller à l'école je *prends le bus.*
> *Comment est-ce que tu vas à l'école?*

1. Mon oncle a *onze* enfants.
2. Jacqueline habite *à Dijon.*
3. La famille prend le dîner *à 8 h 00.*
4. Je reste chez moi *parce que je suis fatigué.*
5. Ils trouvent leur appartement *trop petit.*
6. Ces chaussures coûtent *300 F.*
7. Il fait du jogging *le matin.*
8. Je préfère mon bifteck *à point.*

- interrogative pronouns

 Qui can be either a subject or an object pronoun. When *qui* is the subject, the verb form is always third person singular.

Qui a mangé ma soupe?	Moi, j'ai mangé ta soupe.
Qui va au musée?	Nous y allons.

When *qui* is the direct object, the verb agrees, of course, with the subject of the sentence, as it does in sentences with interrogative adverbs.

Qui est-ce que tu aimes?
 Whom do you love?
Qui est-ce que Denis et Anne attendent?
 Whom are Dennis and Anne awaiting?

In either case the interrogative pronoun *qui* always refers to a person.

Que, on the other hand, refers to a thing and is used only as a direct object. It fits into the pattern you learned with interrogative adverbs.

Qu'est-ce que tu dis?
 What are you saying?
Qu'est-ce que les enfants aiment faire le samedi?
 What do children like to do on Saturday?

The following table summarizes question formation with interrogative adverbs and pronouns.

question word	est-ce que	subject	verb	complement
Quand	est-ce que	tu	pars?	
Pourquoi	est-ce que	M. Dupont	cherche	un appartement?
Combien	est-ce que	cela	coûte?	
-------	-------	Qui	a mangé	ma soupe?
Qu'	est-ce que	tu	dis?	

The word order shown in the table is the common word order for information questions. There are, however, some exceptions to this pattern. One is the use of inversion instead of *est-ce que:*

> Comment allez-vous?
> Où habitez-vous?

Inversion also occurs with subject nouns when there is no verb complement:

> Combien coûte ce manteau?
> Où est le chat?

The other exception is found in informal conversational style:

> Il va où?
> C'est combien par mois?
> Quand tu pars?

All of these sentences can be expressed with *est-ce que:*

> Comment est-ce que vous allez?
> Où est-ce que vous habitez?
> Combien est-ce que ce manteau coûte?
> Où est-ce que le chat est? (very awkward)
> Combien est-ce que c'est par mois? (somewhat awkward)
> Quand est-ce que tu pars?

In this textbook the *est-ce que* pattern is presented as the norm for active use, except in the case of some standard idioms. Other patterns are presented for passive recognition only.

G. Qui ou que?

From the answer provided, decide whether *qui* or *que* is more appropriate in the question.

modèle: Qui est-ce que tu regardes? (Robert)

1. _____ est-ce que tu regardes? (le match de football)
2. _____ porte un chapeau blanc? (Mme Deauville)
3. _____ est-ce qu'il cherche? (son fils)
4. _____ est-ce que tu as? (de la fièvre)
5. _____ est-ce que vous portez? (un pantalon)
6. _____ est-ce que Philippe aime? (Sophie)

H. Who and what?

Make up two questions for each statement according to the model.

modèle: M. Dupont cherche un appartement.

> *Qui cherche un appartement?*
> *Qu'est-ce que M. Dupont cherche?*

1. Mme Dupont achète un journal.
2. M. Dupont regarde les petites annonces.
3. Le concierge montre l'appartement à M. Dupont.
4. M. et Mme Dupont invitent leurs enfants.
5. La famille pose beaucoup de questions.
6. Le concierge offre son aide.
7. Anne cherche son frère.
8. Paul cherche les W.C.

I. A friend is quite proud of his new apartment and has invited you for a visit. To make polite conversation, you show interest in the apartment by asking questions about it and its furnishings. Use the following question words and vocabulary items for inspiration.

qui	le four à micro-ondes
qu'est-ce que	le buffet
pourquoi	le fauteuil
comment	le lit
où	la commode
combien	le salon
quand	l'étagère
est-ce que	la table à café
	les chambres
	les W.C.
	la salle de bains
	le piano
	la télévision
	le téléphone
	l'escalier

modèle: Où est-ce que tu as acheté la jolie table à café?
> *D'habitude, comment est-ce que tu montes à l'appartement?*
> *Tu prends l'ascenseur?*

- interrogative adjective *quel*

As an adjective, *quel* is always used with a noun and agrees with that noun in number and gender, just as other adjectives.

> Quel temps fait-il?
> Quels cours est-ce que tu as?
> Quelle heure est-il?
> Quelles villes est-ce que tu visites?

Sometimes *quel* may be separated from the noun that it modifies by a form of the verb *être:*

> Quelle est la date de ta naissance?
> Quels sont les jours de la semaine?

Since *quel* is an adjective, its sentence position is determined, not by the interrogative pattern presented in the table, but by the noun phrase of which it is a part:

> Quel livre est-ce que l'étudiant lit?
> Quel étudiant lit ce livre?
> Il est à quel étage?

J. Ecrivez la forme correcte de *quel, quels, quelle* ou *quelles*. Puis répondez à la question.

modèle: Quelle heure est-il? Il est 3 h 16.

> *Quels livres est-ce que tu achètes? J'achète des romans.*

1. Dans _____ pièce est-ce qu'on trouve un lit?
2. A _____ étage est le nouvel appartement des Dupont?
3. _____ pièces est-ce qu'on compte pour le titre F4?
4. _____ temps fait-il aujourd'hui?
5. _____ âge est-ce que tu as?
6. _____ est la date aujourd'hui?
7. _____ cours est-ce que tu as?
8. _____ est ta saison favorite?
9. De _____ couleur sont tes chaussures?

K. Quel . . . ?

What *quel*-question would you ask to find out the following pieces of information?

1. today's weather
2. today's date
3. the present time
4. the course your friend has this year (addressing your friend)
5. the hair color of your friend's sister (addressing your friend)
6. a friend's age (addressing the friend)
7. the floor an apartment is on
8. a person's telephone number (addressing the person)

L. You hear one side of a telephone conversation. Tell what questions the other person is asking to evoke these answers.

1. –_____?
   –Non, je ne suis pas Mme Dupont.
2. –_____?
   –C'est M. Dupont qui parle.
3. –_____?
   –Non, Anne ne peut pas parler maintenant.
4. –_____?
   –Elle fait des courses au marché.
5. –_____?
   –Elle rentre vers 5 h 00.
6. –_____?
   –Elle va aller à la réunion de jeunes ce soir.
7. –_____?
   –La réunion commence à 20 h 00.
8. –_____?
   –Elle va prendre le bus.
9. –_____?
   –Oui, je vais dire à Anne que tu as téléphoné.

M. With your partner, imagine a telephone conversation between yourself and the owner of an apartment that you are interested in renting. You will want to find out these things:
   1. location of apartment
   2. the floor that the apartment is on
   3. number of rooms
   4. whether the apartment has a bathroom
   5. the rent per month
   6. when you can look at the apartment
   7. anything else

the conjunction *que*

You have already seen *que* used as an interrogative pronoun. It also serves as a conjunction to introduce a noun clause:

> Alice trouve *que* son appartement est trop petit.
> *Alice finds that her apartment is too small.*

The verb *trouver* tells that Alice is expressing an opinion. The clause introduced by *que* tells what that opinion is. Other verbs that work the same way are *croire* (to believe) and *penser* (to think).

> Annie pense que Paris est magnifique.
> Je crois que Dieu a créé le monde.

N. Tell what you think about the following topics, using either *je trouve que, je pense que* or *je crois que*.
   modèle: le pain français   *Je pense que le pain français est délicieux.*
   1. le français
   2. les escargots
   3. les maths
   4. la glace
   5. le Président
   6. le temps qu'il fait aujourd'hui
   7. ton ami/ton amie
   8. ta voiture
   9. les Tigres de Détroit
   10. la télévision

savoir (to know)

je sais	nous savons
tu sais	vous savez
il, elle, on sait	ils, elles savent

past participle: su

O. Each of these people knows something about an apartment that is for
    rent. Tell what each knows by filling in the appropriate form of *savoir*.
    1. Jean _____ qu'il est toujours libre.
    2. Les enfants _____ qu'il est grand.
    3. Nous _____ où il est.
    4. Je _____ à quel étage il est.
    5. M. Fernandel _____ le loyer.
    6. Tu _____ le nombre de chambres.
    7. Les étudiants _____ réparer les W.C.
    8. _____-vous pourquoi l'appartement est toujours libre?

savoir vs. connaître

You learned in Chapter 13 that *connaître* means to know or to be acquainted
with a person or a place.

Savoir, unlike *connaître,* may be used alone:

Je ne sais pas.

It may also be followed by

- an infinitive, to say that a person knows how to do something.

  Je sais étudier.
  I know how to study.

- the conjunction *que,* to introduce a noun clause.

  Nous savons que la France est en Europe.

- a noun, to indicate the knowledge of some fact.

  Je sais la réponse.
  Mon frère sait la vérité.

P. Fill in the correct form of *savoir* or *connaître,* depending on the context.
   1. Je ne _____ pas.
   2. Est-ce que tu _____ mon cousin?
   3. Pauline _____ la réponse correcte.
   4. Vous _____ Toulouse?
   5. Nous _____ qu'il a beaucoup neigé.
   6. Marc et Hubert _____ faire la cuisine.
   7. Est-ce que tu _____ la vérité?
   8. On _____ l'artiste par son style.
   9. Est-ce que vous _____ jouer du piano?
   10. Mes parents _____ un missionnaire en France.

Q. Chercher un appartement
   Show that you understand the problems involved in renting an apartment by using either *je sais* or *je connais,* as required by each of these
   items.
   1. où l'appartement est situé
   2. le concierge
   3. les voisins
   4. qu'un F4 a quatre chambres
   5. lire les petites annonces
   6. le monsieur qui habite en face
   7. poser de bonnes questions
   8. que le loyer est 2.000 F par mois

R. Describe the location, rooms, furnishings, rent, size, etc., of your ideal
   apartment.
   Mon appartement idéal est . . .

chapitre quatorze

intonation

Intonation is the rise and fall of voice pitch during an utterance. Intonation patterns vary from one language to another and are best demonstrated with actual speech samples. In French it is important to distinguish at least three patterns that correspond to different sentence types.

- Declarative sentences—In general terms the intonation pattern of a declarative sentence rises to a high point within the sentence (often the verb) then falls as the sentence ends to a level below the speaker's average pitch range. Listen to a reading of these declarative sentences:

    Ils vont à la plage.
    Elle va sortir ce soir.
    On traverse le pont pour aller à la banque.
    Il est très grand, mais il n'est pas féroce.

- Yes/no questions—The pattern for yes/no questions is a rising pitch which, at the end of a sentence, stops at a level above the speaker's average pitch range, as illustrated in these sentences:

    C'est mon taxi?
    René est jeune, n'est-ce pas?
    Est-ce qu'il est marié?
    Vous prenez le rôti de bœuf saignant?

- Information questions—Information questions involve a falling pitch pattern that begins with a high level at the initial question word and falls to the lower limit of one's average pitch range at the end of the sentence. The pitch does not fall below the range limit as it does in a declarative sentence.

    Comment allez-vous?
    Qu'est-ce que tu veux?
    Combien de pièces a l'appartement?
    Quel temps est-ce qu'il va faire demain soir?

Few people in French cities and towns live in individual houses. Some live in row houses, which are somewhat similar to townhouses in America. Many others live in apartments or flats. The size of an apartment is indicated with a letter and a number. F3 means that it is for a family (rather than for commercial purposes) and that it has three bedrooms. Land is at a premium, particularly in large cities and in their suburbs, and people must live in *des immeubles* (large apartment buildings) or in *des cités* (apartment complexes). About 65 per cent of the people who live in apartments own them. Some of the older apartment buildings date from as far back as the 1700s and are up to eight or nine stories tall. These older buildings have been modernized with electricity, indoor plumbing, and hot water. Modern apartment buildings are not skyscrapers, but some of them have up to thirty stories. Some of the apartment complexes are quite beautiful, but many of the new structures are harshly criticized by Frenchmen for their ugliness, particularly when the buildings are near lovely, old parts of town. Housing in France is generally less expensive than in America. For families with very modest incomes, the French government has built the *H.L.M. (les habitations à loyer modéré*–moderate rent housing). These apartments are simple but adequate, and the rent is affordable to most people. However, some of the people who live in the *H.L.M.* do not take good care of their surroundings, and the area sometimes becomes run-down.

Some features about French housing are often surprising to an American on his first encounter. When a Frenchman moves into an apartment or a house in France, he knows that he must provide his own kitchen cupboards and light fixtures, even when someone else lived there previously. The former tenant has taken those items with him since he will need them in his new dwelling. Most French homes have the toilet in a room separate from the bathtub and sink, although the *W.C.* does occasionally have a sink as part of its furnishings. French people almost never have screens on their windows. Screens would be difficult, since most French windows swing inward like doors, and since nearly all French dwellings have functioning, not merely decorative, shutters on the windows. Most people close their shutters at night. For some it is a question of privacy or of protection. If an insurance company determines that a robbery victim had not closed and locked his shutters, it will not pay on his claim. For other people, closing the shutters is necessary for better sleeping. Since France is so far north, in the summer it is often still light at 10:00 at night and light again at 4:00 in the morning.

chapitre quinze

les loisirs et les divertissements

Romains 10, 9 Si tu confesses de ta bouche le Seigneur Jésus, et si tu crois dans ton cœur que Dieu l'a ressuscité des morts, tu seras sauvé.

15   15   15   15   15   15   15   15

Anne:	Qu'est-ce que tu as fait ce weekend?
Denis:	Je suis allé dans la montagne pour faire du camping avec mes *copains*.
Anne:	Moi, je préfère rester chez moi pour faire la cuisine.
Denis:	C'est vrai? Eh bien, je reste sûrement en ville le weekend *prochain*. Comme ça tu peux faire la cuisine pour mes copains et moi.
Anne:	*Tu parles!*

buddies

next

You've got to be kidding!

A. Répondez.

1. Qu'est-ce que Denis a fait ce weekend?
2. Est-ce qu'Anne préfère faire du camping?
3. Est-ce que Denis va faire du camping le weekend prochain?
4. Selon Denis, qu'est-ce qu'Anne peut faire pour lui et ses copains?
5. Est-ce qu'elle veut faire de la cuisine pour eux?

vocabulaire

Qu'est-ce que tu aimes faire?

J'aime . . .

lire.　　　　　écrire des lettres.　　　　faire la cuisine.

faire de la peinture. *to paint*
regarder la télévision. *to watch TV*
écouter la radio. *to listen to the radio*

Je vais . . .

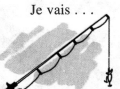  

à la pêche.　　　　à la mer.　　　　　　dans la montagne.

au concert. *to a concert*

Je fais . . .

du camping.
une promenade. *for a walk*
du bateau à voile. *sailing*

du ski.

de la natation.

Je collectionne . . .

des timbres.

des pièces.

des poupées.

Je joue . . .

au football.

au basketball. *basketball*
au rugby. *rugby*
au football américain. *football*
au baby-foot. *foosball*

au tennis.

aux échecs. *chess*
à Mille Bornes. *Mille Bornes*
aux dames. *checkers*

au base-ball

Je joue . . .

du piano.
de la flûte. *flute*
du violon. *violin*

de la guitare.

de la clarinette.

Notez bien: *Jouez* must be followed by the preposition *à* when talking about playing a sport or a game; however, the preposition *de* is used when talking about playing a musical instrument. Compare the following:

jouer au base-ball   jouer de la flute

B. Ask someone in class these questions.
    1. Qu'est-ce que tu aimes faire en été?
    2. A quel sport est-ce que tu joues?
    3. Est-ce que tu préfères le football ou le football américain?
    4. Quel est ton sport favori?
    5. Est-ce que tu joues du piano?
    6. De quel instrument est-ce que tu joues?
    7. Tu aimes la musique classique?

grammaire

y and en

In Chapter 6 you learned that *y* replaces a preposition of location and its object:

Est-ce qu'elle a trouvé son stylo dans le placard?
    Oui, elle y a trouvé son stylo.

Y also replaces the preposition *à* plus a noun referring to a thing:

Répondez-vous à sa lettre?
    Oui, nous y répondons.
Elle sait jouer au rugby?
    Oui, elle sait y jouer.
Est-ce que tu joues au football?
    Oui, j'y joue.

C. Répondez en employant *(using)* le pronom *y* selon le modèle.
    modèle: Est-ce que Michel joue aux dames? *Oui, il y joue.*
    1. Est-ce que ses parents répondent à ses lettres?
    2. Est-ce que M. Savoie travaille à la banque?
    3. Ton frère est allé au concert?
    4. Tu sais jouer au baby-foot?
    5. Voulez-vous jouer au basketball?
    6. Est-ce que Lise va à la pêche?
    7. Est-ce que tu fais souvent du camping dans la montagne?
    8. Avez-vous bien répondu à ces questions?

In Chapter 7 you learned that *en* replaces a partitive:

Est-ce que tu as *de l'argent?*

Non, je n'*en* ai pas.

Combien *de pain* est-ce que Georges a mangé?

Il *en* a mangé beaucoup.

En also replaces the preposition *de* plus a noun referring to a thing:

Est-ce que les Dupont viennent *de Chicago?*

Oui, ils *en* viennent.

Paul joue *du piano?*

Oui, il *en* joue.

D. Répondez en employant le pronom *en* selon le modèle.

modèle: Est-ce que tu achètes beaucoup de croissants?

Oui, j'en achète beaucoup.

1. Est-ce que Mme Poitiers prend du café au lait?
2. Tu viens d'Amérique?
3. Est-ce qu'Alice joue du piano?
4. Rentrez-vous du marché?
5. Tu as un peu d'argent?
6. Est-ce que le médecin prescrit de l'aspirine?
7. Est-ce que Samuel joue de la clarinette?
8. Tu prends de la salade?

les loisirs et les divertissements

217

E. Répondez à l'affirmatif ou au négatif selon le dessin.

modèle:

Hélène joue de la guitare, n'est-ce pas?
Oui, elle en joue.

1. Alfred joue de la flûte, n'est-ce pas?

2. Est-ce que Marcel joue du piano?

3. Claire joue de la clarinette?

4. Est-ce que M. Champs joue du saxophone?

5. Est-ce que Jean-Claude joue de la trompette?

F. Using *y* or *en* tell whether or not you play the following sports or instruments.

   modèle: le base-ball   *J'y joue.*
              le piano   *Je n'en joue pas.*

   1. le tennis
   2. la guitare
   3. le baby-foot
   4. les dames
   5. le rugby
   6. la flûte
   7. le hautbois *(oboe)*
   8. les échecs
   9. le football américain
   10. le violon

direct object pronouns (part I)

Observe the direct objects in these pairs of sentences:

Tu cherches *Michel?*
   Oui, je *le* cherche.
Elle regarde *la télévision,* n'est-ce pas?
   Oui, elle *la* regarde.
Est-ce que les deux pasteurs distribuent *leurs traités?*
   Oui, ils *les* distribuent.

In these sentences, the direct object (that is, the noun or noun phrase that immediately follows the verb) is replaced by a pronoun. The pronoun forms are *le* (him or it), *la* (her or it), and *les* (them). Like *y* and *en,* the direct object pronouns are placed immediately before the verb. If that verb begins with a vowel, *le* and *la* become *l',* and *les* is pronounced /lez/.

Vous écoutez *la radio?*
   Oui, nous *l'*écoutons.
Est-ce qu'elle aide *ses copains?*
   Oui, elle *les*(z)aide.

In negative sentences *ne* precedes the direct object pronoun and the other negative element follows the conjugated verb:

Non, je *ne* la regarde *pas.*
Non, elle *ne* les aide *jamais.*
Non, je *ne* l'ai *pas* mangé.

The third-person direct object pronouns have exactly the same forms as the definite articles *(le, la, les)*. However, you will be able to distinguish what they are since definite articles precede nouns, while direct object pronouns precede verbs.

Je vois *le* garçon. (article)
Je *le* vois. (direct object pronoun)

G. Répondez selon le modèle.
   modèle: Est-ce que tu aimes le football? *Oui, je l'aime.*
   1. Est-ce que M. Dupont écoute la radio?
   2. Voyez-vous les enfants?
   3. Est-ce que tu aides tes parents?
   4. Sylvie regarde la télévision?
   5. Est-ce que tu as mon livre?
   6. Pierre prend le train, n'est-ce pas?
   7. Est-ce que tu lis la Bible chaque jour?
   8. Comprenez-vous le français?

H. Make a statement about each of these objects, using a direct object pronoun and an appropriate verb.
   modèle: la radio   *Je l'écoute.* or *Je ne l'écoute jamais.*
   1. la musique classique
   2. le café au lait
   3. l'autobus
   4. les maths
   5. ton chien
   6. le petit déjeuner
   7. ta lessive
   8. le camembert
   9. tes chaussures

If the verb tense is *passé composé,* the object pronoun is placed before the auxiliary verb:

Est-ce que Daniel a trouvé *son stylo?*
Oui, il *l'*a trouvé.
Si tu confesses de ta bouche *le Seigneur Jésus,* et si tu crois dans ton cœur que Dieu *l'*a ressuscité des morts, tu seras sauvé.

The past participle agrees in number and gender with the preceding direct object pronoun:
Claude a trouvé *ses livres?*
   Oui, il *les* a trouvé*s.*
Est-ce qu'il a perdu *sa cravate?*
   Oui, il *l'*a perdu*e.*
Il a acheté *ses chaussures,* n'est-ce pas?
   Oui, il *les* a achet*ées.*

I. Answer the questions using a form of the verb in parentheses and replacing the direct objects with pronouns. Make changes necessary for the agreement of the past participle with the direct object.

   modèle: Est-ce que Marc a mangé la quiche? (préparer)

   Non, il l'a préparée.

   1. Est-ce que Marie-Flore a perdu ses livres? (trouver)
   2. Est-ce que tu as acheté le piano? (vendre)
   3. Est-ce que Gabrielle et Eugène ont aimé le concert? (détester)
   4. Avez-vous commencé vos exercices (m.)? (finir)
   5. Est-ce que tu as lu la lettre? (écrire)
   6. Est-ce que Papa a préparé les escargots? (manger)
   7. Est-ce que le médecin a pris les médicaments? (donner)
   8. Est-ce que les enfants ont chanté la chanson? (entendre)

If the verb phrase involves an infinitive, the direct object pronoun precedes the infinitive.

   Tu vas porter *ce pull-over?*

   Oui, je vais *le* porter.

   Vous voulez prendre *la voiture?*

   Oui, nous voulons *la* prendre.

   Est-ce qu'il peut repasser *ses vêtements?*

   Oui, il peut *les* repasser.

J. Answer these questions using the subject in parentheses and replacing direct objects with pronouns.

   modèle: Qui veut prendre le train? (nous)   *Nous voulons le prendre.*

   1. Qui sait manger le homard *(lobster)*? (moi)
   2. Qui peut trouver la bonne solution? (Claire)
   3. Qui va aimer le concert? (nous)
   4. Qui aime prendre l'avion? (mes cousins)
   5. Qui préfère lire le journal? (toi)
   6. Qui veut chanter la chanson devant l'église? (eux)
   7. Qui va distribuer les traités cet après-midi? (les jeunes)

K. Answer using a direct object pronoun. Begin your answers with one of the following:

Oui, j'aime . . .   Non, je n'aime pas bien . . .

Oui, j'aime bien . . .   Non, je déteste . . .

modèle: Tu aimes faire la cuisine?

        Non je déteste la faire.

1. Tu aimes écrire les lettres de remerciements?
2. Tu aimes faire les gâteaux?
3. Tu aimes regarder la télévision?
4. Tu aimes vider ta corbeille?
5. Tu aimes faire la vaisselle?
6. Tu aimes repasser tes vêtements?
7. Tu aimes lire ta Bible?
8. Tu aimes étudier le français?

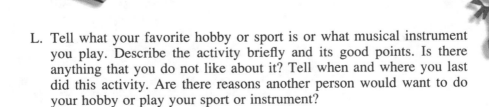

L. Tell what your favorite hobby or sport is or what musical instrument you play. Describe the activity briefly and its good points. Is there anything that you do not like about it? Tell when and where you last did this activity. Are there reasons another person would want to do your hobby or play your sport or instrument?

rhythm and stress

Compared with English, French words are much more evenly stressed. Each syllable is pronounced with the same amount of force so that there is a steadiness in the rhythm that is different from English rhythm. French words pronounced in isolation are stressed on the final syllable. This stress manifests itself as a slight lengthening of the final vowel. Compare the rhythm of these similar English and French words:

English	**French**
Madam	Madame
journal	journal
cousin	cousin
restaurant	restaurant
important	important
telephone	téléphone
exception	exception
conversation	conversation
independent	indépendant
intelligent	intelligent
apartment	appartement
nationality	nationalité
impossibility	impossibilité

Similarly, in a sentence there is a lengthening of the last vowel.

Il part ce *s o i r*.
C'est sa petite am *i e*.
Comment allez *v o u s?*
Qu'est-ce que tu *v e u x?*

France has many holidays, some religious and some civil. The year begins with a holiday, *le jour de l'an* (New Year's Day). The French do more in celebration of New Year's Day than of Christmas. Instead of Christmas cards, most people send New Year's cards, and the best gifts are given then. January 6 is *l'Epiphanie* or *la fête des Rois* (the Feast of the Kings). According to tradition, this is the day that the wise men arrived at the manger. February is the time of *mardi-gras,* which is a day of celebration and feasting before the onset of *le carême* (Lent). Lent is the forty days before *les Pâques*

(Easter), a time when Catholics deny themselves something that they especially enjoy. May is the month with the most holidays. May 1 is *la fête du Travail* (Labor Day in Europe) when all workers are honored with a day off. May 1 is also the day when French people offer their loved ones a sprig of lily of the valley to signify friendship and to bring them "good luck." May 8 is *la fête de la Victoire,* which commemorates the end of World War II in Europe in 1945. *La Pentecôte* (Pentecost), a religious and civil holiday in France, is usually in May. It is a time for family picnics and outings, since spring weather has usually arrived by then. Its date is variable in accordance with the date of Easter that year. *La fête des mères* (Mother's Day) is also in May, and *la fête des pères* (Father's Day) is in June. *La fête nationale* is July 14. It commemorates the taking of the Bastille Prison in 1789 during the French Revolution. The next holidays are *la Toussaint* (All Saints' Day) on November 1 and *le jour des Morts* (All Souls' Day) on November 2. This is a time of remembering dead family members and soldiers slain for France. People decorate graves with flowers, and Catholic masses are offered in profusion. *L'Armistice de 1918* is November 11. At this time people honor soldiers slain during World War I, or *la Grande Guerre* ("The Great War"), as the French refer to it.

Christmas in France is celebrated a little differently than it is in the United States. Many French people who do not go to church any other time of the year attend Midnight Mass. After the church service people gather in the homes of family members for a banquet called *le réveillon.* One part of this celebration is the eating of a piece of *la bûche de Noël,* a chocolate cake roll decorated like a log. Before the children go to bed, they place their well-polished shoes in front of the fireplace or under the *sapin* (Christmas tree). In the morning they find in their shoes little toys and candies from *Père Noël* (Santa Claus). Christmas Day is a restful day spent at home with the family which is recovering from the previous night's party. How sad that the Lord Jesus Christ, whose birthday is being celebrated, is such a little part of their thoughts or traditions. Christmas in France has become just as commercialized as it has in America.

à la campagne

Jean 20, 21 Comme le Père m'a envoyé, moi aussi
je vous envoie.

lecture

vacation
country/farm

during/stay/
discover rural life
thanks to these herds

apple trees
everywhere

C'est le mois d'août. Les Dupont passent leurs *vacances* à la *campagne*. Les parents d'un membre de leur église ont une *ferme* en Normandie. Ils ont invité les Dupont à passer quelques jours dans la ferme. *Pendant* leur *séjour* ils *découvrent la vie rurale*. Ils sont surpris par le grand nombre de vaches, mais ils apprennent que c'est *grâce à ces troupeaux* que la Normandie est riche en fromage. Les noms des animaux de la ferme les amusent beaucoup. Ils sont aussi surpris de voir tant de *pommiers*. Ils apprennent que le cidre de Normandie est apprécié *partout* en France.

A. Répondez.
1. Quel mois est-ce?
2. Où est-ce que les Dupont passent leurs vacances?
3. Pourquoi la Normandie est-elle riche en fromage?
4. Est-ce que le cidre vient des pommes ou des pommiers?
5. Est-ce que le vin de Normandie est apprécié partout en France?

vocabulaire

Quels sont les animaux que l'on trouve à la ferme?
dans la basse-cour?
dans la grange?

What are the animals that one finds on the farm?
. . . in the barnyard?
. . . in the barn?

un cochon   un cheval   un chat   un dindon   une chèvre

un canard   un mouton   une poule   un chien   une vache

chapitre seize

B. Répondez.
1. Quel est l'animal qui donne des œufs?
2. Quel est l'animal qui donne du lait?
3. Quel est l'animal que l'on mange en France mais pas en Amérique?
4. Quel est l'animal que l'on mange en Amérique le jour des actions de grâces *(Thanksgiving)*?
5. Quel est l'animal qui aime l'eau et qui fait "couin-couin"?
6. Quel est l'animal qui mange de presque tout?
7. Quel est l'animal qui aime la boue *(mud)*?
8. Quel est l'animal qui donne de la laine *(wool)* et qui fait "bèèè"?
9. Quel est l'animal qui mange les souris *(mice)* et qui fait "miaou"?
10. Quel est l'animal qui chasse les chats et qui fait "ouah-ouah"?

grammaire

plural of nouns *(révision)*

In spoken French there is no difference in pronunciation between singular and plural forms of most nouns, since the -s that is added to the spelling of the plural noun is silent. Number is indicated often in the spoken form by the article that precedes the noun:

le mouton /lømutɔ̃/	les moutons /lemutɔ̃/
la poule /lapul/	les poules /lepul/

Most nouns ending in -au and -eu add a silent -x in their written plural form.

le tableau	les tableaux
le neveu	les neveux

Most nouns ending in -al form their plural by changing the -l to u and adding -x. This change is also reflected in the pronunciation:

l'animal	/lanimal/	les animaux	/lezanimo/
le cheval	/løšøval/	les chevaux	/lešøvo/

C. Répondez selon le modèle.

modèle: Est-ce que tu as un chien? (2) *Oui, j'ai deux chiens.*

1. Est-ce que tu as une sœur? (3)
2. Est-ce que tu as un cheval? (5)
3. Est-ce que tu as un neveu? (9)
4. Est-ce que tu as une voiture? (2)
5. Est-ce que tu as un chapeau? (4)
6. Est-ce que tu as un bureau? (3)
7. Est-ce que tu as un animal favori? (6)
8. Est-ce que tu as un bon jeu *(game)*? (3)

voir (to see)

je vois	nous voyons
tu vois	vous voyez
il, elle, on voit	ils, elles voient

past participle: vu

croire (to believe)

je crois	nous croyons
tu crois	vous croyez
il, elle, on croit	ils, elles croient

past participle: cru

A common French proverb is *Voir c'est croire.*

D. Substitute the subject in parentheses. Watch tenses!

1. Je vois les cochons dans la basse-cour. (tu)
2. Nous croyons que la Normandie est très jolie. (les Dupont)
3. Il a vu le film hier soir à l'église. (je)
4. Crois-tu en Dieu? (vous)
5. Hassan a cru en Jésus-Christ. (nous)
6. Les enfants voient les animaux à la ferme. (nous)
7. Je crois que ces exercices sont ennuyeux. (Marcelle)
8. A Paris nous allons voir la Tour Eiffel. (elles)

E. *Voir c'est croire?* Tell what each of these people see and then what they believe about what they see. Use a form of *voir* in the first sentence and a form of *croire* and an adjective in the second sentence.
  1. Alain _____ son professeur. Il _____que son professeur est _____.
  2. Je _____ les bébés-chèvres. Je _____qu'ils sont _____.
  3. Mes parents _____ mes notes *(grades)*. Ils _____qu'elles sont _____.
  4. Nous _____ la ferme. Nous _____qu'elle est _____.
  5. Tu _____ cet exercice. Tu _____qu'il est _____.

regular verbs ending in *-yer*

In both *voir* and *croire* the letter *y* occurs instead of an *i* before a pronounced vowel. This same spelling change also occurs in regular verbs ending in *-yer*, like *payer* (to pay), *envoyer* (to send), *nettoyer* (to clean), and *employer* (to use).

j'envoie	nous envoyons
tu envoies	vous envoyez
il, elle, on envoie	ils, elles envoient

Would the past participle have an *i* or a *y?* (For the answer, look at the Bible verse for this chapter.)

F. Complétez les phrases avec la forme du verbe qui convient: *payer, envoyer, nettoyer,* ou *employer.*
  1. Qu'est-ce que tu _____ pour écrire une lettre? Un stylo?
  2. Combien est-ce que tu as _____ pour cette robe? 400 F?
  3. Ma mère _____ la maison tous les jours.
  4. A qui _____-vous cette carte postale?
  5. Je vais _____ 2.200 F par mois pour l'appartement.
  6. Nous avons _____ le salon avec un aspirateur.
  7. On _____ un couteau pour couper la viande.
  8. Il _____ ses dettes.

G. Toi et la voiture familiale
  Répondez aux questions suivantes.
  1. Tu nettoies la voiture de ta famille?
  2. Qu'est-ce que tu emploies pour nettoyer la voiture?
  3. Est-ce que tu es payé(e) pour nettoyer la voiture? Si oui, combien?
  4. Est-ce que tu as jamais envoyé ton frère nettoyer la voiture à ta place?

direct object pronouns (part II)

Comme le Père *m'*a envoyé, moi aussi je *vous* envoie.

In Chapter 15 you learned the third-person direct object pronouns *(le, la, les)*. The Bible verse for this chapter contains two of the remaining four direct object pronouns. Here is the complete list:

me	nous
te	vous
le, la	les

The rules for pronoun placement and verb agreement that you learned in Chapter 15 apply to all the direct object pronouns:

> Anne: Je *t'*ai vu au marché, Denis. Est-ce que tu *m'*as vu*e*?
> Denis: Non, je ne *t'*ai pas vu*e*.

H. Supply either the question or the answer in each of these brief exchanges. Questions could contain either nouns or direct object pronouns, and all answers should contain direct object pronouns.

1. –Tu m'aimes?

   –_____ .

2. –_____ ?

   –Oui, nous la regardons.

3. –Qui a mangé mon sandwich?
   –Ton frère _____.

4. –_____ ?
   –Oui, je t'ai vu hier soir.

5. –Est-ce que votre professeur vous aide?

   –_____ .

6. –Est-ce que tu as ton livre?
   –_____ .

7. –_____ ?
   –Oui, elle les a distribués.

8. –Est-ce que tu portes mes chaussures?
   –Non, _____.

9. –Tu me cherches?
   –_____ .

10. –Est-ce que Dieu nous aime?
    –Oui, _____.

I. Replace the direct objects with pronouns. Be sure to make any necessary agreement.
   modèle: J'ai mangé la pomme. *Je l'ai mangée.*
   1. Tu as mis ton nouveau pantalon.
   2. Mon ami a trouvé ma Bible.
   3. Nous avons perdu nos livres.
   4. Thomas et Suzette ont vu leurs cousines.
   5. Elle a étudié la leçon.
   6. J'ai fait les photos de ma famille.

J. With your partner, play the roles of the various people in these situations, asking the appropriate question and responding affirmatively. Use formal or informal as the situation requires.
   modèle: A boy wants to know if his brother is watching him.
           He turns to his brother and asks: *Tu me regardes?*
           Réponse: *Oui, je te regarde.*
   1. A girl wants to know if her friend is looking for her. She turns to her friend and asks . . .
   2. A young man wants to know if his girlfriend loves him. He turns to his girlfriend and asks . . .
   3. A person wants to know if an elderly man is hearing him. He turns to the older person and asks . . .
   4. A teacher wants to know if her students are listening to her. She turns to the class and asks . . .
   5. A boy wants to know if his parents believe him. He turns to his parents and asks . . .
   6. A woman wants to know if a child knows her. She turns to the child and asks . . .

prepositions of geography (révision)

In Chapter 8 you learned that the preposition *à* precedes the name of a city to express the ideas of *in* or *to* that city:

> Les Plouvin habitent à Toulouse. (in Toulouse)
> Les touristes vont à Toulouse. (to Toulouse)

In English *in* indicates location and *to* indicates destination. In French, however, the choice of the preposition depends on the type of geographical place: a city, a country, or a continent.

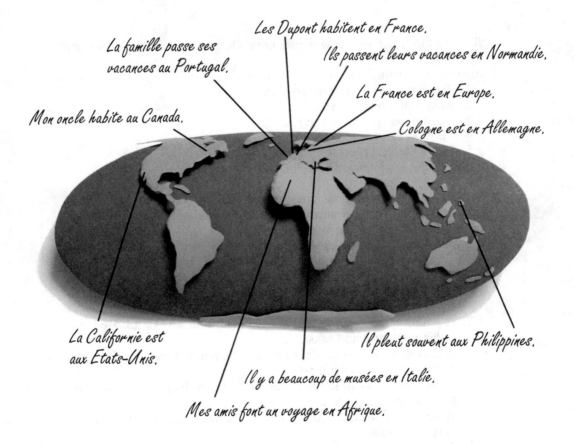

La famille passe ses vacances au Portugal.

Les Dupont habitent en France.

Ils passent leurs vacances en Normandie.

Mon oncle habite au Canada.

La France est en Europe.

Cologne est en Allemagne.

La Californie est aux États-Unis.

Il pleut souvent aux Philippines.

Il y a beaucoup de musées en Italie.

Mes amis font un voyage en Afrique.

The preposition *en* is used with feminine countries and provinces (those ending with *-e*, except *le Mexique*) and with continents. *Au* is used with masculine countries and provinces, and *aux* with plural countries.

K. Tell where each person/family is going to serve as a missionary.
   modèle: les Muller/l'Espagne
         Les Muller vont servir le Seigneur en Espagne.
   1. M. Frankovitch/l'Afrique
   2. Mlle Blough/l'Italie
   3. M. et Mme Gons/la Pologne
   4. les Perry/le Brésil
   5. M. et Mme Banks/Dijon
   6. M. Keppler/l'Allemagne
   7. Mlle Smith/la Bretagne
   8. les Tissot/le Sénégal

vocabulaire

d'autres animaux

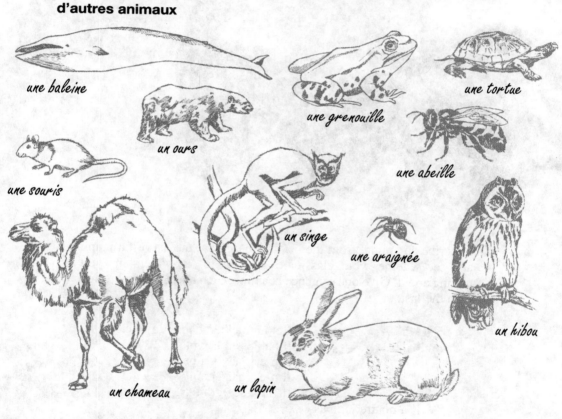

une baleine

un ours

une grenouille

une tortue

une souris

un singe

une abeille

une araignée

un hibou

un chameau

un lapin

Can you guess these . . . ?

un crocodile	une girafe	un hippopotame	un serpent
un éléphant	un gorille	un lion	un tigre

L. Name the animals going into Noah's ark.

M. Describe an animal from the list above or from the list of farm animals and see whether your classmates can figure out which one you are talking about. Give one sentence at a time, each one a little more specific than the last.

> *modèle:* Cet animal est dans la Bible.
> Il habite en Egypte.
> Il n'est pas tres beau.
> Il n'est pas gentil.
> Il est assez grand.
> Il a quatre jambes.
> Il peut voyager longtemps sans prendre de l'eau.
> Il a un gros dos.
> (C'est un chameau.)

N. Describe a place where you have traveled, what you saw, and give your opinion of it all. Include forms of some of the following words: *aller, voyager, voir, croire que, penser que, trouver que, détester, préférer, aimer, parce que.*

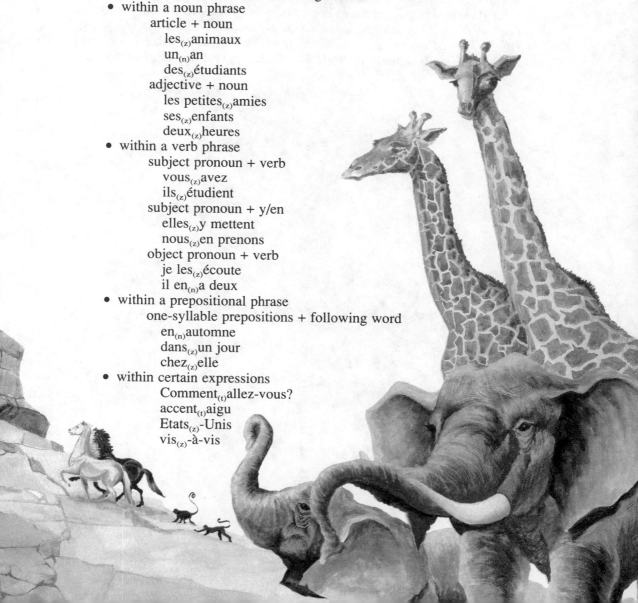

prononciation

liaison summary

Liaison must be made in the following contexts:
- within a noun phrase
    article + noun
        les$_{(z)}$animaux
        un$_{(n)}$an
        des$_{(z)}$étudiants
    adjective + noun
        les petites$_{(z)}$amies
        ses$_{(z)}$enfants
        deux$_{(z)}$heures
- within a verb phrase
    subject pronoun + verb
        vous$_{(z)}$avez
        ils$_{(z)}$étudient
    subject pronoun + y/en
        elles$_{(z)}$y mettent
        nous$_{(z)}$en prenons
    object pronoun + verb
        je les$_{(z)}$écoute
        il en$_{(n)}$a deux
- within a prepositional phrase
    one-syllable prepositions + following word
        en$_{(n)}$automne
        dans$_{(z)}$un jour
        chez$_{(z)}$elle
- within certain expressions
        Comment$_{(t)}$allez-vous?
        accent$_{(t)}$aigu
        Etats$_{(z)}$-Unis
        vis$_{(z)}$-à-vis

Since the time of Napoleon in the early 1800s, France has been divided into 95 administrative regions called *départements*. Each department has a number based on its order in an alphabetical listing. *Ain* is department 01, while *Val-d'Oise* is department 95. This number is used on automobile license plates and as the first two numbers in the postal code. Before Napoleon's time, the regions of France were called *provinces*. French people still use provincial names rather than departmental names when referring to a specific area. The names of some of these areas are familiar to Americans: *la Normandie* (Normandy), *la Bretagne* (Brittany), *l'Alsace* (Alsace), and *la Lorraine* (Lorraine). Each region of France is known for its agricultural products. *La Normandie* is renowned for its cider and its cheeses, especially *le Camembert* and *le Pont l'Évêque*. *La Bretagne* is known for its fish and shellfish. *La Bourgogne* (Burgundy) is world-famous for its vineyards and its mustard.

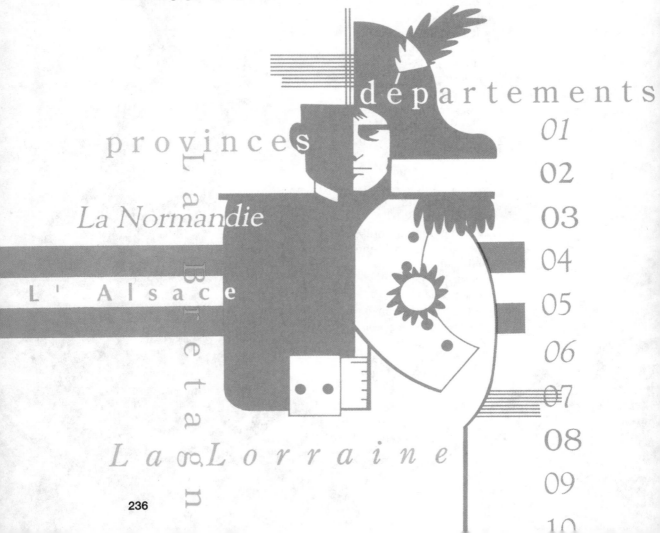

provinces

départements

La Normandie

L' Alsace

La Bretagne

La Lorraine

01
02
03
04
05
06
07
08
09
10

236

à la gare

Ephésiens 2, 8 Car c'est par la grâce que vous êtes sauvés, par le moyen de la foi. Et cela ne vient pas de vous, c'est le don de Dieu.

M. Dupont a fait la connaissance de M. et Mme Johnson, un couple canadien qui étudie le français à l'Université de Toulouse. Ils sont *sur le point* de partir pour la Côte d'Ivoire, un autre pays *francophone*. Les Johnson vont prendre un train pour Paris, et puis un avion pour l'Afrique. M. Johnson est maintenant au guichet pour acheter leurs billets de train.

ready
French-speaking

l'employé:	Monsieur?
M. Johnson:	A quelle heure partent les trains rapides pour Paris?
l'employé:	Il y a un rapide qui part tous les jours à 13 h 24.
M. Johnson:	A quelle heure est-ce qu'il arrive à Paris?
l'employé:	Il arrive à 17 h 39.
M. Johnson:	Est-ce qu'il faut réserver les places?
l'employé:	Bien sûr. Il y a aussi un supplément de 20 F pour le train que vous prenez.
M. Johnson:	D'accord. Je voudrais deux billets aller pour le 28 juin, s'il vous plaît.
l'employé:	Première ou deuxième classe?
M. Johnson:	Deuxième classe.
l'employé:	Ça fait 800 F.

A. Répondez.
1. D'où viennent M. et Mme Johnson?
2. Qu'est-ce qu'ils font à Toulouse?
3. Est-ce que la Côte d'Ivoire est anglophone?
4. Comment est-ce que les Johnson vont voyager à Paris?
5. Où est M. Johnson maintenant?
6. A quelle heure part le rapide pour Paris?
7. Combien est le supplément pour le rapide?
8. En quelle classe voyagent les Johnson?

Qu'est-ce qu'on voit à la gare?

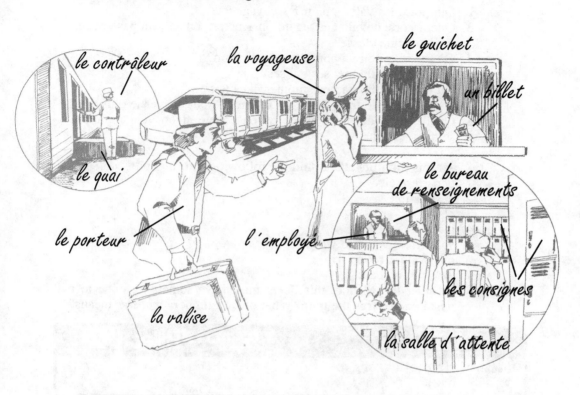

le contrôleur

la voyageuse

le guichet

un billet

le quai

le bureau de renseignements

le porteur

l'employé

les consignes

la valise

la salle d'attente

Quelle sorte de billet voulez-vous?

Je voudrais un billet d'aller.
  I'd like a one-way ticket.

un billet d'aller et retour	prendre le T.G.V. (train à grande vitesse)
round trip ticket	*high-speed train*
voyager en première classe	prendre un train rapide
first class	*nonstop train*
voyager en deuxième classe	prendre un train express
second class	*fast train, but not nonstop*
une voiture non-fumeur	prendre un train omnibus
non-smoking car	*the slow, local train*

B. Répondez.
1. Où est-ce qu'on va pour acheter un billet?
2. Qui porte les valises pour les voyageurs?
3. Quelle sorte de billet est-ce qu'on achète si on ne veut pas voyager en deuxième classe?
4. Où est-ce qu'on va pour attendre le train?
5. Où est-ce qu'on met ses valises?
6. Où est-ce qu'on va pour monter dans le train?
7. Quelle sorte de train est-ce qu'on prend pour arriver le plus vite?
8. Quelle sorte de billet est-ce qu'on achète si on veut rentrer la semaine prochaine?

C. Look at this train ticket and find the following information:
1. departure city
2. destination
3. class
4. price
5. valid from when to when
6. one-way or round trip
7. date of purchase
8. In order to be valid, this ticket must have something done to it when one boards the train. What do you think *composter* means?

A quelle heure part le train?

Throughout Europe, time related to scheduled events is given in official time, or "military time," instead of using A.M. and P.M. as we do in America. This time is based on a 24-hour clock, beginning at midnight (0 h 00). One o'clock in the morning is 1 h 00, whereas one o'clock in the afternoon is 13 h 00. This manner of indicating time is found in travel schedules, the opening and closing times of any place of business, television programming, etc.

Il y a un rapide qui part tous les jours à 13 h 24.
There is a fast train which leaves every day at 1:24 P.M.
Il y arrive à 17 h 39.
It arrives there at 5:39 P.M.

D. A quelle heure part le train? (Indiquez l'heure officielle en français).
    modèle: 5:38 P.M.   *Le train part à dix-sept heures trente-huit.*
    1. 7:21 A.M.   5. 8:17 P.M.
    2. 11:42 P.M.   6. 9:33 A.M.
    3. 10:05 A.M.   7. 6:56 P.M.
    4. 2:29 P.M.   8. 6:15 A.M.

grammaire

relative pronouns

Relative pronouns are used to connect two related sentences. For example, the two sentences

Il y a *un rapide. Ce rapide* part tous les jours à 13 h 24.

could be expressed:

Il y a un rapide *qui* part tous les jours à 13 h 24.

Likewise these sentences

Nous voyons *le professeur.* Tu préfères *ce professeur.*

could be expressed:

Nous voyons le professeur *que* tu préfères.

In each of these sentence pairs, the *italicized* words represent the related element in the two sentences. *Qui* is used to replace the person or thing that served as the subject of the second sentence, whereas *que* replaces a direct object.

E. Join these sentences with the relative pronouns indicated in parentheses.
    1. Nous regardons la télévision. La télévision est au coin. (qui)
    2. Voici ma cousine. Elle aime parler français. (qui)
    3. Je vais lire le livre. Ce livre est sur la table. (qui)
    4. C'est mon oncle. Mon oncle travaille à la banque. (qui)
    5. Il joue avec le ballon. J'ai acheté ce ballon. (que)
    6. Ma mère a fait la robe. Suzanne porte cette robe. (que)
    7. Est-ce que tu aimes le cours? Tu as choisi ce cours. (que)
    8. C'est M. Linard. Nous voyons M. Linard. (que)

F. Decide whether the sentence should contain *qui* or *que*.
1. Le professeur aime le cadeau _____ tu lui as donné.
2. Nous préférons le restaurant _____ est au coin de la rue.
3. C'est un médecin _____ je cherche.
4. C'est un médecin _____ me cherche.
5. Voici le train _____ nous allons prendre.
6. Le billet _____ tu as acheté est aller-retour.
7. Elle téléphone à Rosalie _____ est malade.
8. En France il y a des églises _____ sont très petites.

G. Add a *qui* clause or a *que* clause to each of these sentences.
1. Paris est une ville . . .
2. La chèvre est un animal . . .
3. Le français est la langue . . .
4. Mon oncle est un homme . . .
5. Le petit déjeuner est un repas . . .
6. Le Canada est une nation . . .
7. Le Président des Etats-Unis est une personne . . .
8. Le football américain est un sport . . .
9. Où est le train . . . ?
10. Voici l'employé . . .

chapitre dix-sept

la nationalité et la langue

De quel pays venez-vous?	Quelle est votre nationalité?	Quelle langue parlez-vous?
Je viens de France.	Je suis français(e).	Je parle français.
de Belgique.	belge.	français ou flamand.
d'Allemagne.	allemand(e).	allemand.
d'Italie.	italien(ne).	italien.
de Suisse.	suisse.	allemand, français, italien, ou romanche.
d'Espagne.	espagnol(e).	espagnol.
d'Angleterre.	anglais(e).	anglais.
de Chine.	chinois(e).	chinois.
du Canada.	canadien(ne).	anglais ou français.
du Mexique.	mexicain(e).	espagnol.
des Etats-Unis.	américain(e).	américain.
de Russie	russe.	russe.
du Japon.	japonais(e).	japonais.
du Sénégal.	sénégalais(e).	français.
du Brésil.	brésilien(ne).	portugais.

In Chapter 10 you saw that names of nationality are capitalized only when they are nouns referring to people.

Pierre est un Français.
Suzanne est une Française.
Voici Sophia. C'est une Italienne.

When the noun refers to the language, however, it is not capitalized, and it is usually preceded by the article *le*. The article is not used after the verb *parler* or after the preposition *en*.

Anne étudie l'allemand et elle parle allemand assez bien.
Cette leçon est en anglais.

Nationalities can be used as adjectives, and as such, they show agreement, follow the nouns they modify, and are not capitalized. When the nationality is preceded by *il est* or *elle est,* it is an adjective, and the indefinite article is dropped.

Carlos est *un* garçon *mexicain.*   Maria est *une* fille *mexicaine.*
Elle est mexicaine. (Compare with "C'est une Mexicaine.")

H. Quelle est la nationalité?
   modèle: Choon-Fong habite en Chine.
         Elle est chinoise. or *C'est une Chinoise.*
   1. Léopold habite au Sénégal.
   2. Maria habite en Italie.
   3. Thomas habite en Angleterre.
   4. Patricia habite au Brésil.
   5. Pedro habite au Mexique.
   6. John habite aux Etats-Unis.
   7. Petrovitch habite en Russie.
   8. Madeleine habite en Belgique.

I. Answer this question about each person in exercise H: Quelle langue est-ce qu'il/elle parle?
   modèle–Quelle langue est-ce qu'elle parle?   *Elle parle chinois.*

dialogue

C'est aujourd'hui le 28 juin. Les Johnson partent pour Paris par le train. Les Dupont les accompagnent à la gare pour les aider à porter leurs valises et leur dire au revoir.

Mme Dupont:	Avez-vous vos billets et vos passeports?
Mme Johnson:	Attends. Je vais regarder. Oui, ils sont dans mon sac.
M. Johnson:	Vite, chérie. Le train va partir dans deux minutes.
M. Dupont:	Eh bien, au revoir.
M. Johnson:	Au revoir. *Que Dieu vous bénisse* dans votre travail ici à Toulouse!
M. Dupont:	Bon voyage! Au revoir.

May the Lord bless you

(dans le train)

M. Johnson:	Mais, Sonia, quel est ce *paquet?*
Mme Johnson:	C'est un *cadeau* qu'Alice m'a donné.
M. Johnson:	*Quelle gentillesse.*

package
gift
How nice

J. Répondez.
1. Quelle est la date aujourd'hui?
2. Pourquoi est-ce que les Dupont vont à la gare?
3. Où sont les billets et les passeports des Johnson?
4. Est-ce qu'ils ont beaucoup de temps avant le départ du train?
5. Quel est le prénom de Mme Johnson?
6. Qui a donné le cadeau à Mme Johnson?

grammaire

indirect object pronouns

Alice *m'*à donné un cadeau.

The word *m(e)* is an indirect object pronoun telling to whom Alice has given the gift.

In the sentence, *Les Dupont leur disent au revoir,* the word *leur* is an indirect object pronoun telling to whom the Duponts say good-bye. Note the complete list of indirect object pronouns.

me *to me*	nous *to us*
te *to you*	vous *to you*
lui *to him or to her*	leur *to them*

The pronouns *me, te, nous,* and *vous* serve as either direct or indirect object pronouns, depending on the grammatical context:

Je *t'* aime. ("you"–direct object)
Je *te* donne un cadeau. ("to you"–indirect object)
Dieu *nous* aime. ("us"–direct object)
Dieu *nous* donne la vie éternelle. ("to us"–indirect object)

Third person indirect object pronouns replace *à* + a person, which in French grammar is considered an indirect object. The singular *lui* ("to him" or "to her") does not distinguish between the masculine and the feminine:

J'ai envoyé une lettre *à mon grand-père.*
   Je *lui* ai envoyé une lettre.
J'ai envoyé une carte postale *à ma tante.*
   Je *lui* ai envoyé une carte postale.

Note that the past participle does not agree with an indirect object pronoun as it would with a direct object pronoun. Indirect object pronouns also follow all the rules of placement that you have already learned with direct object pronouns. (See pages 219 and 230.)

à la gare

245

K. Answer each of these questions, replacing the indirect objects with pronouns.

modèle: Est-ce que Dominique téléphone à ses parents?

　　　　Oui, elle leur téléphone.

1. Est-ce que les jeunes donnent les traités aux voyageurs?
2. Est-ce que Marc obéit à son père?
3. Est-ce que Pauline a envoyé la lettre à son ami?
4. Est-ce que les élèves répondent à leur professeur?
5. Est-ce que tu as montré les photos à Gaston?
6. Est-ce que vous allez parler aux visiteurs?
7. Est-ce que tu as téléphoné à Robert et Alice?
8. Est-ce qu'elles ont demandé le prix au vendeur?

L. Répondez.

modèle: Qu'est-ce qu'elle t'a donné? (un livre) *Elle m'a donné un livre.*

1. Qu'est-ce que le professeur vous a montré? (un film)
2. Qu'est-ce que Matthieu m'a envoyé? (un paquet)
3. Qu'est-ce qu'Irène nous a donné? (une chèvre)
4. Qu'est-ce que les Jourdain t'ont dit? (le secret)
5. Qu'est-ce que votre père veut vous acheter? (une voiture)
6. Qu'est-ce que tu vas me préparer? (un bon repas français)

M. Restate each of these sentences, replacing the *à* and its object with *y, lui,* or *leur.*

1. Les Johnson vont à la gare.
2. M. Johnson achète les billets au guichet.
3. Il pose des questions à l'employé.
4. L'employé donne les billets aux voyageurs.
5. Mme Dupont offre un paquet à son amie.
6. Ils vont ensemble au quai pour monter dans le train.
7. Ils donnent leurs billets au contrôleur.
8. Ils vont arriver à Paris ce soir.

N. You are at a train station. You need to buy tickets from Paris to Bordeaux. Since you will be returning next week, you need to buy round-trip tickets. Write a conversation between you and the ticket vendor. Include departure and arrival times, price, type of train, and the type of car in which you wish to travel.

semivowels: /w/, /j/, and /ɥ/

Semivowels are produced in the same area of the mouth as their correspond-ing pure vowel sounds. However, they do not represent a separate syllable as do vowels, but rather they are merely glides onto or off of a vowel sound. Notice the following contrasts:

/u/	/w/
ou	oui
doux	doué
loup	louange
joue	jouer
moue	mouette

/y/	/ɥ/
tu	tué
hue	huit
pu	puis
lu	luire
mue	muet

/i/	/j/ glide + vowel
lit	lion
si	sillon
fit	fier
dis	diacre
vie	vient

vowel sound	vowel + /j/ glide
a	ail
fit	fille
aller	soleil
mit	famille
nous	nouille

Notice that *-il* and *-ill* are normally pronounced /ij/ or /j/, except for these three words and their derivatives:

mille villes tranquilles   *1,000 calm cities*

France is a world leader in many areas of transportation. Its public mass transit system is extremely well developed, and the S.N.C.F. *(la Société nationale de chemins de fer français*–the National Railroad System) prides itself in its punctuality. Tourists learn quickly that when the schedule indicates that a train will leave at 15 h 32, it will be gone if they show up at 15 h 33. Many French people travel by train instead of by car when taking a long trip–some because they do not own a car, but others mostly because they do not want to drive to their destinations. For them it is much more restful to sit on the train, read a novel or magazine, and get up for a little walk to stretch their legs while someone else does the driving. Trains are plentiful, and the train lines go to just about any destination that one could desire. Not only is the train system efficient, but France also boasts one of the fastest trains in the world. The *train à grande vitesse (T.G.V.)* averages 168 miles per hour. New T.G.V. lines are opening all the time. A tunnel is being dug under the English Channel to link Paris and London by the T.G.V. Its completion is scheduled for 1993.

France is also actively involved in air and space travel. The city of Toulouse is known for the manufacture of the Airbus, which many airlines buy for their overseas flight service. The *Concorde* of *Air France* is the fastest passenger jet in the world. It flies its passengers from Paris to New York in under four hours. Another jet in the planning stages now will make that flight in an even shorter time. The major cities in France are linked by the French airline *Air Inter*. On Christmas Eve, 1979, France launched its first rocket, *Ariane,* from the Kourou Space Center in French Guiana. Since then Ariane rockets have been used to launch many satellites, with many more launchings contracted for the future. France has launched space probes, and several French astronauts have been a part of teams of astronauts for both America and the U.S.S.R. France even has plans to launch a European space shuttle called *Hermès* in 1998.

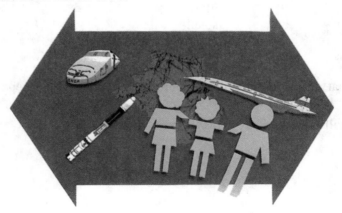

chapitre de révision

2 Timothée 4, 7 J'ai combattu le bon combat, j'ai
achevé la course, j'ai gardé la foi.

Paris

The Dupont family has decided to spend their vacation in Paris to familiarize themselves with the capital. They soon learn that Paris, the capital of France, is a city of contrasts–the very old and the ultra-modern, the typically French and the cosmopolitan, the beautiful and the dirty. The original settlement in the third century B.C. was called Lutèce, which means "midwater dwelling." It was called that because it was located on *Ile de la Cité,* an island in the Seine River. As the town grew, it expanded onto the mainland along the river. A wall was built as a protection for the town. As Paris continued to grow, new walls were built, and the old walls were leveled to build streets. Thus many of the major streets in Paris are concentric circles radiating out from *Ile de la Cité.* The Seine River divides present-day downtown Paris into two distinct parts. The area south of the Seine is called *la Rive Gauche* (the Left Bank). It is known for its picturesque, narrow streets that have not changed in centuries, as well as the many bookstores, sidewalk cafés, and antique shops. Part of *la Rive Gauche* is called *le Quartier Latin* (the Latin Quarter). This district is so named because Latin was for centuries the language of the classroom at the University of Paris located there. *La Sorbonne* is the oldest part of the university, dating from the Middle Ages. The area north of the Seine, known as *la Rive Droite* (the Right Bank), is the chic, commercial part of Paris. In this part of town, one would find well-dressed businessmen, banks, and large department stores. The famous *Champs-Elysées* is the magnificent boulevard lined with elegant boutiques, airline offices, fancy restaurants, as well as fast-food restaurants such as Burger King and McDonald's.

chapitre de révision

Although the city is over 2,000 years old, with many buildings dating from the Middle Ages still in use today, Paris has many modern features as well. Some of the most notable are the 56-story Montparnasse Tower, the Georges Pompidou Center (also called *Beaubourg*), and *le Forum des Halles*. *Beaubourg*, with its shops, bookstores, art exhibits, and lending library, looks like a building turned inside out because of its architectural style, deplored by many French people. *Le Forum des Halles* is an underground, four-story commercial center. It houses 180 shops specializing in fashion, sporting goods, recreational items, and home accessories. There are also public service agencies such as banks and transportation information offices.

A tourist's "must-see" list of Parisian landmarks would include *la Tour Eiffel, l'Arc de Triomphe, l'Arc de Triomphe du Carrousel, le Louvre, Notre Dame, la Sainte Chapelle, Montmartre, le Sacré Cœur, l'Opéra, les Bateaux-Mouches, le Palais de Justice, le Panthéon, la Madeleine, l'Hôtel des Invalides, la Place de la Concorde,* and *le Jardin du Luxembourg.*

la Tour Eiffel

Plus de quatre millions de touristes visitent la Tour Eiffel chaque année. Visible jour et nuit de toutes parties de Paris, ce monument a 320,75 mètres de haut. On est obligé de changer deux fois d'ascenseur pour monter jusqu'au sommet de la tour. Appelée laide et monstrueuse par ses détracteurs au moment de sa construction en 1889, elle symbolise aujourd'hui la ville de Paris et l'esprit de ses habitants. Elle joue aussi un rôle très pratique: elle porte une antenne qui sert de relais de télévision.

Répondez:
1. Que font quatre millions de touristes chaque année?
2. Pourquoi est-ce que la Tour Eiffel est visible de toutes parties de Paris?
3. Quand est-ce qu'on a construit la Tour Eiffel?
4. Est-ce qu'on doit prendre l'escalier pour arriver au sommet de la tour?
5. Qu'est-ce que la Tour Eiffel symbolise?
6. Quel rôle pratique joue la tour?

In the following exercises you will experience some of the same situations the Duponts might encounter in Paris. As you role-play with your classmates or with your teacher in these situations, use language structures that you have learned. If you cannot remember certain words or phrases, use other structures that you do remember to make yourself understood and to communicate your needs, wants, or opinions.

A. You need to buy a train ticket from Toulouse to Paris. Imagine that you are in a train station in Toulouse and you are purchasing a ticket at the *guichet*.

B. Once you arrive in Paris, you take the *métro* to the *Opéra* and begin looking for *la rue du Helder*. You ask a pedestrian for help. He refers to a map (of Paris) to give you directions to the street.

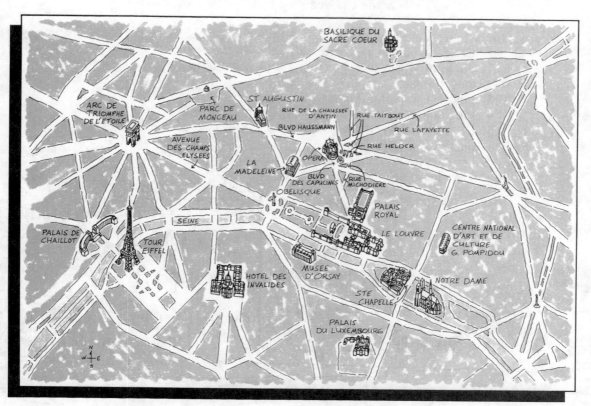

C. You find the hotel and go in to inquire about a room. Find out the following information:
1. whether they have a room for four people
2. how much it costs per night (300 F)
3. whether the price includes breakfast (20 F extra)
4. whether it has a bathroom
5. what floor it is on

D. You go into a restaurant with several other people.
1. Discuss several items on the menu.
2. Decide on the 50 F dinner.
3. Tell the waiter/waitress what each of you would like to choose for your meat, vegetable, and beverage.
4. Ask what the soup of the day is.
5. Later order cheese, dessert, and coffee.
6. Tell how much you enjoyed your meal, or how good a dish was.

E. In the hotel lobby you begin a conversation with a couple seated there.
1. Greet the couple appropriately.
2. Find out where they are from, their nationality, what languages they speak.
3. Find out what their professions are.
4. Find out about their children–ages, schooling, etc.
5. Discuss any favorite leisure-time activities (sports, games, music, reading, etc.).
6. Share opinions about Paris.
7. Take leave of them appropriately.

chapitre de révision

F. On another occasion you encounter the same couple you had met in the hotel lobby. Bring the conversation around to spiritual things.
   1. Find out what religion they believe.
   2. Tell about your own personal beliefs.
   3. Give a simple presentation of the plan of salvation.

G. In your hotel room in the evening, plan your activities for the next day.
   1. Discuss what the weather will be like according to the weather report.
   2. Tell what places in Paris you will visit and why.
   3. Decide what you will wear.
   4. Tell when you plan to do certain activities.

H. Either to a friend in person or in a letter, tell what you did the previous day.
   1. Tell when you did things (specific times).
   2. Relate the places you visited and what you saw.
   3. Tell where and what you ate for your meals and snacks.

Reference Tables

regular -er verbs

parler

je parle	nous parlons
tu parles	vous parlez
il, elle, on parle	ils, elles parlent

Other examples: *regarder, dîner, écouter, travailler, chercher*

-ir verbs like *dormir*

dormir

je dors	nous dormons
tu dors	vous dormez
il, elle, on dort	ils, elles dorment

Other examples: *sortir, partir, servir, mentir*

-ir verbs like *finir*

finir

je finis	nous finissons
tu finis	vous finissez
il, elle, on finit	ils, elles finissent

Other examples: *obéir, polir, punir, choisir, maigrir*

regular -re verbs

attendre

j' attends	nous attendons
tu attends	vous attendez
il, elle, on attend	ils, elles attendent

Other examples: *répondre, entendre, perdre, vendre, descendre*

irregular verbs (in this book)

	je	tu	il, elle, on	nous	vous	ils, elles
aller	vais	vas	va	allons	allez	vont
avoir	ai	as	a	avons	avez	ont
connaître	connais	connais	connaît	connaissons	connaissez	connaissent
croire	crois	crois	croit	croyons	croyez	croient
dire	dis	dis	dit	disons	dites	disent

	je	tu	il, elle, on	nous	vous	ils, elles
écrire	écris	écris	écrit	écrivons	écrivez	écrivent
être	suis	es	est	sommes	êtes	sont
faire	fais	fais	fait	faisons	faites	font
lire	lis	lis	lit	lisons	lisez	lisent
mettre	mets	mets	met	mettons	mettez	mettent
pouvoir	peux	peux	peut	pouvons	pouvez	peuvent
prendre	prends	prends	prend	prenons	prenez	prennent
savoir	sais	sais	sait	savons	savez	savent
venir	viens	viens	vient	venons	venez	viennent
voir	vois	vois	voit	voyons	voyez	voient
vouloir	veux	veux	veut	voulons	voulez	veulent

tense formation

présent

(See Verb Conjugations, Present Tense, p. 256.)

futur proche

present tense of *aller* + infinitive

> *Je **vais partir** ce soir.*
> *Le concierge **va fermer** la porte.*
> *Ils **vont prendre** le train.*

passé composé

present tense of *avoir* or *être* + past participle
> *Tu **as trouvé** ton chien?*
> *Mon frère **a dormi** tout l'après-midi.*
> *Mes amis **ont attendu** au magasin.*
> *Je **suis venu** en retard.*

verbs (in this book) conjugated with *être:*

aller	entrer	partir	revenir
arriver	monter	rentrer	tomber
descendre	mourir	rester	sortir
devenir	naître	retourner	venir

verbs with irregular past participles:

avoir	eu	mettre	mis
connaître	connu	pouvoir	pu
croire	cru	prendre	pris
dire	dit	savoir	su
écrire	écrit	venir	venu
être	été	voir	vu
faire	fait	vouloir	voulu
lire	lu		

pronouns

subject pronouns

je	nous
tu	vous
il, elle, on	ils, elles

Usage: used only in connection with a verb

stress pronouns

moi	nous
toi	vous
lui, elle	eux, elles

Usage: used only in certain contexts, such as
- emphasis: *Lui, il s'appelle Marc.*
- after a preposition: *Je vais chez toi.*
- alone: *Qui est là?–Moi.*
- in compounds: *Alice et moi, nous venons ce soir.*
  etc.

object pronouns

direct pronouns

me	nous
te	vous
le, la	les

Usage:
- replaces direct object noun
- comes before verb:
  Tu lis ta Bible?
  –Oui, je la lis.

indirect pronouns

me	nous
te	vous
lui	leur

Usage:

- replaces indirect object noun, that is, noun preceded by the preposition *à*
- comes before verb:
    Tu écris à tes parents?
    —Oui, je leur écris.

y

Usage:

- replaces *à* plus a thing:
    Tu réponds à ses questions?
    —Oui, j'y réponds.
- replaces a prepositional phrase of location:
    Tu es dans le salon?
    —Oui, j'y suis.

en

Usage:

- replaces *de* plus a thing:
    Tu prends du thé?
    —Oui, j'en prends.
- replaces anything after an expression of quantity:
    Tu as deux sœurs?
    —Non, j'en ai trois.

interrogative pronouns

qui

Usage:

- refers to a person
- used as a subject or as a direct object:
    Qui parle?—Claude.
    Qui est-ce que tu regardes?—Les enfants.

que

Usage:

- refers to a thing
- used as a direct object:
    Que cherchez-vous?—Mes chaussures.

relative pronouns

qui

Usage:
- refers to a person or a thing
- used as a subject of a clause:
    C'est ma fille qui est malade.
    Je prends le train qui part à 8 heures.

que

Usage:
- refers to a person or a thing
- used as a direct object of a clause:
    J'ai les billets que tu cherches.
    C'est Pierre qu'elle aime.

determiners

	singular masculine	*singular feminine*	*plural*
indefinite articles	un	une	des
definite articles	le (l')	la (l')	les
partitives	du (de l')	de la (de l')	des
demonstrative adjectives	ce (cet)	cette	ces
possessive adjectives	mon	ma	mes
	ton	ta	tes
	son	sa	ses
	notre	notre	nos
	votre	votre	vos
	leur	leur	leurs

Glossary

French / English

à (prep) to, at

abeille (f) bee

accent (m) accent

accomplir (*-ir* verb like *finir*) to accomplish

accordéon (m) accordion

acheter (regular *-er* verb) to buy; (conjugation irregularity: *achète, achètes, achète, achetons, achetez, achètent*)

acteur, actrice (noun) actor

activité (f) activity

addition (f) bill (in a restaurant)

adresse (f) address

afin de (prep) in order to; **afin que** (conj) in order that

Afrique (f) Africa

âge (m) age; *Quel âge avez-vous?* How old are you?

âgé, âgée (adj) old

agent (de police) (m) policeman

agneau (m) lamb

aider (regular *-er* verb) to help

aigu, aigue (adj) acute, sharp; **accent aigu** acute accent: *é*

aimer (regular *-er* verb) to love, to like

Ain (m) Ain (department in eastern France)

air (m) air; *avoir l'air* to look, to seem

Airbus (m) Airbus (jet airliner manufactured in France)

alcool (m) alcohol

algèbre (m) algebra

Allemagne (f) Germany

allemand, allemande (adj and noun) German

aller (irregular verb) to go

aller-retour (m) round-trip ticket

allocation (f) allotment (of money); **allocutions familiales** (f, pl) government grants to families with dependents

alors (adv) then, at that time, well then

Alpes (f, pl) Alps (mountains in southeastern France)

Alsace (f) Alsace (province in eastern France)

américain, américaine (adj and noun) American

Amérique (f) America

ami, amie (noun) friend

amitié (f) friendship; **mes amitiés** best regards (complimentary closing at end of a friendly letter)

amour (m) love

amusant, amusante (adj) amusing, funny

an (m) year; *Elle a trois ans.* She is three years old.

âne (m) donkey

anglais, anglaise (adj and noun) English

Angleterre (f) England

anglophone (adj and noun) English-speaking, English-speaking person

animal (m) animal; (pl) **animaux**

année (f) year; *Quels sont les mois de l'année?* What are the months of the year?

anniversaire (de naissance) (m) birthday

annonce (f) announcement; **petites annonces** classified ads

antenne (f) antenna

antibiotique (adj and masc noun) antibiotic

août (m) August

appareil (photographique) (m) camera (for taking snapshots)

apparenté, apparentée (adj) related

appartement (m) apartment

appeler (regular *-er* verb) to call; (conjugation irregularity: *appelle, appelles, appelle, appelons, appelez, appellent*)

apprécier (regular *-er* verb) to appreciate

apprendre (irregular verb) to learn

après (adv) after

après-midi (m) afternoon

araignée (f) spider

argent (m) money

Ariane (f) Ariane (French satellite-launching rocket)

armée (f) army

armoire (f) wardrobe, closet

arrêt (m) stop; **arrêt d'autobus** bus stop

arriver (regular *-er* verb) to arrive, to happen

art (m) art

artichaut (m) artichoke

article (m) article

artiste (m and f) artist

ascenseur (m) elevator

asperge (f, pl) asparagus
aspirateur (m) vacuum cleaner
aspiré, aspirée (adj) aspirate(d); *h*-**aspiré** (m) *h* that blocks liaison and elision
aspirine (f) aspirin
assez (adv) rather, fairly; enough (as an expression of quantity)
assiette (f) dinner plate
athée 1.(adj) atheistic; 2. (m and f) atheist
attendre (regular -*re* verb) to wait (for)
attentivement (adv) attentively
atterrissage (m) landing (of an aircraft)
au (contraction) *à* plus *le*
au revoir (m) goodbye
aujourd'hui (adv) today
aussi (adv) also
auto (-mobile) (f) automobile, car
autobus (m) bus
automne (m) autumn, fall
autre (adj and pron) other
aux (contraction) *à* plus *les*
avance (f) advance; **être en avance** to be early, ahead of time
avant (adv), **avant de** (prep), **avant que** (conj) before
avec (prep) with
avion (m) airplane
avocat, avocate (noun) lawyer
avoir (irregular verb) to have
avril (m) April

baby-foot (m) foosball
bac, bachot, baccalauréat (m) final examination for studies in the *lycée*
baguette (f) long, thin loaf of French bread
baignoire (f) bathtub
bain (m) bath; **la salle de bains** room with a bathtub
baleine (f) whale
ballon (m) balloon; (inflatable) ball
banane (f) banana
banque (f) bank
bas, basse 1. (adj) low; 2. (adv) low, below; **là-bas** over there
bas (m) stocking
basse-cour (f) farmyard
Bastille (f) Bastille (Parisian prison attacked at the beginning of the French Revolution)
bateau (m) boat

bateau-mouche (m) riverboat for tourists; (pl) **bateaux-mouches**
bavard, bavarde (adj) talkative
beau, bel, belle (adj) beautiful, handsome; (pl) **beaux, belles**
beau-fils (m) son-in-law, stepson; (pl) **beaux-fils**
beau-frère (m) brother-in-law, stepbrother; (pl) **beaux-frères**
beau-père (m) father-in-law, stepfather; (pl) **beaux-pères**
beaucoup (adv) much, a lot
bébé (m) baby
belge (adj and noun) Belgian
Belgique (f) Belgium
belle-fille (f) daughter-in-law, stepdaughter; (pl) **belles-filles**
belle-mère (f) mother-in-law, stepmother; (pl) **belles-mères**
belle-sœur (f) sister-in-law, stepsister; (pl) **belles-sœurs**
bénisse (subjunctive of *bénir*) bless; *Que Dieu vous bénisse.* May God bless you.
besoin (m) need; **avoir besoin de** to have need of, to need
bête 1.(adj) stupid; 2. (f) beast, animal, insect
beurre (m) butter
bibliothèque (f) library
bien (adv) well; very (as an intensifier)
bientôt (adv) soon
bienvenu, bienvenue (adj) welcome
bifteck (m) (beef)steak
billet (m) ticket
biologie (f) biology
biscotte (f) melba toast
bise (f) kiss
blanc, blanche (adj) white
bleu, bleue (adj) blue
blond, blonde (adj) blond
blue-jean (m) jeans; (pl) **blue-jeans**
boisson (f) beverage, drink
bol (m) bowl
bon, bonne (adj) good
bonhomme (m) fellow, guy; **bonhomme de neige** snowman
bonjour (m) hello, good day
boîte (f) box, can
bouche (f) mouth
boucherie (f) butcher's shop
boue (f) mud

boulanger, boulangère (noun) baker
boulangerie (f) bakery
boulevard (m) boulevard
Bourgogne (f) Burgundy (province in eastern France)
bouteille (f) bottle
bras (m) arm
Brésil (m) Brazil
brésilien, brésilienne (adj and noun) Brazilian
Bretagne (f) Brittany (province in western France)
brie (f) Brie (a variety of cheese, made from cow's milk)
brioche (f) yeast roll
brouillard (m) fog; *Il fait du brouillard.* It's foggy.
brun, brune (adj) brown
bûche (f) log; **bûche de Noël** yule log, yule cake in the form of a log
buffet (m) sideboard, buffet
bureau (m) desk, office

cabine (téléphonique) (f) telephone booth
cacher (regular -*er* verb) to hide
cadeau (m) gift
café (m) coffee, café
cage (f) cage
cahier (m) notebook, workbook
camembert (m) Camembert (a variety of rich, yellowish cheese)
caméra (f) movie camera
canadien, canadienne (adj and noun) Canadian
canard (m) duck
carême (m) Lent
carte (f) map, card, menu
cassette (f) cassette (audio) tape
cathédrale (f) cathedral
catholique (adj and noun) Catholic
ce, cet, cette (demonstrative adj) this (or that), **ces** these (or those)
cédille (f) cedilla (ç—mark placed under the letter *c* that gives it the sound /s/)
cela (pron) that
célibataire (adj and noun) unmarried, single (person)
celui, celle (demonstrative pron) the one, **celles, ceux** those
cent (number) hundred

centime (m) centime (one hundredth of a *franc*)
certain, certaine (adj) certain
ces *See* **ce.**
cet *See* **ce.**
cette *See* **ce.**
chaise (f) chair
chameau (m) camel; (pl) **chameaux**
champignon (m) mushroom
chanson (f) song
chanter (regular -*er* verb) to sing
chapeau (m) hat; (pl) **chapeaux**
chaque (adj) each
charcuterie (f) pork butchery
chasse (f) hunting
chat, chatte (noun) cat
chaud, chaude (adj) hot
chaussée (f) pavement; **rez-de-chaussée** (m) street level, first floor
chaussette (f) sock
chaussure (f) shoe
chemin (m) way, road
chemise (f) shirt
chemisier (m) blouse
cher, chère (adj) dear, expensive
chercher (regular -*er* verb) to look for
cheval (m) horse; (pl) **chevaux**
chevalin, chevaline (adj) pertaining to a horse; **boucherie chevaline** (f) horse-butcher's shop
chèvre (f) goat
chez (prep) at the house of, at the office of
chien, chienne (noun) dog
chimie (f) chemistry
chinois, chinoise (adj and noun) Chinese; Chinese person
chocolat (m) chocolate
choisir (-*ir* verb like *finir*) to choose
chose (f) thing; **quelque chose** (pron) something
chou (m) cabbage; (pl) **choux**
chou-fleur (m) cauliflower; (pl) **choux-fleurs**
chrétien, chrétienne (adj and noun) Christian
cidre (m) cider
ciel (m) sky, heaven; (pl) **cieux**
cinq (number) five
cinquième (adj and noun, m) fifth
circonflexe (adj) circumflex; **accent circonflexe** (m) circumflex accent: â, ê, î, ô, û

cité (f) large town; **cité universitaire** student residences

clarinette (f) clarinet

classe (f) class

cochon (m) pig

cœur (m) heart

coiffeur, coiffeuse (noun) hairdresser

coin (m) corner

collège (m) secondary-level school

commander (regular -er verb) to order (i.e., food in a restaurant)

commencer (regular -er verb) to begin (first-person plural form: *commençons*)

commerçant (m) shopkeeper, small businessman

complet, complète 1. (adj) complete; 2. (m) (man's) suit

composter (regular -er verb) to stamp, punch (a ticket)

comprendre (irregular verb) to understand (conjugated like **prendre**)

comprimé (m) medicine tablet, pill

comptable (m) accountant

compter (regular -er verb) to count

concierge (m and f) doorkeeper, caretaker

Concorde (f) Concorde (supersonic commercial airliner)

confesser (regular -er verb) to confess

confiance (f) confidence, faith

confortable (adj) comfortable

conjuguer (regular -er verb) to conjugate

connaissance (f) acquaintance, knowledge

connaître (irregular verb) to know, to be acquainted with

consigne (f) checkroom

contrôleur, contrôleuse (noun) conductor (on a train)

copain (m) pal, buddy

corbeille (f) basket (as in wastebasket, breadbasket)

correspondre (regular -re verb) to correspond, to write letters

côte (f) coast

côté 1. (m) side; **à côté de** (prep) beside, next to

côtelette (f) cutlet (lamb chop, pork chop)

couchage (m) lying in bed; **sac de couchage** (m) sleeping bag

couleur (f) color, paint

couloir (m) corridor, hall

coup (m) hit, blow, knock

cour (f) court, courtyard

cours (m) course, class (in school)

course (f) race, racing; **faire des courses** to go shopping, to run errands

cousin, cousine (noun) cousin

coût (m) cost, price

couteau (m) knife

coûter (regular -er verb) to cost

couvert 1. (m) covering; place setting (at a table); 2. (past participle of **couvrir**) covered

couvrir (irregular verb) to cover; *See* **ouvrir**

craie (f) chalk

cravate (f) tie

crayon (m) pencil

création (f) creation

crème (f) cream

crémerie (f) dairy, dairy store

crevette (f) shrimp

croire (irregular verb) to believe

croix (f) cross

croque-monsieur (m) toasted ham and cheese sandwich

croyant, croyante 1. (noun) believer; 2. (present participle) believing

cru, crue (adj) uncooked, raw

crudités (f, pl) raw vegetable hors d'œuvres

cuiller (f) spoon (also spelled *cuillère*)

cuisine (f) kitchen; cooking, **faire la cuisine** to do the cooking

cuisinière (f) stove

cuisse (f) thigh; **cuisses de grenouilles** frogs' legs

cuit, cuite (adj) cooked; **bien cuit** well done

culte (m) worship; church service

d'abord (adv) first, in the first place

d'accord (adv) in agreement; (interj) yes, O.K.

dame (f) lady, married woman; **jeu de dames** game of checkers

dans (prep) in

date (f) date

de 1. (prep) of, from; 2. (partitive) any

décembre (m) December

découverte (f) discovery

découvrir (irregular verb) to discover; *See* **ouvrir.**

dédicace (f) dedication (of a building, book, etc.)

défini, définie (adj) definite; **article défini** (m) definite article

déjeuner 1. (m) noon meal, lunch; **petit déjeuner** breakfast; 2. (regular -*er* verb) to have lunch, to have breakfast

déjà (adv) already, ever

délicieux, délicieuse (adj) delicious

demain (adv) tomorrow

demander (regular -*er* verb) to ask (however: **poser une question** to ask a question)

demi (adj) half *quatre heures et demie* 4:30, or four and a half hours; **une demi-heure** a half hour

dent (f) tooth

dentiste (m and f) dentist

départ (m) departure

département (m) department; governmental subdivision of France

dernier, dernière (adj) last

des *See* **de.**

descendre (regular -*re* verb) to go down, descend

désirer (regular -*er* verb) to desire, to want

désobéir (*ir* verb like *finir*) to disobey

dessert (m) dessert

dessin (m) drawing, sketch, design

détester (regular -*er* verb) to detest, to hate

détracteur, détractrice (noun) detractor

deux (number) two

deuxième (adj and noun, m) second

devant (prep) in front of

devenir (irregular verb) to become

devenu (past participle of **devenir**) became

devoir 1. (m) duty; (pl.) **devoirs** homework; 2. (irregular verb) should, ought

Dieu (m) God

dimanche (m) Sunday

dindon (m) turkey (rooster); **dinde** (f) turkey hen

dîner 1. (m) dinner; 2. (regular -*er* verb) to have dinner

dire (irregular verb) to say

discuter (regular -*er* verb) to discuss

distribuer (regular -*er* verb) to distribute, to hand out

dit *See* **dire.**

dix (number) ten

dixaine (f) a group of ten

dix-huit (number) eighteen

dix-neuf (number) nineteen

dix-sept (number) seventeen

dixième (adj and noun, m) tenth

docteur, doctoresse (noun) doctor (having a doctorate)

doigt (m) finger

don (m) gift

donc (conj) therefore, thus, so

donner (regular -*er* verb) to give

doré, dorée (adj) golden

dormir (-*ir* verb) to sleep

dos (m) back

douche (f) shower (i.e., bath)

doué, douée (adj) gifted, talented

doux, douce (adj) sweet, soft

douzaine (f) dozen

douze (number) twelve

droguerie (f) housewares shop (selling cleaning items, kitchen utensils, shelf paper, etc.)

droit, droite 1. (adj) right; straight; 2. (adv) in a straight line, directly; 3. **droite** (f) right (hand side); *Tournez à droite.* Turn right.

droitement (adv) uprightly, justly

du, de la, des 1. (prep) of the, from the; 2. (partitive) some.

eau (f) water

échecs (m, pl) chess

école (f) school

écolier, écolière (noun) schoolboy, schoolgirl

écouter (regular -*er* verb) to listen

écrire (irregular verb) to write

écureuil (m) squirrel

éducation (f) education, upbringing

église (f) church

Egypte (f) Egypt

éléphant (m) elephant

élève (m and f) pupil, student in elementary school

elle (subject pron) she, it; (stress pron) her, it; (pl) **elles** they

employé, employée (noun) employee

employer (regular -*er* verb) to use, to utilize; (conjugation irregularity: *see* **envoyer**)

emprunter (regular -*er* verb) to borrow

en 1. (pron) of it, of them, some of it, some of them, from it, from them; 2. (prep) in, to

enchanté, enchantée (adj) charmed, delighted (in a greeting)

énergique (adj) energetic
enfant (m and f) child
enfer (m) hell
enfin (adv) at last, finally, after all
ennuyeux, ennuyeuse (adj) boring, tiresome
enseignement (m) teaching, education
enseigner (regular -*er* verb) to teach
ensemble (adv) together
entendre (regular -*re* verb) to hear
entre (prep) between
entrecôte (f) ribsteak
entrée (f) entrance
entrer (regular -*er* verb) enter
enveloppe (f) envelope
envers (prep) toward
environ (adv) about
envoyer (regular -*er* verb) to send (*y* changes to *i* before unpronounced endings: *envoie, envoies, envoient*)
épaule (f) shoulder
épice (f) spice
épicerie (f) grocery store
épicier, épicière (noun) grocer
Epiphanie (f) Epiphany
éprouver (regular -*er* verb) to test, to try; to feel, to experience
es See **être.**
escalier (m) stairs
escargot (m) snail
Espagne (f) Spain
espagnol, espagnole (adj and noun) Spanish; Spaniard
esprit (m) spirit
est See **être.**
estomac (m) stomach
et (conj) and
établir (-*ir* verb like *finir*) to establish
étage (m) floor, story (of a building)
étagère (f) rack, set of shelves
Etats-Unis (m, pl) United States
été 1. (m) summer; 2. (past participle of **être**) been
éternel, éternelle (adj) eternal
éternité (f) eternity
êtes See **être.**
étiquette (f) label; etiquette
être (irregular verb) to be
étude (f) study; **faire des études** to study
étudiant, étudiante (noun) student
étudier (regular -*er* verb) to study

eu (past participle of **avoir**) had
eux (stress pron, m, pl) them
évangile (m) gospel
évier (m) (kitchen) sink
examen (m) test, examination
exemple (m) example
exercice (m) exercise
expérience (f) experience; experiment
express (m) express train

facteur, factrice (noun) postman
faim (f) hunger; **avoir faim** to be hungry
faire (irregular verb) to do, to make
falloir (irregular verb) to be necessary; **il faut** it is necessary
fameux, fameuse (adj) famous
familial, familiale (adj) family; (pl) **familiaux, familiales**
famille (f) family
fatigué, fatiguée (adj) tired
faut See **falloir.**
fauteuil (m) armchair, easy chair
faux, fausse (adj) false
favori, favorite (adj) favorite
femme (f) woman, wife
femme-agent (f) policewoman
fenêtre (f) window
fer (m) iron; **fer à repasser** laundry iron
ferme (f) farm
féroce (adj) ferocious, fierce
feront (third-person plural future of **faire**) (they) will do, will make
fête (f) festival, celebration, holiday
février (m) February
fier, fière (adj) proud
fièvre (f) fever
filet (m) 1. fillet (of fish, etc.); 2. net
fille (f) daughter; girl; **jeune fille** girl, young woman
fils (m) son
finir (-*ir* verb, with -*iss* in plural forms) to finish
fixer (regular -*er* verb) to make firm, to set (a date, a meeting)
flamand, flamande (adj and noun) Flemish; Fleming
flûte (f) flute
foi (f) faith
foie (m) liver
fois (f) time, occasion
font See **faire.**

forme (f) form, shape
fort, forte 1. (adj) strong; 2. (adv) strongly; very (as an intensifier)
foulard (m) scarf
foule (f) crowd
four (m) oven
fourchette (f) fork
frais, fraîche (adj) fresh; cool
franc (m) franc (French monetary unit)
français, française (adj and noun) French; Frenchman
France (f) France
francophone (adj and noun) French-speaking; French-speaking person
frère (m) brother
frites (f, pl) French fried potatoes
froid, froide (adj) cold
fromage (m) cheese
fruit (m) fruit
futur (m) future (a verb tense)

gant (m) glove
garage (m) garage
garçon (m) boy; waiter (in a café)
garder (regular -er verb) to keep
gare (f) (railroad) station
gâteau (m) cake; (pl) **gâteaux**
gauche 1. (f) left; clumsy; 2. (f) left (hand side); *Tournez à gauche.* Turn left.
geler (regular -er verb) to freeze; (conjugation irregularity: *see* **acheter**)
genou (m) knee: (pl) **genoux**
gens (m, pl) people, folks
gentil, gentille (adj) pleasing, nice
gentillesse (f) graciousness, kindness
géographie (f) geography
géométrie (f) geometry
gigot (m) leg of lamb
girafe (f) giraffe
glace (f) mirror; ice; ice cream
gloire (f) glory
gorge (f) throat
gorille (m) gorilla
goûter 1. (m) afternoon snack; 2. (regular -er verb) to taste
gouvernement (m) government
grâce (f) grace; thanks
grammaire (f) grammar
grand, grande (adj) tall, large, big
grand-mère (f) grandmother; (pl) **grand-mères**

grand-père (m) grandfather; (pl) **grands-pères**
grands-parents (m, pl) grandparents
grange (f) barn
gras, grasse (adj) fat, fatty, rich (food, meat, etc.)
gratin (m) cheese topping; **au gratin** (cooked) with grated cheese
gratuit, gratuite (adj) free, at no cost
grave (adj) serious, grave
grenadine (f) pomegranate (syrup)
grenouille (f) frog
griller (regular -er verb) to grill, to toast; **pain grillé** (m) toast
gros, grosse (adj) big, stout, heavy, fat
grossir (-ir verb like *finir*) to enlarge, to get fat
guichet (m) (ticket, box office) window, gate
guitare (f) guitar

Words beginning with an aspirate **h** *are indicated by an asterisk.*
habitant, habitante (noun) inhabitant
habiter (regular -er verb) to inhabit, to live in (a place)
***haricot vert** (m) green bean
***haut, haute** (adj) high, tall; (m) height; *Le monument a vingt mètres de haut.* The monument is 20 meters tall.
***hautbois** (m) oboe
heure (f) hour; *Quelle heure est-il?* What time is it?
heureux, heureuse (adj) happy
***hibou** (m) owl; (pl) **hiboux**
hier (adv) yesterday
hippopotame (m) hippopotamus
histoire (f) story; history
hiver (m) winter
***homard** (m) lobster
homme (m) man
hôpital (m) hospital; (pl) **hôpitaux**
horloge (f) clock (i.e., a large clock on a building)
***hors (de)** (prep) outside of; **hors de la ville** outside of town; **hors d'œuvre** appetizer served before a meal
hôtel (m) hotel
***huit** (number) eight
***huitième** (adj and noun, m) eighth
huître (m) oyster

hypermarché (m) combination supermarket and department store

ici (adv) here
idéal, idéale (adj) ideal
il (subject pron, m) he, it; (pl) **ils** they
il y a (pron plus impersonal verb) there is, there are
immédiatement (adv) immediately
immeuble (m) apartment building
immobile (adj) motionless, fixed, immobile
impair, impaire (adj) odd (as opposed to even; e.g., number)
imperméable (m) raincoat
important, importante (adj) important; considerable (amount of goods, etc.)
impossibilité (f) impossibility
indépendant, indépendante (adj) independent
infirmier, infirmière (noun) nurse
ingénieur (m) engineer (as electrical engineer, etc.)
inspiration (f) inspiration
instituteur, institutrice (noun) elementary school teacher
instruction (f) instruction, education, schooling
intelligent, intelligente (adj) intelligent
intéressant, intéressante (adj) interesting
invité, invitée (noun) guest
Italie (f) Italy
italien, italienne (adj and noun) Italian

jamais (adv) ever; **ne . . . jamais** never
jambe (f) leg
jambon (m) ham
janvier (m) January
Japon (m) Japan
japonais, japonaise (adj and noun) Japanese
jardin (m) garden
jaune (adj) yellow
je (subject pron) I
Jéhovah (m) Jehovah
Jésus-Christ (m) Jesus Christ; **570 avant J.-C.** 570 B.C.; **570 après J.-C.** 570 A.D.
jeu (m) game
jeudi (m) Thursday
jeune (adj) young; *jeune fille* girl, young woman
jeunesse (f) youth, childhood

joli, jolie (adj) pretty
jouer (regular -*er* verb) to play; **jouer à** (followed by a game or sport); **jouer de** (followed by a musical instrument)
jour (m) day
jour de l'an (m) New Year's Day
journée (f) day (time); **toute la journée** all day long
juif, juive (adj and noun) Jewish, Jew
juillet (m) July
juin (m) June
jupe (f) skirt
Jura (m) **le Jura** the Jura Mountains (in eastern France)
jus (m) juice
jusque (prep) as far as, up to; *jusqu'à onze heures* until eleven o'clock
juste (adj) just, right; (adv) exactly; *commencer à dix heures juste* to begin at ten o'clock exactly

kilo, kilogramme (m) kilogram

la *See* **le.**
là (adv) there; **là-bas** (adv) over there
laid, laide (adj) ugly
laine (f) wool
lait (m) milk
laitier, laitière (adj and noun) dairy; dairyman, dairywoman
lampe (f) lamp
langue (f) tongue; language
lapin (m) rabbit
lard (m) bacon
lavabo (m) (bathroom) sink; washroom
laver (regular -*er* verb) to wash
lave-vaisselle (m) dishwasher
le, la 1. (definite article) the, (pl.) **les**; 2. (direct object pron) him, her, it, (pl.) **les**
leçon (f) lesson
lecture (f) reading
légume (m) vegetable
les *See* **le.**
lessive (f) washing; **faire la lessive** to do the wash
lettre (f) letter
leur 1. (poss adj) their; (pl) **leurs**; 2. (indirect object pron) to them
liaison (f) liaison (pronouncing the final consonant of a word preceding a word beginning with a vowel sound)

librairie (f) bookstore
ligne (f) line
lion, lionne (noun) lion, lioness
lire (irregular verb) to read
litre (m) liter
livre (m) book
logement (m) lodging, housing
loger (regular *-er* verb) to lodge, to live
loin (adv) far
loisir (m) leisure
long, longue (adj) long
longtemps (adv) a long time
Lorraine (f) Lorraine (province in eastern France)
lorsque (conj) when
louange (f) praise
louer (regular *-er* verb) 1. to rent; 2. to praise
loup (m) wolf
loyer (m) rent, rental
lu (past participle of *lire*) read
lui 1. (stress pron) him; 2. (indirect object pron) to him, to her
luire (irregular verb) to shine, to glow
lumière (f) light
lundi (m) Monday
lune (f) moon
Luxembourg (m) Luxemburg
lycée (m) high school

ma *See* **mon.**
madame (f) Mrs.; madam; (pl) **mesdames**
mademoiselle (f) Miss; (pl) **mesdemoiselles**
magasin (m) store; **grand magasin** department store
magazine (m) magazine
magnifique (adj) magnificent
mai (m) May
maigrir (*-ir* verb like *finir*) to get thin, lose weight
maintenant (adv) now
mais (conj) but
maïs (m) corn
maison (f) house
mal 1. (m) evil, harm; 2. (adv) badly, ill; **avoir mal** to be sick
malade (adv) ill, sick; **être malade** to be sick
mandat (m) money order
manger (regular *-er* verb) to eat (first-person plural form: *nous mangeons*)

manteau (m) coat, cloak; (pl) **manteaux**
marchand, marchande (noun) merchant
marché (m) market
marcher (regular *-er* verb) to walk; (idiomatic use) *La machine ne marche pas.* The machine is not working.
mardi (m) Tuesday
mardi-gras (m) Shrove Tuesday (the Tuesday before Ash Wednesday, the beginning of Lent)
mari (m) husband
marié, mariée (adj and noun) married person
mars (m) March
Massif Central (m) Massif Central (mountains in south central France)
maternel, maternelle (adj) maternal
maths (f, pl) math
matin (m) morning
matinée (f) morning (time); **faire la grasse matinée** to sleep in; **toute la matinée** all morning long
mauvais, mauvaise (adj) bad
mécanicien, mécanicienne (noun) mechanic
méchant, méchante (adj) spiteful, mean; vicious
médecin (m) medical doctor
médecine (f) medicine (refers to both the art and medical treatments)
médicament (m) medicine, drug, medical treatment
membre (m) member
même 1. (adj) same; 2. (adv) even
ménage (m) housekeeping; **faire le ménage** to do the housework
ménagère (f) housewife
mener (regular *-er* verb) to lead; (conjugation irregularity: *see* **acheter**)
mentir (*-ir* verb like *dormir*) to lie
menu (m) menu, dinner special (in a restaurant)
mer (f) sea
merci (adv) thank you
mercredi (m) Wednesday
mère (f) mother
mes *See* **mon.**
météo (f) weather forecast
mètre (m) meter
métro (m) subway

mettre (irregular verb) to put, to place; to put on

mexicain, mexicaine (adj and noun) Mexican

Mexique (m) Mexico

micro-onde (f) microwave (oven); (pl) **micro-ondes**

midi (m) noon

mil (alternate spelling of **mille** in a date)

mille (number) thousand

million (m) million; *deux millions de citoyens* two million citizens

mince (adj) thin, slender

minéral, minérale (adj and noun, m) mineral; **eau minérale** mineral water; (pl) **minéraux, minérales**

ministère (m) ministry

minuit (m) midnight

missionnaire (m and f) missionnary

modéré, modérée (adj) moderate, reasonable

moderne (adj) modern

moi (stress pron) me

moins (adv) less, *Il est trois heures moins dix.* It is ten to three.

mois (m) month

mon, ma, mes (poss pron) my

monde (m) world

monnaie (f) change; *Avez-vous la monnaie de dix francs?* Do you have change for ten francs?

monsieur (m) Mr.; man, gentleman; (pl) **messieurs**

monstreux, monstreuse (adj) monstrous, huge, dreadful

montagne (f) mountain

monter (regular -*er* verb) to ascend, to go up

montre (f) (wrist)watch

montrer (regular -*er* verb) to show

monument (m) monument

morceau (m) piece; (pl) **morceaux**

mort 1. (f) death; 2. (past participle of *mourir*) dead, died

mot (m) word

moto (f) motorbike

moue (f) pout; **faire la moue** to pout

mouette (f) sea gull

moule (f) mussel

mourir (irregular verb) to die

mouton (m) sheep

moyen (m) means

muet, muette (adj) dumb, mute, silent

musée (m) museum

musique (f) music

naissance (f) birth

nappe (f) tablecloth

natation (f) swimming

nationalité (f) nationality

naître (irregular verb) to be born

ne (adv) (first of two elements in negative formation); **ne . . . pas** not; **ne . . . jamais** never; **ne . . . personne** no one; **ne . . . plus** no longer; **ne . . . rien** nothing

né, née (past participle of **naître**) born

négatif, négative (adj) negative

neige (f) snow

neiger (regular -*er* verb) to snow

nettoyer (regular -*er* verb) to clean; (conjugation irregularity: *see* **envoyer**)

neuf 1. (number) nine; 2. (adj) new, brand-new (f, **neuve**)

neuvième (number and noun, m) ninth

neveu (m) nephew; (pl) **neveux**

nez (m) nose

nièce (f) niece

Noël (m) Christmas (f in the expression **à la Noël** at Christmas time)

noir, noire (adj) black

nom (m) name

nombre (m) number

nombreux, nombreuse (adj) numerous, large

non (adv) no

non-compris, non-comprise (adj) not included

non-fumeur (adj) non-smoking

Normandie (f) Normandy (province in northwest France)

nos *See* **notre.**

notre, nos (possessive pron) our

nourriture (f) food, nourishment

nous (subject pron) we; (stress pron) we, us; (direct object pron) us; (indirect object pron) to us

nouveau, nouvel, nouvelle (adj) new; (pl) **nouveaux, nouvelles**

novembre (m) November

nuit (f) night

numéro (m) number

obéir (-*ir* verb like *finir*) to obey
obligé, obligée (adj) obligated
occultiste (m and f) occultist
océan (m) ocean
octobre (m) October
œil (m) eye; (pl) **yeux**
œuf (m) egg
œuvre (f) work
officiel, officielle (adj) official
offrir (irregular verb) to offer; *See* **ouvrir.**
oignon (m) onion
oiseau (m) bird; (pl) **oiseaux**
omelette (f) omelet
omnibus (m) bus; slow train that stops often
on (subject pron) one (also, we, you, or they, depending on context: *On parle français en France.* They speak French in France.)
oncle (m) uncle
or 1. (m) gold; 2. (adv) now then, well then
oral, orale (adj) oral; (pl) **oraux, orales**
orange (adj and noun) orange (m=color, f=fruit)
orangeade (f) carbonated orange drink
ordinateur (m) computer
oreille (f) ear
où (adv) where (interrogative)
oui (adv) yes
ours (m) bear
ouvert (past participle of *ouvrir*) open
ouvrier, ouvrière (noun) worker
ouvrir (irregular verb) to open *(j'ouvre, tu ouvres, il ouvre, nous ouvrons, vous ouvrez, ils ouvrent)*

paie (f) pay
pain (m) bread
pair, paire (adj) even (as opposed to odd; e.g., number)
pantalon (m) (pair of) pants
papier (m) paper
pâque (f) Passover
Pâques (f, pl) Easter
paquet (m) packet, package
par (prep) by; per; through
parapluie (m) umbrella
parce que (conj) because
pardon (m) pardon; *Pardon.* Excuse me, I'm sorry.
parent (m) parent
parler (regular -*er* verb) to talk

parole (f) word; **la parole de Dieu** the word of God
participe (m) participle
partie (f) part (of a whole)
partir (-*ir* verb like *dormir*) to leave, depart (followed by *de* plus noun)
partitif (m) partitive
partout (adv) everywhere
passé composé (m) compound past tense, corresponds to English present perfect and simple past; *J'ai travaillé.* I have worked. I worked.
passeport (m) passport
passer (regular -*er* verb) to pass, to go (by, through, on); to spend (time)
pasteur (m) pastor
pâte (f) pastry, mixture; **pâte à tartiner** chocolate-hazelnut spread
pâté (m) (meat) paste; **pâté de fois gras** goose liver pâté
pâtisserie (f) pastry; cake shop
pauvre (adj) poor
payer (regular -*er* verb) to pay; (conjugation irregularity: *see* **envoyer**)
pêche (f) 1. peach; 2. fishing; **aller à la pêche** to go fishing
péché (m) sin
pécheur, pécheresse (noun) sinner
peinture (f) painting (art); picture; paint
pendule (f) clock
penser (regular -*er* verb) to think
Pentecôte (f) Pentecost
perdre (regular -*re* verb) to loose
père (m) father
périr (-*ir* verb like *finir*) to perish
périsse (subjunctive of **périr**) perish
personne (f) person; **ne . . . personne** no one, nobody
personnel, personnelle (adj) personal
personnellement (adv) personally
petit, petite (adj) small, little, short
petit-fils (m) grandson; (pl) **petits-fils**
petite-fille (f) granddaughter; (pl) **petites-filles**
peu (adv) little, few
peur (f) fear; **avoir peur** to be afraid
peut *See* **pouvoir.**
peuvent *See* **pouvoir.**
peux *See* **pouvoir.**
pharmacie (f) pharmacy

pharmacien, pharmacienne (noun) pharmacist

photo(graphie) (f) photograph

phrase (f) sentence

physique (f) physics

pièce (f) piece; (theater) play; room (of a house, apartment, etc.)

piano (m) piano

pied (m) foot

pile (f) 1. battery, cell; 2. reverse (of a coin toss); **pile ou face** heads or tails

piqûre (f) injection, shot; sting, bite (of an insect)

placard (m) cupboard

plafond (m) ceiling

plage (f) beach

plaît (third-person singular of *plaire*, to please); **s'il vous plaît** (if you) please

plan (m) plan, map

plancher (m) floor

plante (f) plant

plat, plate (adj) flat

plein, pleine (adj) full

pleut See **pleuvoir.**

pleuvoir (irregular verb) **Il pleut.** It is raining.

pluriel, plurielle (adj) plural

plus (adv) more; **ne . . . plus** no longer

plusieurs (adj and pron) several

plutôt (adv) rather

poème (m) poem

point 1. (m) period; 2. (adv) **ne . . . point** not (at all)

poire (f) pear

pois (m) pea

poison (m) poison

poisson (m) fish

poissonnerie (f) fish market

poivre (m) pepper

polir (*-ir* verb like *finir*) to polish

Pologne (f) Poland

polonais, polonaise (adj and noun) Polish; Pole

pomme (f) apple

pommier (m) apple tree

pont (m) bridge

porc (m) pork; hog

porte (f) door

porter (regular *-er* verb) to wear; to carry

porteur, porteuse (noun) carrier; messenger

portugais, portugaise (adj and noun) Portuguese

Portugal (m) Portugal

poser (regular *-er* verb) to pose, to rest on; **poser une question** to ask a question

poste (f) post, post office; **mettre une lettre à la poste** to mail a letter

pouce (m) thumb

poule (f) hen

poulet (m) chicken

poupée (f) doll

pour (prep) for

pourboire (m) tip

pourquoi (adv and conj) why

pouvoir (irregular verb) to be able

pratique 1. (adj) practical; 2. (f) practice

prêcher (regular *-er* verb) to preach

préférer (regular *-er* verb) to prefer; (conjugation irregularity: *préfère, préfères, préfère, préférons, préférez, préfèrent*)

premier, première (adj and noun) first

prendre (irregular verb) to take; **prendre le dîner** to have dinner

prénom (m) first name

préparer (regular *-er* verb) to prepare

près (prep) near (followed by *de* plus noun)

présent, présente (adj) present

présenter (regular *-er* verb) to introduce; to present

presque (adv) almost, nearly

prier (regular *-er* verb) to pray

primaire (adj) primary

printemps (m) spring

pris (past participle of **prendre**) taken

prix (m) price, cost; prize

problème (m) problem

prochain, prochaine (adj) next, nearest

proche (adj and adv) close, nearby

prof, professeur (m) teacher

programme (m) program

projet (m) plan, project

pronom (m) pronoun

prononciation (f) pronunciation

protestant, protestante (adj and noun) Protestant

prouver (regular *-er* verb) to prove

pu (past participle of **pouvoir**)

public, publique 1. (adj) public; 2. (m) public; **le grand public** the general public

puis (adv) then

pull-over (m) pullover (sweater)

punir (-*ir* verb like *finir*) to punish
pupitre (m) desk
pyjama (m) pajamas
Pyrénées (f, pl) Pyrenees Mountains (located on the border between France and Spain)

Québec (m) Quebec; *à Québec* to, in Quebec City; *au Québec* to, in Quebec Province
quai (m) platform, wharf
quand (adv and conj) when
quarante (number) forty
quart (m) quarter; *Il est six heures moins le quart.* It is quarter to six.
quatorze (number) fourteen
quatre (number) four
quatre-vingts (number) eighty
quatre-vingt-un (number) eighty-one
quatrième (adj and noun, m) fourth
que 1. (relative pron) that, whom, which; *Voici le livre que tu cherches.* Here is the book that you are looking for. 2. (interrogative pron) what; *Que voulez-vous?* What do you want? 3. (conj) that (often omitted in English); *Je sais que tu viens.* I know (that) you are coming.
quel, quelle, quels, quelles (interrogative adj) what, which; *Quel temps fait-il?* What is the weather like? *Quelle heure est-il?* What time is it? *Quels livres est-ce que tu préféres?* Which books do you prefer?
quelque chose (pron) something
quelquefois (adv) sometimes
quelque part (adv) somewhere
quelque (adj) some, any; **quelque jour** some day; **quelques traités** some tracts
quelqu'un (pron) someone
question (f) question
queue (f) tail, line; *faire la queue* stand in line
qui (interrogative and relative pron) who, whom
quiconque (pron) whoever
quinze (number) fifteen
quitter (regular -*er* verb) to leave (can take a direct object)
quoi (interrogative pron) what

radio (f) radio
raisin (m) grape

raison (f) reason
rapide 1. (adj) rapid, fast; 2. (m) express train
rare (adj) rare
rarement (adv) rarely
ravi, ravie (adj) delighted
rebours (m) wrong way; **à rebours** backward
réfrigérateur (m) refrigerator
regarder (regular -*er* verb) to look at, to watch
règle (f) rule
regretter (regular -*er* verb) to regret
rejeter (regular -*er* verb) to throw back, to reject (conjugation irregularity: *see* **appeler**)
relais (m) relay, relay broadcasting station
religieuse (f) cream éclair
religieux, religieuse (adj) religious
religion (f) religion
remède (m) remedy, cure
rendez-vous (m) appointment, meeting; **fixer un rendez-vous** make an appointment
rentrée (f) return, return home; beginning of school term
rentrer (regular -*er* verb) to go (come) in again, re-enter; to return home; to return to school
réparer (regular -*er* verb) to repair, to fix
repas (m) meal
repasser (regular -*er* verb) 1. to pass by again; 2. to iron (clothes)
répondre (regular -*re* verb) to answer
réponse (f) answer
responsable (adj and noun, m) responsible; person responsible, person in charge
ressuscité (past participle of *ressusciter*) resuscitated; risen (from the dead)
restaurant (m) restaurant
rester (regular -*er* verb) to stay, to remain
retard (m) delay; **être en retard** to be late
retourner (regular -*er* verb) to return, to go back
réunion (f) reunion; joining up again; meeting
réussir (-*ir* verb like *finir*) to succeed
révéler (regular -*er* verb) to reveal, to disclose
revenir (irregular verb: *see* **venir**) to come back
révision (f) review

revoir (irregular verb) to see again; **au re-voir** goodbye

rez-de-chaussée (m) street level, first floor

rhume (m) cold

riche (adj) rich

rideau (m) curtain; (pl) **rideaux**

rien (indefinite pron) **ne . . . rien** nothing

robe (f) dress

rôle (m) role, part (in a play)

romanche (adj and noun) Romansh

roman (m) novel

roquefort (m) Roquefort (a blue cheese made with sheep's milk)

rose 1. (f) rose; 2. (adj) pink

rôti (m) roast

rouge (adj) red

rougeole (f) measles

rougir (*-ir* verb like *finir*) to grow red; to blush

roux, rousse (adj) reddish-brown; redhaired

rue (f) street

russe (adj and noun) Russian

Russie (f) Russia

sa *See* **son.**

sac (m) sack, bag, purse

sachet (m) sachet, packet

saignant, saignante (adj) bleeding; rare (meat)

saison (f) season

salade (f) salad

salaire (m) wages

salle (f) room

salon (m) parlor, living room

salut (m) 1. salvation; 2. Hi! (as an informal greeting)

samedi (m) Saturday

sang (m) blood

sans (prep) without

sapin (m) fir, pine (tree)

s'appeler (regular *-er* verb, reflexive) to call oneself; *je m'appelle* my name is; *tu t'appelles* your name is; *il s'appelle* his name is; *Comment vous appelez-vous?* What is your name?

sardine (f) sardine

satellite (m) satellite

saucisson (m) sausage (cooked)

sauté (adj and noun, m) sauté (cooking)

sauter (regular *-er* verb) to jump, to leap

sauvé (past participle of **sauver**) saved, rescued

sauver (regular *-er* verb) to save, to rescue

Sauveur (m) Saviour

savoir (irregular) to know, to have knowledge about

savon (m) soap

scène (f) stage, scene

scolaire (adj) scholastic

secrétaire (m or f) secretary

Seigneur (m) Lord

Seine (f) Seine River (in northern France, flowing through Paris)

seize (number) sixteen

séjour (m) stay; **salle de séjour** living room

sel (m) salt

self-service (m) cafeteria-style restaurant

selon (prep) according to

semaine (f) week

Sénégal (m) Senegal

sénégalais, sénégalaise (adj and noun) Senegalese

sensible (adj) sensitive

sentier (m) path

sept (number) seven

septembre (m) September

septième (adj and noun, m) seventh

seras (second-person singular, future tense of **être**) (you) will be

sérieux, sérieuse (adj) serious

serpent (m) snake

service (m) service (in a hotel, restaurant: implies the offering of a gratuity)

serviette (f) napkin

servir (*-ir* verb like *dormir*) to serve

ses *See* **son.**

seul (adj) alone, sole, single, only

si 1. (conj) if; 2. (adv) so, so much; yes (as a positive response to a negative question)

silencieux, silencieuse (adj) silent

sillon (m) furrow

sincère (adj) sincere, frank, honest

singe (m) monkey

situé, située (adj) situated

six (number) six

sixième (adj and noun, m) sixth

sœur (f) sister

soif (f) thirst; **avoir soif** to be thirsty

soir (m) evening

soirée (f) evening (the events, viewing the duration of the evening) *passer une soirée* to spend an evening

soixante (number) sixty

soixante-dix (number) seventy

sole (f) sole (fish)

soleil (m) sun

sommeil (m) sleep; **avoir sommeil** to be sleepy

sommes *See* **être.**

sommet (m) top, summit

son, sa, ses (possessive adj) his, her

sont *See* **être.**

sortir (*-ir* verb like *dormir*) to go out, to leave (followed by *de*)

souhait (m) wish, desire; **à tes (vos) souhaits** Bless you (said when someone sneezes)

soupe (f) soup

souris (f) mouse

sous (prep) under

souvent (adv) often

spirituel, spirituelle (adj) 1. spiritual; 2. witty

sportif, sportive (adj) athletic, sporting

station (f) station (taxi, subway)

style (m) style

stylo (m) pencil

sucre (m) sugar

suggérer (regular *-er* verb) to suggest (conjugation irregularity: *see* **préférer**)

suis *See* **être.**

Suisse (f) Switzerland

suisse (adj and noun) Swiss

suite (f) following, continuation

suivant, suivante (adj) following

supermarché (m) supermarket

supplément (m) supplement; additional (i.e., fee)

sur (prep) on

sûr, sûre (adj) sure

sûrement (adv) surely

surpris, surprise (adj) surprised

sympa (sympathique) (adj) likeable, nice

ta *See* **ton.**

tabac (m) tobacco; tobacco shop

table (f) table

tableau (m) (black)board; painting; (pl) **tableaux**

tailleur (m) woman's suit

tant (adv) so much

tante (f) aunt

tapis (m) carpet

taquin, taquine (adj) teasing; (noun) a tease (a person)

tard (adv) late

tarte (f) tart, pie

tartine (f) slice of bread with butter, jam

tartiner (regular *-er* verb) to spread bread with jam or butter

tasse (f) cup

tee-shirt (m) T-shirt; (pl) **tee-shirts**

tel, telle (adj) such

télégramme (m) telegram

téléphone (m) telephone

téléphoner (regular *-er* verb) to telephone

télévision (f) television

témoignage (m) testimony

témoigner (regular *-er* verb) to witness, to testify

témoin (m) witness

température (f) temperature

temps (m) time; weather; **Quel temps fait-il?** What is the weather like?

terre (f) earth, world, ground

tes *See* **ton.**

tête (f) head

têtu, têtue (adj) stubborn

T.G.V. (m) train à grande vitesse (high-speed train)

thé (m) tea

théâtre (m) theater

tigre (m) tiger

timbre (m) stamp

timide (adj) timid, shy

titre (m) title

toi (stress pron) you

toilette (f) washstand, restroom, toilet; **faire sa toilette** to wash and dress

tomate (f) tomato

tomber (regular *-er* verb) to fall

ton, ta, tes (possessive pron) your

tort (m) wrong; **avoir tort** to be wrong

tortue (f) tortoise

toujours (adv) always

tour 1. (f) tower; 2. (m) circuit, tour

touriste (m and f) tourist

tourner (regular *-er* verb) to turn

Toussaint (f) All Saints' Day

tousser (regular *-er* verb) to cough

tout, toute, tous, toutes (adj and pron) all

train (m) train

traité (m) treatise; (religious) tract; **distri-buer des traités** to hand out tracts
tranche (f) slice
tranquille (adj) calm
travail (m) work
travailler (regular -er verb) to work
traverser (regular -er verb) to go across
treize (number) thirteen
trente (number) thirty
très (adv) very
triste (adj) sad
trois (number) three
troisième (adj and noun, m) third
trompette (f) trumpet
trop (adv) too
troupeau (m) herd; (pl) **troupeaux**
trouver (regular -er verb) to find
truite (f) trout
tu (subject pron) you
tuer (regular -er verb) to kill

un, une (indefinite article) a; (pl) **des**
unique (adj) only, sole; *sens unique* one-way (street)
université (f) university

va *See* **aller.**
vacances (f, pl) vacation
vache (f) cow
vais *See* **aller.**
vaisselle (f) dishes; **faire la vaisselle** to do the dishes
valise (f) suitcase
vanille (f) vanilla
varicelle (f) chicken pox
vas *See* **aller.**
veau (m) calf; veal; (pl) **veaux**
vélo (m) bicycle
vélomoteur (m) lightweight motorcycle
vendeur, vendeuse (noun) salesman; saleswoman
vendre (regular -re verb) to sell
vendredi (m) Friday
venir (irregular verb) to come
vent (m) wind
venu (past participle of **venir**) come
verbe (m) verb
vérité (f) truth
verre (m) glass
vers 1. (m) verse, line of poetry; 2. (prep) toward

verset (m) verse (of Scripture)
vert, verte (adj) green
vertige (m) dizziness; **avoir des vertiges** to have dizzy spells
veste (m) jacket
vêtement (m) coat, garment; (pl) **clothing**
veulent *See* **vouloir.**
veut *See* **vouloir.**
veux *See* **vouloir.**
viande (f) meat
vide (adj) empty
vider (regular -er verb) to empty
vie (f) life
viens *See* **venir.**
vient *See* **venir.**
vierge (f) virgin
vieux, vieil, vieille (adj) old; (pl) **vieux, vieilles**
village (m) village
ville (f) city, town
vin (m) wine
vinaigrette (f) vinaigrette (French salad dressing)
vingt (number) twenty
vingt et un (number) twenty-one
violet, violette (adj) violet, purple
violon (m) violin
visible (adj) visible
visiter (regular -er verb) to visit (a place)
visiteur, visiteuse (noun) visitor
vite (adv) quickly
vitesse (f) speed
vocabulaire (m) vocabulary
voici (prep, adv) here is, here are
voient *See* **voir.**
voilà (prep, adv) there is, there are
voile (f) sail
voir (irregular verb) to see
voisin, voisine (noun) neighbor
voit *See* **voir.**
voiture (f) vehicle, car, automobile
voler (regular -er verb) 1. to fly; 2. to steal
vont *See* **aller.**
vos *See* **votre.**
Vosges (f, pl) Vosges (mountains in eastern France)
votre, vos (possessive pron) your
voudrais (first- and second-person singular conditional tense of **vouloir**) would like
voudrions (first-person plural conditional tense of **vouloir**) would like

vouloir (irregular verb) to want, to will, to wish
voulu (past participle of **vouloir**) wanted
vous (subject pron, stress pron, direct object pron) you; (indirect object pron) to you
voyage (m) trip, journey
voyager (regular -er verb) to travel
voyageur, voyageuse (noun) traveler
voyez See **voir.**
vrai, vraie (adj) true
vu (past participle of **voir**) seen

wagon (m) car (of a train)
w.c. (m/pl) restroom, toilet
western (m) western (movie or book)

y (pron) there (replacing a prepositional phrase of location); to it (replacing à plus a noun)
yaourt (m) yogurt; **le yaourt** (no elision or liaison)
yeux See **œil.**

zéro (m) zero
zoo (m) zoo

Index

Din, Din, C'est la Cloche du Matin

Traditional French Round

Din, din, din, din c'est la clo - che du ma - tin,

qui sonne au re - tour du jour: bon - jour, bon - jour!

Frère Jacques

Traditional French Round

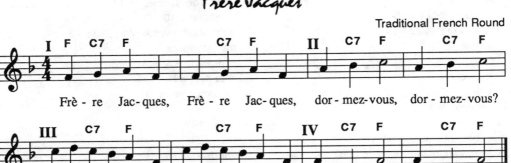

Frè - re Jac- ques, Frè - re Jac- ques, dor - mez-vous, dor - mez-vous?

Sonnez les ma-ti - nes, sonnez les ma-ti - nes, din, din, don, din, din, don!

Un, Deux, Trois

Traditional French Round

I — Un, deux, trois, nous i - rons au bois,

II — quat', cinq, six, cueil - lir des ce - ris';

III — sept, huit, neuf, dans mon pan - ier neuf;

IV — dix, onz', douz', el - les sont tout' roug's.

Quel ami fidèle et tendre

C. C. Converse

Quel a-mi fi-dèle et ten-dre Nous a-vons en Jé-sus- Christ,

Tou - jours prêt à nous en - ten - dre, A ré - pondre à no - tre
Tou - jours prêt à nous com - pren - dre Quand nous som - mes en sou -
Tou - jours prêt à nous dé - fen - dre Quand nous pres - se l'en - ne -

cri! Il con - naît nos dé - fail - lan - ces,
ci! Di - sons - lui tou - tes nos crain - tes,
mi! Il nous suit dans la mê - lé - e,

Nos chu - tes de cha - que jour. Sé - vère en ses ex - i -
Ou - vrons - lui tout no - tre cœur. Bien - tôt ses pa - ro - les
Nous en - tou - re de ses bras, Et c'est lui qui tient l'é -

gen - ces, Il est riche en son a - mour.
sain - tes Nous ren - dront le vrai bon - heur.
pé - e Qui dé - ci - de des com - bats.

La B-I-B-L-E

1. La B - I - B - L - E, quel liv - re mer - veil - leux Je
2. Par son S - A - N - G, Jé - sus m'a lib - é - ré Car
3. Sa G - R - A - C - E, me S - A - U - V - E le

m'y tiens fer - me, je crois tou - jours à la B - I - B - L - E.
sur la croix, il est mort pour moi Son__ sang m'a rach - et - é.
moy - en, c'est par la F - O - I Dit la B - I - B - L - E.

Dans la Forêt Lointaine

Traditional French Round

Dans la fo - rêt loin - tai - ne on en - tend le cou - cou;
du haut de son grand chê - ne il ré - pond au hi - bou:

Cou - cou, cou - cou, cou - cou, cou - cou, cou - cou!

Merci, Seigneur

Mer - ci, Seig - neur, Tu m'as sau - vé,

Mer - ci, Seig - neur, Tu m'as don - né

La vic - toi - re sur le pé - ché,

Prends- moi, car en Toi j'ai tout trou - vé!

Sur le pont d'Avignon

French Folk Song

Sur le pont d'A - vi - gnon, l'on y dan - se, l'on y dan - se.

Sur le pont d'A - vi - gnon, l'on y dan - se tout en rond.

1. Les beaux mes - sieurs font comm' ça (salut)
2. Les bell's da - mes font comm' ça (révérence)
3. Les of - fi - ciers font comm' ça (salut militaire)

D. C. al fine

et puis en - cor' comm' ça. (salut)
et puis en - cor' comm' ça. (révérence)
et puis en - cor' comm' ça. (salut militaire)

Jésus aime tous les enfants

Jé - sus ai - me tous les en - fants,

Les pe - tits en - fants du monde. Rou - ges,

jau - nes, noirs, et blancs Il les ai - me con - stam - ment, Jé - sus

ai - me les pe - tits en - fants du monde.

Au clair de la lune

French Folk Song

1. Au clair de la lu - ne, mon a - mi Pier - rot,
2. Au clair de la lu - ne Pier - rot ré - pon - dit:

prê - te - moi ta plu - me pour é - crire un mot.
Je n'ai pas de plu - me, je suis dans mon lit;

Ma chan - delle est mor - te, je n'ai plus de feu,
va chez la voi - si - ne, je crois qu'elle y est;

ou - vre - moi ta por - te je te prie, mon vieux.
car dans sa cui - si - ne on bat le bri - quet.

L'Alouette

French Canadian Folk Song

A - lou - et - te, gen - tille a - lou - et - te,

a - lou - et - te, je te plu - me - rai. *fine*

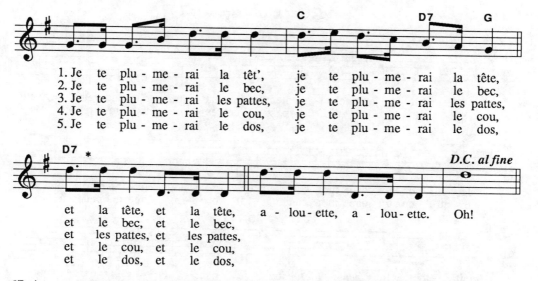

1. Je te plu - me - rai la têt', je te plu - me - rai la tête,
2. Je te plu - me - rai le bec, je te plu - me - rai le bec,
3. Je te plu - me - rai les pattes, je te plu - me - rai les pattes,
4. Je te plu - me - rai le cou, je te plu - me - rai le cou,
5. Je te plu - me - rai le dos, je te plu - me - rai le dos,

et la tête, et la tête, a - lou - ette, a - lou - ette. Oh!
et le bec, et le bec,
et les pattes, et les pattes,
et le cou, et le cou,
et le dos, et le dos,

*During verse 2, repeat this measure, singing the words from verse 1. During verse 3, repeat this measure twice, first singing the words from verse 3, then the words from verse 2, and then the words from verse 1. Continue in the same manner for verses 4 and 5.

En passant par la Lorraine

French Folk Song

1. En pas - sant par la Lor - rai - ne a - vec mes sa - bots,
2. Ren - con - trai trois ca - pi - tai - nes a - vec mes sa - bots,
3. Ils m'ont ap - pe - lée vi - lai - ne a - vec mes sa - bots,
4. Je ne suis pas si vi - lai - ne a - vec mes sa - bots,

ren - con - trai trois ca - pi - tai - nes, a - vec mes sa-
ils m'ont ap - pe - lée vi - lai - ne, a - vec mes sa-
je ne suis pas si vi - lai - ne, a - vec mes sa-
puis - que le fils du roi m'ai - me, a - vec mes sa-

bots, Don - dai - ne, Oh! Oh! Oh! a - vec mes sa bots!

Merveilleux changement

1. Mer - veil - leux chan - ge-ment, je na - quis de nou-veau, Quand
2. Je jou - is d'u - ne paix d'un es - poir as - su - ré, De-

Jé - sus en - tra dans mon cœur. Quel grand jour lu - mi-neux, tout fut
puis qu'il en - tra dans mon cœur. Il ban - nit tou - te peur et toute

clair, tout fut beau, Quand Jé - sus en - tra dans mon
obs - cu - ri - té, De puis qu'il en - tra dans mon

coeur. Quand Jé - sus en - tra dans mon cœur, Quand
coeur.

Refrain

Jé - sus en - tra dans mon cœur, Ce fut joie et fer-veur, in - ef-

fa - ble bon - heur, Quand Jé - sus en - tra dans mon cœur.

Savez-vous planter les choux?

Traditional

1. Sa - vez - vous plan - ter les choux, à la
2. On les plante a - vec la main, à la
3. On les plante a - vec les pieds, à la

mo - de, à la mo - de, sa - vez vous plan - ter les
mo - de, à la mo - de, On les plante a - vec la
mo - de, à la mo - de, On les plante a - vec les

choux, à la mo - de de chez nous?
main, à la mo - de de chez nous.
pieds, à la mo - de de chez nous.

Jésus m'aime

William Bradbury

Jé - sus m'ai - me, je le sais Car la Bi - ble me le dit.

Chaque en - fant est son tré - sor Je suis fai - ble, Lui est fort.

Oui, Jé - sus m'ai - me, Oui, Jé - sus m'ai - me,

Oui, Jé - sus m'ai - me, La Bi - ble me le dit.

Car Dieu m'a tant aimé

Frances Townsend

Al Smith

Car Dieu m'a tant ai - mé Qu'Il a don - né son

Fils Pour Mour - ir sur la croix Me sau - ver du pé-

ché. Un jour Christ re - vien - dra Pour mon cœur quel - le

joie Mer - veil - leux jour ce se - ra.

Il était une bergère

Traditional

1. Il___ é - tait un' ber - gè - re, et
2. El - le fit un fro - ma - ge, et
3. Le___ chat qui la re - gar - dait, et
4. "Si___ tu y mets la pat - te, et
5. Il___ n'y mit pas la pat - te, et
6. La ber - gè - re en col - è - re, et

ron, ron, ron, pe - tit pa - ta - pon, il___
ron, ron, ron, pe - tit pa - ta - pon, el -
ron, ron, ron, pe - tit pa - ta - pon, le
ron, ron, ron, pe - tit pa - ta - pon, si___
ron, ron, ron, pe - tit pa - ta - pon, il___
ron, ron, ron, pe - tit pa - ta - pon, la ber-

é - tait un' ber - gè - re qui
le fit un fro - ma - ge du
chat qui la re - gar - dait d'un
tu y mets la pat - te, tu
n'y mit pas la pat - te, il
gè - re en col - è - re, a

gar - dait ses mou - tons. (ron, ron) qui
lait de ses mou - tons. (ron, ron) du
pe - tit air fri - pon. (ron, ron) d'un
au - ras du bâ - ton." (ron, ron) tu
y mit le men - ton. (ron, ron) il
tu - é son cha - ton. (ron, ron) a

gar - dait ses mou - tons._____
lait de ses mou - tons._____
pe - tit air fri - pon._____
au - ras du bâ - ton."_____
y mit le men - ton._____
tu - é son cha - ton._____

La Marseillaise

French National Anthem

Al - lons, en - fants de la Pa - tri - e, le jour de

gloire est ar - ri - vé. Con - tre nous de la ty - ran -

ni - e l'é - ten - dard sang - lant est le - vé, l'é - ten -

dard_____ sang - lant est le - vé. En - ten - dez - vous dans les cam -

pa - gnes mu - gir ces fér - o - ces sol - dats? Ils

vien - nent jus- que dans nos bras, é - gor - ger nos fils, nos com -

pa - gnes! Aux ar - mes, cit - oy - ens! For -

mez___ vos ba - tail - lons! Mar - chons, mar - chons,

qu'un sang im - pur a - breu - ve nos sil - lons.

Entre le bœuf

Traditional

1. En - tre le bœuf et l'â - ne gris,
2. En - tre les ro - ses et les lys,

dors, dors, dors le pe - tit fils: Mil - le anges di -
dors, dors, dors le pe - tit fils: Mil - le anges di -

vins, mil - le sé - ra - phins, vo - lent à l'en -

tour de ce grand Dieu_____ d'a - mour.

Un flambeau, Jeannette, Isabelle

Traditional French Carol

1. Un flam - beau,_____ Jean - nette, I - sa - bel - le!
2. C'est un tort,_____ quand l'en - fant som - meil - le,

Un flam - beau,_____ cou - rons au ber - ceau.
c'est un tort_____ de cri - er si fort.

C'est Jé - sus, bon - nes gens du ha - meau;_____
Tai - sez - vous, l'un et l'au - tre d'a - bord!

le Christ est né, Ma - rie ap - pel - le.
Au moin - dre bruit Jé - sus s'é - veil - le.

Ah!   Ah!   Ah, que la mè - re est bel - le!
Chut!   Chut!   Chut, il dort à mer - veil - le!

Ah!   Ah!   Ah, que l'en - fant est beau.
Chut!   Chut!   Chut, voy - ez comme il dort.

Il est né, le divin Enfant

Traditional French Carol

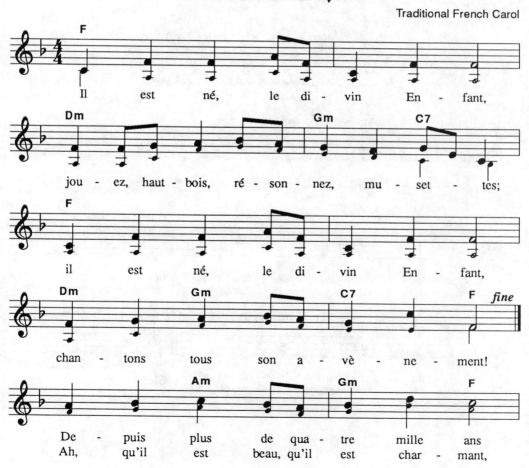

Il est né, le di - vin En - fant,

jou - ez, haut - bois, ré - son - nez, mu - set - tes;

il est né, le di - vin En - fant,

chan - tons tous son a - vè - ne - ment!

De - puis plus de qua - tre mille ans
Ah, qu'il est beau, qu'il est char - mant,

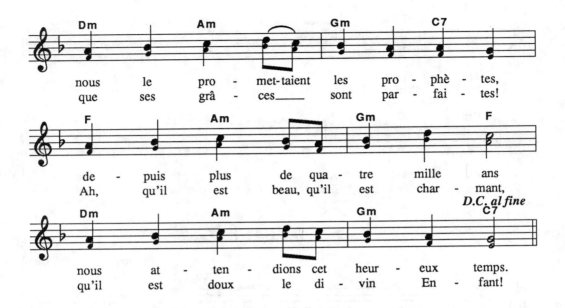

nous le pro - met-taient les pro - phè - tes,
que ses grâ - ces___ sont par - fai - tes!

de - puis plus de qua - tre mille ans
Ah, qu'il est beau, qu'il est char - mant,

D.C. al fine

nous at - ten - dions cet heur - eux temps.
qu'il est doux le di - vin En - fant!

Les anges dans nos campagnes

Traditional French Carol

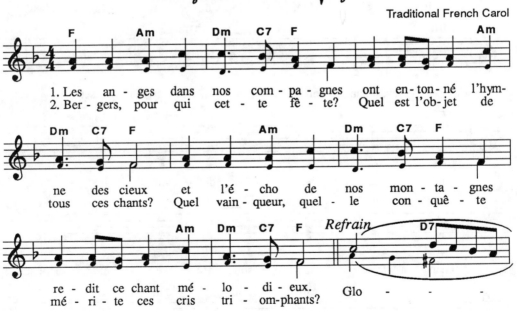

1. Les an - ges dans nos com - pa - gnes ont en - ton - né l'hym-
2. Ber - gers, pour qui cet - te fê - te? Quel est l'ob- jet de

ne des cieux et l'é - cho de nos mon - ta - gnes
tous ces chants? Quel vain - queur, quel - le con - quê - te

Refrain

re - dit ce chant mé - lo - di - eux. Glo - - -
mé - ri - te ces cris tri - om-phants?

- - - - - - - - - - - - - - ri - a

in ex - cel - sis De - o! Glo - - -

- - - - - - - - - - - - - ri - a

in ex - cel - sis De - - o!

Sainte nuit

Franz Grüber

Sain - te nuit! À____ mi - nuit

le ha - meau dort sans bruit;

dans l'é - ta - ble re - pos' un en - fant

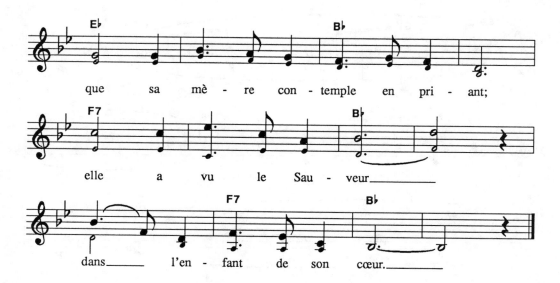

que   sa   mè - re   con - temple   en   pri - ant;

elle   a   vu   le   Sau - veur_____

dans_____   l'en - fant   de   son   cœur._____

Cantique de Noël

Cappeau de Roquemaure

Adolph Adam

Mi - nuit Chré - tiens,_____ c'est l'heu - re so - len - nel - le Où l'hom - me

Dieu des - cen - dit jus - qu'à nous,   Pour ef - fa-

cer_____ la tache o - ri - gi - nel - le, Et de son Père ar - rê - ter le cour-

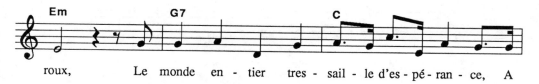

roux,   Le monde en - tier tres - sail - le d'es - pé - ran - ce,   A

cet - te nuit qui lui donne un Sau - veur. Peuple à ge - noux, at -

tends____ ta dé - li - vran - ce, No - ël!____ No -

ël! voi - ci____ le Ré - demp - teur! No -

ël! No - ël! Voi - ci le Ré - demp - teur!

Acknowledgments

A careful effort has been made to trace the ownership of selections included in this textbook in order to secure permission to reprint copyright material and to make full acknowledgment of their use. If any error or omission has occurred, it is purely inadvertent and will be corrected in subsequent editions, provided written notification is made to the publisher.

"For God So Loved the World" by Alfred B. Smith and Frances Townsend. Copyright © 1938 by Singspiration Music/ASCAP. All Rights Reserved. Used By permission of The Benson Co., Inc., Nashville, TN.

"Merveilleux Changement" from *Cantharmonie* with permission granted from La Voix de L'Evangile, a ministry of Global Outreach Mission, Inc., Box 711, Buffalo, NY.

"Thank You, Lord" by Bessie Sykes and Seth Sykes. Copyright © 1940 by Singspiration Music/ASCAP (chorus), and Copyright 1945 by Singspiration Music/ASCAP (verses). All Rights Reserved. Used By permission of The Benson Co., Inc., Nashville, TN.

Photo Credits

Suzanne R. Altizer: 10 (both), 173 (bottom), 174, 175, 181
Clare Baughman: 258 (left)
Edith Boyd: ii (top left, bottom), iii (top), 23 (left), 41, 126, 134, 137, 167, 186, 191, 206, 208, 210, 217
Grace C. Collins: 93, 118 (right), 119
G. David Koonts: ii (top right), 1, 24, 25, 29 (right), 48, 53 (top), 55, 69, 83, 107, 112, 148, 183, 195, 202, 213, 225, 237, 249, 215 (bottom)
Rob Loach: 11, 23 (right), 29 (left), 45 (both), 53 (bottom), 56, 67, 70, 71 (all), 72, 98, 91, 118 (left), 136 (both), 143, 173 (top), 258 (right)
Courtesy of Rob Loach: 13 (all), 14-15 (all), 36 (all)
NASA: 111
Sarah Reid: iii (bottom), 92
Ed Richards: 251 (top)
John Weeks: 73, 151
Unusual Films: 176, 177